Praise for *Good Book*

A smart, fearless deconstruction of evangelical attempts to "save" the Bible, *Good Book* is compellingly written, persuasively argued, and brilliantly feminist. Jill Hicks-Keeton has written a necessary book for our moment.

—Rhiannon Graybill, Rhodes College

Good Book is essential reading for anyone who struggles with the logic of evangelical biblical interpretation and can't quite put their finger on why. Hicks-Keeton lays bare the rhetoric of self-salvation that threads through New Testament interpretation in evangelical circles to reveal the sheer political power that generates enormous economic benefit for purveyors and sows social discord in faith communities. *Good Book* is a timely intervention when people need spiritual connection and meaning-making—but for whom "the Bible-benevolence script" offers neither.

—Katherine A. Shaner,
Wake Forest University School of Divinity

Evangelicals have long engaged in the ruse of selective literalism, but Jill Hicks-Keeton's remarkable book demonstrates the many ways "Bible redeemers" have twisted the Scriptures to their own purposes. "It takes a lot of work to make Jesus good for women," the author argues, and Paul is even more of a challenge. The author's obvious command of the Bible makes her arguments difficult to refute. This is a wise and provocative—not to mention controversial—book, one that every Christian should take seriously.

—Randall Balmer, author of *Saving Faith:
How American Christianity Can Reclaim Its Prophetic Voice*

The Bible looms large in our society and casts a long shadow. Hicks-Keeton sheds light on shadow by examining how the insistence that the Bible is *good* serves other agendas that perpetuate harm. This book is for anyone who wants to wrestle with the Bible's complex legacy and continued influence in our lives.

—Blake Chastain, host of *Exvangelical* and author of
The Post-Evangelical Post (Substack)

Hicks-Keeton's *Good Book* is a magnificent critique of the toxicity of White evangelical apologetics—"Bible benevolence." Hicks-Keeton deftly analyses some of the most quoted, and most contentious, biblical passages as they are used by those who would contort them into something they're not: in this case, good for women. The book exposes just how intertwined—and dangerous—the policing of gender performance and attempts to save the Bible really are. It is a must-read for anyone who wants to add to their feminist research and teaching arsenal.

—Meredith J. C. Warren, University of Sheffield

GOOD BOOK

JILL HICKS-KEETON

GOOD BOOK

HOW WHITE EVANGELICALS SAVE THE BIBLE TO SAVE THEMSELVES

FORTRESS PRESS

Minneapolis

GOOD BOOK
How White Evangelicals Save the Bible to Save Themselves

Copyright © 2023 Fortress Press, an imprint of 1517
Media. All rights reserved. Except for brief quotations
in critical articles or reviews, no part of this book may
be reproduced in any manner without prior written
permission from the publisher. Email copyright@1517.
media or write to Permissions, Fortress Press, PO Box
1209, Minneapolis, MN 55440-1209.

Library of Congress Control Number: 2023933461 (print)

Cover design: Kristin Miller
Cover image: Detail of front of Scottish Victorian family
Bible with text removed, ©abzee | Getty Images

Print ISBN: 978-1-5064-8585-0
eBook ISBN: 978-1-5064-8587-4

Printed in China.

For Eurydice

Contents

Acknowledgments........................ *ix*

1. The Business of Bible Benevolence
   The White Evangelical Script for Saving Scripture... 1

2. Making Jesus Good
   Sacrificing Women for the Sake of the Bible...... 21

3. Making Paul Less Bad
   The Fantasies of White Evangelical Men 67

4. Making Paul Less Bad, Again
   The Complicity of White Evangelical Women.... 119

5. The Cost of Bible Benevolence
   The Harms of White Evangelical Power........ 161

Notes 169
Bibliography.................. 209
Index of Scriptures............... 227
Subject Index 231

Acknowledgments

This was a hard book for me to write.

Analysis is never dispassionate. My own reckoning with this was hard-earned because of how I was trained, as a woman in white evangelical Christianity in the American South, and as a believer in the myth that historical criticism is *the* tool for revealing truth. Becoming an expert practitioner of both taught me to deny my own experience as trustworthy or as potentially revelatory. And, further, not to really think about the consequences to other people.

The worlds of possibility that I now see when it comes to what questions can be asked and what tools are helpful for seeking and speaking answers have been shaped by engaging the words of many others, some in personal conversation, but many more encountered by reading and thinking with their published work. They are more than footnotes to me—but by convention that is where I have endeavored to recognize and appreciate their influence. Kate Manne's books on misogyny gave me the transformative gift of language to use in naming the phenomena I have sought to describe. The scholarship of pioneers and practitioners of womanist and feminist criticism of the Bible, including especially Renita Weems, Wil Gafney, Elisabeth Schüssler Fiorenza, Rhiannon Graybill, Kat Shaner, and Jenny Knust, has helped me think better about what counts as harm and, further, what kinds of reading are promising for tackling the hard parts of the Bible without rejecting or dismissing it entirely. Mine is ultimately not a book about *the*

Bible, after all, but about a certain brand of biblicism—one whose characteristics and claims are usually either too easily taken as axiomatic or summarily dismissed as hypocritical or ludicrous. The work of Vincent Wimbush and Timothy Beal helped me appreciate that studying biblicism is doing biblical studies. I am glad for those in the field who have cheered me on by affirming that this project was worth doing, including especially Mark Leuchter and Ben Wright.

Thanks for support in acquiring materials are due to Rebecca Hall-Davis in the Department of Religious Studies at the University of Oklahoma. This project was supported by grants from the Arts & Humanities Forum at the University of Oklahoma, helmed by Kimberly Marshall, as well as the Dodge Family College of Arts & Sciences and the Research Council of the University of Oklahoma Norman Campus. Financial support was also provided from the Office of the Vice President for Research and Partnerships and the Office of the Provost, University of Oklahoma.

I am grateful to my editor at Fortress Press, Carey Newman. He did all the things good editors do. And more things, too, things to which I am keenly attentive given the contents of this book, and which I regard as deserving of higher praise: he presumed I was entitled to expertise even as he helped me envision how to execute this project. He trusted rather than regulated me, even as his recipe for book-cooking helped make this one better. He listened, *really listened*, when I asked for what I needed, even as his voice—"be a better poet"—yet resounds in my mind.

More than anyone, Cavan Concannon has enabled me to push this book forward and pull myself back from the brink as I have worked to shape fear and fury into critical curiosity. I probably could have done it without him—I like to think so, on principle—but I never would have wanted to.

ONE

The Business of Bible Benevolence

The White Evangelical Script for Saving Scripture

A talking cucumber, French peas in Roman headdresses, and flying purple slushies. These cute fruits and other foods populate the desert-set battle of Jericho in *VeggieTales*, a white evangelical media empire whose animations have shaped how a generation or more of evangelicals have viewed the Bible.

The biblical source text is the book of Joshua, a story of how the ancient Israelites, under God's command, conquered the land of Canaan. God promised the Israelites this land as the place they will live after their rescue from enslavement in Egypt, narrated in Exodus. In Deuteronomy (7:1–5), God commands the Israelites to annihilate the existing inhabitants of Canaan when they get there. "When the Lord your God gives them over to you and you defeat them, then you must utterly destroy them," the Bible reads.[1] "Make no covenant with them," God commands, "and show them no mercy."[2]

No mercy.

Mercifully, though, *VeggieTales* viewers are spared images of carnage. There are no dead children, no raped women as spoils of war, no signs of the human cost of conquest. In "Josh and the Big Wall," Larry the Cucumber, in the role of Joshua, leads a smattering of tomatoes, asparagus, and other salad ingredients in a march around Jericho with the animated ark of the covenant in tow. The moral of the story centers on their obedience to a command from God even though it felt, well, silly. God told them to march around the walls of Jericho for seven days, and on the seventh to blow horns and to shout. This, God says, will bring down the city's walls.

The Israelite veggies do it—even as the French peas lining the top of Jericho's walls move quickly from confusion to derision, musically mocking their opponents in an overwrought French accent. Insult becomes injury—sort of—when the peas begin to launch purple slushies at the Israelites. Larry and his botanic friends dutifully continue their march. At the climax, the priestly peas in the Israelite contingent blast their horns. As the jazzy rendition of "When the Saints Go Marching In" turns to silence, the cucumber and his compatriots yell. For a moment nothing happens. But then the walls begin to come down, brick by brick. In the end the walls implode entirely. After the destruction, a few surprised French peas, now slushie-less, disperse from the rubble. And they all live happily ever after.

Some questions viewers might pose to *VeggieTales* are difficult to answer. Why does the anthropomorphism include speech but not arms and legs? Why exactly are there pirates? *Where is my hairbrush?*[3]

But the answer to the question of why an animated show aimed at children would avoid depicting mass killing is obvious. Some parts of the Bible do not commend themselves to silly songs.

This is true, too, of Shechem's rape of Dinah, narrated in Genesis 34.[4] The violation against Jacob's family leads in turn to a bloodbath, as her brothers Simeon and Levi trick and murder the Shechemites in retaliation. This Bible story closes in a question mark. Readers are left with moral ambiguity as the men in Dinah's family argue with one another about whether her brothers should have taken such revenge. "Should our sister be treated like a whore?" Simeon and Levi challenge, claiming the last word. The narrator does not resolve the tension.

Yet other violence in the Bible is neither commanded by God nor ignored by God. It is, rather, perpetrated by God. The prophets Hosea, Jeremiah, and Ezekiel develop a trope of the deity as a cuckolded husband whose wife, representing God's people, must be punished for infidelity to him.[5] She is beaten, abused, and sexually assaulted. Hosea 2, for example, portrays the jealous husband, who represents God, violently stripping his wife naked to punish her. In Ezekiel 16, the whoring woman is excoriated repeatedly as justification for her subsequent rape. "I will satisfy my fury on you," God threatens. Readers of the New Testament frequently claim that God is therein depicted as kinder, gentler, less violent. But such a characterization of the deity can only be wrought when Bible readers overlook or put a rosy filter over, for example, divinely authorized violence in the gospel stories or divinely perpetrated violence in Revelation's frightful sexual assault scene.[6]

Such scenes in biblical texts are difficult for readers in the contemporary US to grapple with and to reconcile, often, with their expectations of what the Bible is supposed to be. Readers who understand the Bible to be benevolent have a puzzle to solve, a problem to tackle: how to deal with what feels bad when it comes to scriptural texts deemed fundamentally good.

MISCHIEF ENOUGH?

The Bible is the Good Book. Everyone knows it. Or, in the US, everyone knows at the very least that the Bible enjoys this nickname as a result of its broad popularity.

The Good Book commands this reputation for good reason. Millions of Americans report understanding the Bible as the Word of God, that is, gracious communication from a beneficent deity whose care and concern for humanity saturate its pages. The Bible has furnished fuel for social reformers and provoked courage among, and provided comfort to, those fighting against oppression in a variety of contexts. The Good Book has sparked the imaginations of beloved artists, musicians, writers, and home decor designers. For some influential Bible devotees, the Good Book is so good as to constitute a necessary ingredient for goodness to exist in the world at all. Convictions about the Bible's universal benevolence regularly combine with capital to influence American politics, law, and textbooks. The Good Book garners such popularity in the US that in the last century the Bible has become a commodified good successful enough to be "the best-selling book" in this country, year after year. People want it on their shelves—whether they crack it open or not. Yet many do regularly, seeking on or through their Bibles' pages moral guidance, inspiration, answers, and a connection to their community and their God.

Not everyone experiences the Bible as fundamentally good, though. For some, the Bible's benevolence is not immediately available. Many enslaved and formerly enslaved African Americans in the nineteenth century, for example, had to work hard to make the book of their white Christian slavers into one that spoke goodness into their lives. The Bible was good for them, but only because they struggled to make it so.[7] Such negotiations took the form of resisting or rejecting outright parts of the Bible that endorsed slavery,[8] freely changing inherited translations to make the words of the Bible more easily cohere with their experiences and aims,[9] and managing access to the Bible because of its oppressive potential.[10] Frederick Douglass, the self-liberated Black man who became a famous Christian abolitionist, loved the Bible and simultaneously was wary of supporting efforts to distribute Bibles to enslaved people in the American South. He worried, in part, that the liberative message he wrestled from the Bible would not be obvious enough to others.[11] Like medicine, the Bible could be both balm and poison.[12] For it to be beneficial, it must be carefully managed.

In the same century, women's rights proponents in the US alternately approached the Bible with trust, suspicion, or sheer pragmatism.[13] They did not agree about whether the Good Book was good for their cause, and their internal disagreements about the Bible's usefulness reveal that the Bible's benevolence was not universally agreed on. Many passionately recruited the Bible. With a wry nod to traditionalist renderings of Eve as primal provocateur, Sojourner Truth pointed to the Genesis protagonist to motivate women auditors to act for their own interests when she addressed the attendees of the 1851 Women's Rights Convention in Akron, Ohio.[14] If a woman had caused all the trouble in the first place, she reportedly reasoned, then the women around her should be able to make it right.[15] White abolitionist and suffragist Sarah Grimké argued that patriarchal social order was not mandated by the Bible, squarely putting the Good Book on the side of the controversy that she deemed the right one.

But others were wary. Some women's rights activists sought to push the Bible out of the conversation entirely, refusing to accept their comrades' optimism that the Bible is fundamentally liberative if only read rightly and applied well. Nineteenth-century Jewish feminist Ernestine Rose argued that the Bible had done "mischief enough."[16] In 1852 Rose successfully blocked a proposal at a women's rights convention that would have centered the Bible as an authority and ally in the cause. Still others saw the Bible not as irrelevant but as blameworthy. Elizabeth Cady Stanton famously viewed the Bible as a cause of women's oppression, even as she used the Bible as a battleground by publishing her own version. Her collaborative and highly controversial project *The Woman's Bible* (1895, 1898) sought to expose the degree to which patriarchy is encoded in the Bible in an effort to unseat patriarchy as a normative framework. The Bible had such the reputation as the Good Book, however, that even Stanton balked at the idea that a guest in her home might reach for a nearby Bible to raise their seat at the table.[17] The Bible would boost no one.

For others, the Bible's benevolence is a curiosity, more entertaining than embattled. Contemporary American journalist David Plotz, for example, narrates his bewilderment at reading some boring, impish, or even wicked parts of the Hebrew Bible in his *Good Book: The Bizarre, Hilarious, Disturbing, Marvelous, and Inspiring Things I Learned When I Read Every Single Word of the Bible* (2010). He wonders at God's "lax parenting" in the creation story in Genesis. The deity threatened Adam and Eve with death if they ate of the fruit but then did not follow through, he observes. Plotz is surprised that rape is a plot device and that famous biblical characters like Abraham and Jacob are not really moral exemplars by his accounting. They manipulate and lie, and "the Lord seems to love it," he points out playfully.[18] These are not reasons, for Plotz, to stop reading the Bible or teaching its contents to his kids, even as he reports that his fidelity is borne of pragmatism and respect for Jewish tradition and community. If nothing else, the Bible is a good read.

For many, though, the Bible's benevolence is a ruse. The Bible is bad, full stop. New Atheists such as Christopher

Hitchens and Richard Dawkins, for example, have lambasted the Bible as an evil book.[19] The Bible's god, they claim, is a "moral monster"—vindictive, fickle, selfish, and a genocidal maniac. Even if the Bible is a divine word from such a deity, the word is compromised because God himself is morally suspect. The Bible's sanction of slavery, bride-price, child murder, and other evils provides more evidence for such critics that the Bible is in fact a bad book. For biblical scholar and evangelical-turned-agnostic Bart Ehrman, the Bible is a failure. The Good Book does not satisfactorily explain, for him, why humans suffer.[20] For many, it is their own suffering at the hands of Bible-believers that has led them to reject the goodness of the Bible. How can the Bible be benevolent, they reasonably challenge, if it has been a source of such harm? Some in the thriving, diverse movement of "Exvangelicals" in the US today might fall into this category, since some who embrace the label have experienced deep trauma in Christian contexts where the Bible forms the basis not only of moral formation but also of world building. In their experience, the authority of the Bible is inextricably tied to powerful Bible-wielders who deny their ability to thrive or even exist.

The goodness of the Good Book is not a given.

THE BUSINESS OF BIBLE BENEVOLENCE

The Bible's goodness is also not an illusion. Better, its goodness is a construct. The Bible's benevolence, like the Bible itself,[21] is made and remade.

White evangelicals, through *VeggieTales*, make smooth biblical rough edges when it comes to Jericho and the conquest of Canaan by eliminating entirely the divine command to kill. Doing so saves viewers from having to confront difficult moral questions. *Doing so saves the Bible from potential critique.* Eliminating the bad makes the Book good. The problem that this animated show resolves—how to square

God's command to Israel to destroy the Canaanites with expectations that the Bible is good—is a common one that Bible-redeemers must tackle. This work becomes especially important when strident Bible-rejectors indict the Bible as a violent book. Eradicating the divinely directed death instead of eradicating the Canaanites is a convenient and economical solution. But while purple slushies may satisfy literal thirst, or even a thirst for fun if that's one's thing, they will not satisfy Bible readers, whether insiders or outsiders to Christianity, who attend closely to the text of their printed Bibles.

Enter the business of Bible benevolence—the intellectual, rhetorical, and moral work of rendering the Bible the Good Book. Such labor is often accomplished through clever use of building materials and production techniques spanning the gamut from strategic translation and definition to historical contextualization and creative invention. Bible benevolence is not the exclusive domain of any group in particular. Lots of people are invested in this project, across religious traditions, denominations, educational backgrounds, and the political spectrum.[22] Almost anyone who reads a Bible devotionally, even privately, is engaged in a Bible benevolence project. Any time debates populate the national news wherein commentators argue about "what the Bible actually says" about an issue, the Bible's goodness is at stake. In the wake of SCOTUS's overturn of *Roe v. Wade* in 2022, for example, both progressives and conservatives argued fervently and earnestly about what the Bible says about abortion. The thing all these Bible readers could agree on is that, when it comes to developing and defending one's views, the Good Book is a good resource.

White evangelical Protestants, a subset of religious adherents who render the Bible the Good Book, have risen prominently to public scrutiny and academic analysis in recent years because of their outsize political influence in the United

States.[23] In a time of broad national reckoning with systemic harms such as racism and sexism, white evangelicals in the US have labored steadfastly to commend their Bible as an authoritative guide that—ever the Good Book—provides liberty and justice for all. White evangelical Protestants have publicly engaged in a series of creative negotiations to square a commitment to the Bible as an unassailable good with historical realities and biblical contents that could pose a challenge to the Bible's benevolence. It is now difficult to deny, for example, that white Christians historically mobilized the Bible to support institutions that are now near-universally condemned, including slavery and racial segregation.[24] Bible benevolence projects in this vein must simultaneously redeem the Bible-redeemers themselves, as they put themselves on the side of Bible wars (and military wars) that contemporary society deems the moral one. The fruits of such labor frequently take the form of books and other print media, which is the arena through which evangelicals in the US have long forged, publicized, and protected their religious authority.[25]

THE SCRIPT OF BIBLE BENEVOLENCE

White evangelical Bible-redeemers have a standard, if not official, set of Bible benevolence moves they employ to address the violence of the biblical conquest of Canaan.[26] Book after book, blog post after blog post, they all tackle the nature and extent of the violence, the context of the violence, and the motivations behind the violence in order to make the Bible's conquest narratives more palatable to modern readers. This set of common rhetorical tactics can be called, for short, a script.[27] The arguments in the script do not always appear in the same order, with the same language, or with the same tone—but the basic lines are generally the same. Significantly, the claims in the script cannot all be true at the same time. Fascinatingly, apologists present them as though they are. Rather than accept a paradox that the Good Book is bad sometimes, Bible benevolence apologists create different, more elaborate paradoxes in which a whole system of competing and even contradictory notions must be held simultaneously. What can never be in the script is that the Bible is potentially flawed. Further, while apologists present their arguments as reasonable and historically-sound, the script does not follow the rules of logic or standard practices of historical reconstruction—because neither of those is providing the actual rules Bible benevolence laborers are following. Biblicism is.

The white evangelical Bible benevolence script presents the biblical conquest violence as both time-bound and timeless. Arguments move quietly, if not smoothly, between these depending on which is more advantageous for the benevolence work. The violence is time-bound, for example, when Bible-redeemers justify the conquest by highlighting that it only happened once, and only to a limited number of people. "Most of the violent battles initiated by God occur during one generation," writes one apologist.[28] The violence of the conquest is time-bound, too, when apologists suggest that a better understanding of the historical context promises to help modern readers with modern moral sensibilities about killing make sense of the Bible's conquest. Antiquity was violent, they reason. A contemporary expectation that the Bible should not be violent will inevitably be met with disappointment. "Warfare was a way of life—and often a matter of survival—in the ancient Near East," writes one apologist as a way of explaining the mass death.[29]

The violence is time-bound, further, when Bible-redeemers reckon it as unique not merely to antiquity but specifically to one moment in the ancient biblical story, or the ancient history of Israel. The conquest killing was not precedent-setting, neither repeated nor repeatable. It was never intended to be, in the words of one Bible redeemer, "a permanent fixture in Israel's story."[30] The "Yahweh warfare," he goes on, "wasn't the standard for other stages in Israel's history."[31] Relegating the uncomfortable killing to a single instance is intended to make the violence feel more palatable. "God was ordering" the battles and "encouraging violence," another apologist puts it, "for a specific situation during a specific time period."[32] God is not a serial killer. He only did it once.

But, also, he would—and he might—do it again. The Bible benevolence script frames the violence of the biblical conquest as simultaneously time*less*. It wasn't just the Canaanites who were the targets of divine wrath and violence in the Bible. God punished Israel too. And he threatened other nations as well (in, for example, Amos 1–2). Even as apologists narrow the scope of the violence by limiting the number of people affected and confining the chronological relevance, they simultaneously mobilize a defense of God that hinges on expanding the scope of the violence. "The very language of 'dedication to destruction/ the ban [*herem*]'," one apologist writes, "could be applied equally to Israel as well as to a Canaanite city (Deut. 13:16)."[33] Apologists make this point as a way of saving the biblical deity from charges of race-based violence. "These battles were not based on ethnicity," one Bible-redeemer writes, "so this is not 'genocide'."[34] The Canaanites were not killed as a result of their ethnic identity, since God also threatened Israel, his own people.[35] Israel too faced divine violence, often framed as exile rather than exter-mination, when they deserved it. God threatened everyone. He is an equal opportunity punisher. God is not a racist killer. He will kill anyone.

Moderns can feel better about the violence, then, because it was relegated to one specific historical moment—but also not. This script simultaneously makes the conquest violence, interpreted as divine punishment, repeatable. In fact, Bible apologists who marshal the time-bound-violence argument frequently go on to suggest or imply that it might happen again today. One writer warns: "we moderns shouldn't think that severe divine judgment was only for biblical times, as though God no longer judges nations today."[36] "We may resemble the Canaanites more than we realize," he suggests ominously.

The divine violence in the Bible may be both time-bound and timeless, limited and expansive, unique and replicable, but it can never be random.[37] In Bible benevolence projects, purposed killing is obviously preferable to other types of killing. Articulating God's motivations for commanding the killing further helps Bible-redeemers temper the trouble of the text. God only commanded the annihilation of the Canaanites because the Canaanite victims deserved it, or because he was protecting Israel, or because it was part of a more long-range plan to save everyone in the world, including—no one really appreciates the irony—the Canaanites. When the victim-blaming motivation takes center stage, the Canaanites become the target of severe invective as interpreters describe them as so morally corrupt that any modern reader should understand why they had to go.[38] They were "cancerously immoral."[39] They sacrificed their children, they had weird sex, and they did not stop it and start worshipping Israel's God when they had the chance.[40] They were worth targeting. Moderns are expected to be more comfortable with their divinely directed deaths because they were *really bad people*. God is not an indiscriminate killer. He only does it in service of an agenda.

When the script expands on the proposed divine agenda, Bible-redeemers assert that it was not the badness of the people but rather of their behavior that solicited divine violence. The Canaanites themselves were not the true target, by this logic. They were just collateral damage in God's quest to eliminate behaviors he did not accept. "The conquest," suggests one writer, "was more about ending the Canaanites' religious and cultural practices than ending their lives."[41] "The problem wasn't the people," he goes on, "but idolatry." With this move, the violence becomes acceptable because God had good intentions: he was protecting the Israelites from Canaanite practices that might lead them astray. The battles in Joshua functioned as "part of God's plan to cleanse the land of evil practices and push back the dark spiritual powers that had enslaved the people of Canaan."[42] The people were not the point. Yet if the people were just collateral damage, why would apologists spill so much ink describing how terrible they must have been? The answer must be that doing so makes them *acceptable* collateral damage.

The Bible benevolence script further alternates between reckoning the biblical conquest violence as real and thoroughgoing and pitching the violence either as not real or as exaggerated. When they explain the violence by defending God's motivations, the killing must be real. Men, women, and children all died. If the deity's goal was to protect Israel from influences deemed corrupting, or to clear the land for Israel to make good on his word and set in motion events that would eventually benefit the world (except for the dead Canaanites?), then God *did* command their utter annihilation. (This would be true whether or not the Israelites completely obeyed God's command, which, as apologists rightly point out, the biblical text itself contests.) When it comes to evaluating whether such violence is morally palatable, apologists switch to downplay the violence as murder of real people. "God's commands to Israel," as one writer frames it, were "to wipe out Canaan's idols and false, immoral worship" as part of a cosmic battle in which God fought otherworldly "dark powers."[43] Spiritualizing the violence makes it easier to overlook actual deaths. The identity of the people who died is very important, because they must be presented as so bad as to deserve punishment—but the people who died are simultaneously insignificant as people. A win-win argument for the Bible-redeemers makes for a lose-lose situation for the Canaanites who died: they get excoriated as terrible people so that others will understand why they had to die, but then their deaths do not really count. It is outside the bounds of the white evangelical Bible benevolence script to empathize with the Canaanites.[44]

The same apologists offer arguments that render the biblical violence unreal, or less real. Apologists play with translations and definitions to make this argument, recruiting supporting material from outside the Bible, including archaeological records, insights from historical criticism, and literary remains of other ancient civilizations. After explaining why the conquest violence was necessary, the script goes on to suggest that the conquest was not actually quite as violent as a "surface reading" of the Bible would indicate. Israel was exaggerating their victory in a form of ancient "trash talk." This argument that relies on strategically comparing the Bible to other ancient literature in which other people groups bragged about military conquests.[45] At the same time, the Bible-redeemers do not consider that the biblical descriptions of Canaanites' bad behavior might also be exaggerated or otherwise conditioned by conventions of polemic. That cannot be part of the script because it would undercut the reason the Canaanite deaths are tolerable.

Or perhaps, Bible-redeemers argue, God meant something other than "destroy" when he gave the Israelites commands about how to execute the conquest. One apologist asserts, for example, that "phrases like 'completely destroy' (often the Hebrew words *herem* or *ban*, which are translated into English as 'completely destroy') didn't actually mean completely destroy as we think of it today."[46] Perhaps God meant "drive out" when he said "destroy," since clearing the land was the intended purpose of the killing anyway.[47] God is a killer in the way that a winning basketball team is when contemporary sports fans say one team *annihilated* the other.[48]

Each of these arguments depends on extrabiblical evidence. Yet it is a standard part of the script—so common one would think it required—to give the Bible itself credit.[49] One Bible redeemer shares of his own personal experience: "In digging deeper into these verses and studying the violence of the Bible, I have maintained my faith and love in God. In fact, somewhat ironically, it has been in studying these violent passages that I have come to understand even more of God's great love, patience, and compassion."[50] "Knowing that the difficult parts have not been edited out" helps him to "trust the Bible more."[51] The violence is necessary for a different reason in this case—to demonstrate the truthfulness, and therefore benevolence, of the Bible.

Another means of reckoning the violence as less real is to posit that only men, and specifically military and political leaders, were killed. Biblical writers exaggerated not only the destruction but also the population. Apologists suggest in this vein that Canaanite "cities" were more like military outposts than centers of civilian life full of women, children, and other non-combatants. In this accounting, Rahab, the Canaanite woman who cooperates with Israelite spies and thereby ensures her own survival (Josh 2), becomes the lone woman in Jericho because she ran an inn at the military outpost.[52] "So when Israel 'utterly destroys' a city like Jericho or Ai," suggests one writer, "we should picture a military fort being taken over—not a civilian massacre."[53] He envisions God's violence as "pulling down the Great Wall of China, not demolishing Beijing" or "taking out the Pentagon, not New York City."[54] God is not a mass killer. He only kills influential people.

At least one white evangelical apologist follows up this argument with a base-covering return to the moral culpability defense, in case Canaanite women really were there after all.[55] "Women may not have been combatants," he states, "but they were hardly innocent."[56] The evidence he provides—as often happens in white evangelical Bible benevolence projects— has to do with sex. Women were prostitutes, he observes. Pointing to Numbers 25, further, he enjoins his reader to "notice how readily the Midianite women sought to seduce Israelite men."[57] The passage to which he points describes, disapprovingly, sexual relationships between Israelite men and Midianite women. But the Bible passage does not blame the women. Rather, Israelite men are the initiators: "While Israel was staying at Shittim, the people began to have sexual relations with the women of Moab" (Num 25:1 NRSVUE); or, more viscerally: "While Israel lived in Shittim, the people began to whore with the daughters of Moab" (ESV). It takes an extra level of victim blaming to recruit *this* story as evidence that Canaanite women deserved to die. It is telling, perhaps, that Numbers 25 culminates in a moment of biblical violence that these apologists feel no need to explain. A Midianite woman named Cozbi, whom an Israelite man has brought before his family, is impaled to death by another Israelite man who sticks a spear through her belly at God's behest. Some biblical violence is naturalized among white evangelical Bible readers—particularly violence against women. What a Bible benevolence script leaves out is just as important as what it includes.

GOOD GRIEF

In recent years, though, many white evangelical Christians in the US have indeed advanced Bible benevolence projects that make the Good Book good for women.[58] They seek to redeem biblical passages that sanction violence against women and those that ground oppression of women in many forms and fora. The Christian Old Testament is a big topic of discussion. Usually Bible-as-good-for-women redeemers make distinctions between what they see as normative, and therefore prescriptive, and what they see as merely descriptive in the text.[59] The troubling gang rape and subsequent dismemberment of the woman in Judges 19, for example, becomes easily explicable with this benevolence strategy because the Bible redeemer can say that the narrative is not setting a pattern that people should, or do, follow. What the men did was obviously bad, the logic goes, but the Bible is not bad just because it narrates it.

In fact, Christians have a grand narrative, which they locate in the Bible itself, that invites evil content while simultaneously explaining it: what is usually called "the Fall," that is, Adam's and Eve's disobedience in the Garden of Eden that sets off a human rebellion against God, leading to their separation from God and plunge into sin. With the Fall, Christians get sin as a sorting device. They can ascribe bad things, even in the Bible, to bad people in a bad world that is made bad because of sin. In this paradigm, the violence against the unnamed woman in Judges 19 is not only acceptable but expected. Dinah in Genesis 34 gets the same treatment. "Dinah's story is a case study," writes one Bible redeemer, "in the issue of oppression between the sexes in God's fallen world."[60] The Fall introduced inequality. Sin is what explains, too, why slavery and polygamy are in the Bible. "We see," writes one Bible apologist, "a world of pain and mess due to human pride, ego, power, and control—everything that was beautiful in the original creation is reversed."[61]

Bad stories—the worse, the better—are necessary for the grand narrative of the Good Book to mean much at all.

"Good" is a relative term. It exists in definitional relationship to what is bad. These troubling passages about women are recruited as evidence for how much the world needs Jesus. "Many stories simply *reinforce our need for a Savior*," one Bible apologist writes.[62] "Stories such as the rape and dismemberment of the concubine of an unnamed Levite in Judges 19," she goes on, "reinforce the Israelites' warped sense of right and wrong, inability to be righteous on their own, and need for salvation through Christ."

The sin-and-salvation paradigm becomes a mechanism by which Bible-redeemers can create standards for divine behavior in the Old Testament that do not match up with contemporary ethical expectations. Anytime Bible-redeemers claim, for example, that the ancient Israelite laws that God gave in the Bible were good for the ancients even if they offend contemporary moral sensibilities, they are assessing God with a meager benchmark. The law commands a rapist to marry the woman he assaulted, for example. In this day and age, seeing this as a positive rather than as a doubling of trauma, or as a denial of the woman's agency, requires lowering the bar for what counts as good. Apologists make the Bible benevolent on this point by viewing God as working within "fallen" human systems that are marred by sin. God gave this order "to *protect* the woman."[63] "Without marriage," writes one apologist, "she would likely end up neglected and impoverished."[64] Sin as a concept allows Bible-redeemers to envision a bad more bad, often mapped onto other ancient peoples by negative comparison, and then favorably compare God's command to that bad. To be good, the Good Book has to be only incrementally better than the bad they envision. The white evangelical Bible benevolence script cannot tolerate wondering whether the bar is too low.

For such Bible-redeemers, God's revelation in the New Testament fixes any problem. It is a new era, an era with a solution to sin. *Jesus* fixes the problem. With Jesus, the Book is always Good—but only because Jesus, too, is a product of the Bible benevolence business.

"Above all else, we must search the attitudes & practices of Christ Jesus himself toward women. HE is our Lord. He had women followers!"

—Beth Moore[1]

"Whether it's conscious or not, we want women to take care, but we want men to take charge."

—Therese Huston[2]

TWO

Making Jesus Good

Sacrificing Women for the Sake of the Bible

The latest installation of the conservative Christian *God's Not Dead* film franchise (2021) repeats a formula that has worked well for the series. Caricatured enemies persecute US Christians. Christians defend themselves. Their detractors do not prevail.[3] The 2014 original film, in which a college student successfully challenged a belligerent atheist college professor's assertion that "God is dead," was a surprise box office hit, pulling in $9 million on opening weekend and nearly $65 million in total. In the fourth installation, the perceived threat is no longer to an individual in a university classroom. This time, persecution suddenly enters a home in the heartland, ultimately sending Christians to the nation's capital in a quest to defend themselves from secularizing onslaught. At stake, fundamentally, is the Bible's reputation.

A dour social services representative knocks on the door of a white Christian family in Hope Springs, Arkansas, performing an unannounced inspection of their church-affiliated homeschooling co-op. She observes Pastor Dave, the series' hero, teaching students with the Bible as a textbook. After she reports the co-op for failing to conform to district norms, a local family court judge finds that if they refuse to modify their curriculum, they must enroll the children in an accredited school or face fines, jail time, and maybe even loss of custody. Determined to fight, the group of parents travels with Pastor Dave to Washington, DC, to testify at a congressional subcommittee hearing and argue their case. The primary issue at hand shifts from parental rights to religious freedom to the respectability of Christianity in the US and, finally, to the goodness of the Bible.

An antagonistic congresswoman challenges the group by challenging the Bible. It is intolerant and oppressive, she suggests, asking pointedly, "surely you recognize how offensively patriarchal and sexist the Bible is?" Pastor Dave fires back: "Is that a legitimate question? Or is that just your chance at a sound bite?" Auditors laugh until a gavel sounds. The congresswoman cries, "Excuse me?" in disbelief. And then Pastor Dave gets serious. "Considering the time when it was written," he tells her, "the Bible is one of the most pro-feminist documents in history."

One could be forgiven for thinking it was a legitimate question, of course. The Bible famously contains disturbing stories of violence against women (Gen 34, Judg 19, Rev 2). The Bible's androcentric commands frequently assume women to be the sexual property of men. Numbers 5, for example, outlines a torture routine through which a suspicious man can determine if his woman has been entered by another man. The Ten Commandments presume an audience of men. The Bible says that women should be silent, in two different passages in the Pauline epistles. The Good Book is not short on content for Bible-redeemers to redeem.

Yet Pastor Dave faces the congresswoman's critique with such confidence, with such conviction that she is ridiculous, that viewers might miss the rhetorical work that enables him to claim the Bible as superlatively "pro-feminist." Seven words, quickly delivered: *"Considering the time when it was written,"* he says. Not even in the evangelical Christian fantasy world of *God's Not Dead* can the Bible be represented as obviously good for women without qualification. Pastor Dave cannot get around the fact that the Bible was written in antiquity, and times have changed.

"Jesus Loves the Ladies"

Sexism is not cool anymore, and US evangelicals know it. In a time when misogyny sparks scrutiny, outrage, and exposés, anyone who abuses or disdains women at the very least has to call it something else. Sexism and misogyny must be rooted out or rebranded. US evangelicals in the Bible benevolence business must render the Bible good for women if the Bible is to be good for everyone. In an era of #MeToo and #ChurchToo, in the wake of revelations of rampant sex abuse and cover-ups in the Southern Baptist Convention, in a time when evangelical sex scandals attract national media attention, white evangelicals are keenly aware that distancing the Good Book from charges of misogyny is essential.[4] The story of white evangelicalism and gender is ripe for redemption projects, in which Bible-redeemers creatively defend the Bible from charges of harm.[5]

White evangelicals in the US are internally divided when it comes to normative claims around the place of women in the church, society, families, and the world—and therefore as to what counts as harm to women. Evangelicals typically identify themselves as "complementarian" or "egalitarian" and then argue with each other—not about whether the Bible is good for women but rather what *good* really means. The intensity of the internal argument means they argue less with outsiders, even as the very nature of Bible benevolence work is to render the Bible good for everyone, including outsiders whom evangelicals (as their very name implies) would be happy to evangelize. In other words, the internal conversation has consequences for outsiders, even as evangelicals for the most part aim their arguments about the Bible and women at each other.

Their debate turns on whether the Bible authorizes or resists patriarchy as a good way to organize society.[6] So-called complementarians read the Bible and conclude that men and women are existentially equal but designed for separate, complementary roles within a patriarchal hierarchy. So-called egalitarians push back with biblical warrants for their conviction that women should be accorded the same degree of authority, decision-making, and access to leadership opportunities that men have. For complementarians, the Bible mandates patriarchal social order, which in turn must be good for women because it is biblical. For egalitarians, who reject patriarchal social order as normative, the Bible resists or outright upends patriarchy.

Those who read the Bible as enforcing patriarchal hierarchy must defend patriarchy from criticism that sees its social order as bad for women. To save the Bible, they save patriarchy, disentangling both from the negative cultural valences associated with the word "misogyny." Harms against women, in this schema, are conceived not as the result of biblical patriarchy but rather as a result of its misapplication or its absence altogether. Patriarchy, properly practiced, protects women. The patriarchal Bible, properly applied, is good for women. The Bible, therefore, is not misogynistic. Members of the egalitarian camp, by contrast, typically argue along lines that the Bible does not denigrate or demean women because the Bible does not normalize patriarchal social order. Patriarchy is a condition from which God wants humans redeemed, and the Bible, when read properly with the right egalitarian theological and historiographical controls, is the primary evidence. The Bible, therefore, is not misogynistic. These Bible-is-good-for-women redemption projects forge diverging paths toward the same destination, even as their practitioners argue bitterly with one another about which path is the best way to get there.

There is one major intersection, though, and it's the Sunday School answer: Jesus. Virtually all white evangelical Bible benevolence scripts offer readings of Jesus in the New Testament gospels that see him as a special ally of women. Complementarians point to Jesus as pro-women as they defend their men-over-women hierarchy from charges of sexism, while egalitarians point to Jesus as pro-women in the course of arguing, against complementarians, that women should not be excluded from positions of leadership.

North Carolina pastor Kevin DeYoung, to take an example of a patriarchy-reputation-manager, claims Jesus as both patriarchal and anti-misogynist. DeYoung writes for conversative Christian outlet *The Gospel Coalition* that "Jesus boldly affirmed [women's] worth and gladly benefited from their vital ministry."[7] DeYoung points out that Jesus speaks to women, like the Samaritan woman at the well in John 4. Jesus heals women, including Peter's mother-in-law in Mark 1. Jesus meets women's needs, such as those of the Syrophoenician woman in Mark 7 and the woman with a flow of blood in Matthew 9. The gospels depict Jesus, further, accepting financial support from women. "Underlying Jesus's ministry," DeYoung argues, "was the radical assumption that women have enormous value and purpose." But there is no biblical evidence, for DeYoung, that such affirmations of women empower them to be leaders or equal partners. Complementarian Bible-redeemers are pro-Jesus, pro-women, and pro-patriarchy.

Baylor University professor Beth Allison Barr, author of the best-selling book *The Making of Biblical Womanhood* and staunch egalitarian advocate, argues the opposite: Jesus is pro-women because he is *anti*-patriarchal.[8] She equates "complementarianism" with patriarchy and claims Jesus as evidence that patriarchy is not what God wants for women. She asserts that the modern evangelical "biblical woman-hood" movement that constrains opportunities for women is antithetical to "the freedom offered by Jesus."[9] Oppression of women is "contrary to everything Jesus did and taught."[10] Barr points to Jesus's interactions with women in the gospels, including the Samaritan woman at the well and Mary of Bethany, as biblical subversions of traditional gender roles.[11] For Barr, the subjugation of women is unbiblical. Christians should not, she warns, "model our treatment of women after the world around us instead of the world Jesus shows us is possible."[12]

In his recent book *How (Not) to Read the Bible: Making Sense of the Anti-Women, Anti-Science, Pro-Violence, Pro-Slavery and Other Crazy-Sounding Parts of Scripture*, California pastor Dan Kimball goes further. He makes a bold claim about the origins of modern gender equity expecta-tions. "The world we live in today, with our cultural values of equality for both men and women," he writes, is "the product of Jesus and his followers."[13] Readers of the New Testament gospels, he goes on, "see Jesus striving to change the culture he lived in through the way he treated women—with respect, dignity, and equality."[14] In her book *Jesus Feminist*, to take another example, popular author Sarah Bessey writes:

> After years of reading the Gospels and the full canon of Scripture, here is, very simply, what I learned about Jesus and the ladies: he loves us. He loves us. On our own terms. He treats us as equals to men around him; he listens; he does not belittle; he honors us; he challenges us; he teaches us; he includes us—calls us all beloved.[15]

Jesus loves the ladies. On each of these Bible benevolence journeys, Jesus is a rest stop.

Resting is not a helpful description for what these interpreters are doing, though. Reading Jesus in the New Testament gospels as a special friend of or advocate for women requires creative rhetorical and historiographical work. It requires Bible benevolence labor. When it comes to making Jesus good for women, the work involved is harder to see, owing in no small part to the pristine reputation that Jesus enjoys in popular parlance, culture, and beyond. Calling Jesus compassionate, kind, and welcoming to all-comers does not raise many eyebrows, even among outsiders to Christianity.

Bringing the benevolence work to light requires pushing past Jesus's popular reputation. Seeing how the Bible redemption script operates to make the New Testament Jesus good for women requires asking different questions.

Is Jesus a Misogynist?

White evangelical Bible benevolence scripts work with a strategic definition of misogyny. For those engaged in Bible benevolence projects, misogyny is found where the misogynists are. And misogynists are woman-haters. This definition is not *wrong* so to speak, particularly if one is strident about etymology. After all, the word "misogyny" is built from the Greek words for "hatred" (*misos*) and "woman" (*gunē*). Defining misogyny simply as woman-hating makes it easy to locate, easy to decry, and easy to demarcate as an attitude unworthy of oneself or one's heroes. This narrow understanding of misogyny makes a Bible benevolence script easy to write: Jesus did not hate women, and neither do the evangelicals who follow him. Defining misogyny as woman-hating puts the bad in a box. With Jesus in a separate box, there is no overlap. But the Bible benevolence script does not rely on the claim that the Bible, along with Jesus on its pages, is merely *not*-misogynistic. A standard line in the script is that the Good Book is *anti*-misogynistic. If the Bible does not hate women, Bible-redeemers reason, it is anti-misogynistic and therefore good for women.

Attention to recent conversations about misogyny in the field of moral philosophy reveals just how narrow, and therefore useful for the success of Bible benevolence labor, this definition is. The work of philosopher Kate Manne in particular provides valuable analytical tools for thinking both more expansively and more precisely about misogyny and its effects on women. In her book *Down Girl: The Logic of Misogyny*, Manne disentangles the words "patriarchy," "sexism," and "misogyny."[16] Manne does not write about the Bible or Christianity or religion, but her conceptual paradigm applied to New Testament gospel texts opens up new questions and possibilities that are foreclosed when Bible readers use these terms interchangeably.

In Manne's schema, patriarchy is a social system. Sexism is an ideology, a belief system justifying patriarchal social order.[17] Misogyny is the environment women encounter that regulates their behavior within patriarchal norms.[18] In contrast to patriarchy, misogyny is not a social order.

In contrast to sexism, misogyny is not a belief system. It is not made of ideas. Misogyny is not, for example, a *belief* that women are lesser than men or that women should be subject to men or that women should be paid less or hurt more. Misogyny, further, is not made of emotions. It is not a *feeling* of animosity toward women. Misogyny is not something that is perpetrated, by men or anyone else.[19] Instead, it is something experienced—by women and girls.[20]

Manne describes misogyny as "the law enforcement branch" of patriarchy.[21] The environment women and girls face within a patriarchal social system rewards them for playing by the rules of patriarchy, for complying with gendered expectations of their behavior. Misogyny punishes women and girls who do not comply with patriarchal norms, disincentivizing them from stepping outside the bounds.[22] Misogyny is like a shock collar, teaching women the boundaries of acceptable behavior.[23]

The primary norms to which women are held to account, Manne argues, have to do with gendered "goods."[24] Goods that are conceived to properly belong to men include, for example, status, authority, and power; entitlement to sex; claims to knowledge; prestige, recognition, and a positive reputation. Misogyny punishes women who encroach on such territory, as women who "take" or try to "take" such goods are frequently blamed, belittled, (de)sexualized, vilified, silenced, and/or mocked.[25] Such women are often portrayed as attention-seeking, drama-bringing, over-sexed, or under-sexed.[26]

Feminine goods, by contrast, are those that a patriarchal society assigns to women, who are fundamentally conceived as *givers*. Women are expected to give to men, and in particular to designated men or dominant men within a patriarchal hierarchy wherein men compete with other men for power. These goods include such things as respect, sex, domestic labor, care, nurturing, and reproductive labor.[27] Misogyny is what rewards women for according such goods to the proper man or men. Misogyny punishes women who accord these goods to other women, or to the wrong man or men.[28] Misogyny regulates behavior by sorting women into compliant—good—women and non-compliant—bad—women. "Good" women learn not to encroach on masculine domains, not to take from men what is properly considered theirs, and further not to withhold what they are expected to owe to the right man or men. Misogyny thereby constrains possibilities for women and deprives them of goods to which they actually should be entitled.[29]

With this definition, misogyny can exist without misogynists.[30] Misogyny exists without any particular individual or group hating women. As Manne points out, a major benefit of her definition is that misogyny becomes empirically recognizable through attention to the experiences of women and girls. Identifying misogyny does not entail the impossible task of reading someone's mind to assess whether or not they hate women. Nor does it require scrutinizing behavior to determine someone's motivations. Motivations are immaterial.[31] The effect, and particularly the regulatory effect, on women is what matters most. Hostility, unequal opportunities, and behavioral regulation faced by women and girls can be taken seriously without pointing out any particular woman-hater. The experiences of women take center stage.

Reading misogyny not as hatred of women but as the "law enforcement" branch of patriarchy that regulates women's behavior transforms the questions available to pose to the New Testament regarding its portrayal of Jesus. Not "Does Jesus hate women and girls?" but rather "Does Jesus participate in a social environment in which the behavior of women and girls is regulated by patriarchal norms?" Not "Does Jesus believe in the full humanity of women?" but rather "Do Jesus's words and actions direct women's humanity within patriarchally-conditioned expectations?" Not "Does

Jesus treat women as able to think and reason?" but rather "To what ends are women's thinking and reasoning ultimately put?" Not "Does Jesus value women?" but rather "What are they valued *for*?" When women interact with Jesus, does their encounter with him empower them or police them? When women interact with Jesus, are they constrained by or forced to resist male entitlement to power, to knowledge, to control of their bodies? What do the women in this man's world face? What is expected of them? Of their behavior, their labor, their lives?

Reading Jesus in the New Testament with these questions in mind reveals just how much work Bible-redeemers have to do to construct Jesus as anti-misogynistic. Doing so reveals that Bible-redeemers read Jesus in the New Testament gospels with "good goggles," special lenses that help them transform what is on the page into benevolence. The Jesus they describe far exceeds the textual raw materials of Bible stories. Interpreters who read Jesus as an ally to women are being *very creative*, even if they do not realize or acknowledge it. They combine such creative interpretation with a limited definition of "misogyny" to conclude that the Bible is anti-misogynistic.

Bible-redeemers take for granted that they themselves are not misogynistic either. Yet perhaps the greatest irony is that as white evangelicals labor to disentangle Jesus and the Bible from misogyny, they themselves perpetuate misogyny. Thinking with Manne's definition of misogyny allows for the possibility that misogyny can thrive in biblical interpretations even when the interpreters are not woman-haters. Interpretations of biblical texts can be deemed misogynistic without simultaneously accusing the interpreter of being a misogynist. Regardless of whether any interpreter in question feels disdain for women and girls, their interpretation could function to regulate the behavior of women within a patriarchal order. Sometimes interpreters who self-describe as feminist or pro-women produce misogynistic interpretations. As they baptize the misogyny in the biblical text, they put serious limits on what can be thought of as *good* for women—and they define what *good women* must do and not do to remain good. Along the way, white evangelical Bible benevolence projects sacrifice women to save the Bible.

Jesus without Good Goggles

The earliest account of Jesus in the New Testament is the gospel of Mark. Without "good goggles," this gospel can very naturally be read as a story featuring a powerful man jostling for power with other powerful men. The Jesus of Mark is obsessed with demonstrating and exerting power within a patriarchal system organized by hierarchy. Reading without "good goggles" shows that women in Mark's gospel in no way have equal access to markers of Jesus's power, including healing and teaching. Women's lives and labor are directed toward supporting the interests of men, and women who comply are rewarded. Those who do not are punished. Women in Jesus's orbit work harder, get less, and suffer more. The earliest Jesus available in the Bible does not combat or transform patriarchy. He masters it.

Once Jesus enters the scene in the gospel of Mark, he almost immediately collects followers (1:16–20) in a hierarchical relationship with himself at the top.[32] In quick succession Jesus exorcises a demon from a man in a Capernaum synagogue and relieves Simon's mother-in-law from a fever. Observers in the narrative interpret Jesus's actions as demonstrations of power. They are amazed, specifically at Jesus's *authority* (1:27). Jesus is competing with others—and winning. His number of disciples grows. Jesus chooses to associate with people who are weak (2:15–17) and deferential

(3:31–35)—those who pose little threat to his consolidation of power and platform-building.[33] In one instance, Jesus rejects his own mother and brothers, family members who have sought him out, in favor of the people currently sitting around him, the ones quietly listening (3:31–35). Jesus prefers supplicants.

Jesus becomes increasingly famous despite his mysterious attempts to silence both demons and people. He continues to heal—as much as to demonstrate his power to others as for any other reason. His treatment of the so-called "paralyzed man" in Mark 2 fits this mold. In this passage, a group of men goes to extreme lengths to solicit Jesus to heal their friend. They even remove the roof of a home and lower the man down in front of Jesus, hoping against hope that Jesus will heal him. Jesus praises the friends' "faith" but then does not heal the man. Instead, he does something that thousands of years of theological discourse have smoothed over for modern gospel readers: Jesus says to the man, "Child, your sins are forgiven."[34]

Readers accustomed to a sin-forgiveness discourse might not pause long enough to appreciate that Jesus has done something in this moment that no one asked him to do. Neither the man nor his friends have sought forgiveness. Whereas the man's friends see paralysis as the problem and healing as the solution, Jesus transforms the problem into something else and then fashions himself the problem-solver of *that* problem. Jesus demeans the friend of these supplicants to advance his own authority. Some observers of this event in the gospel narrative recognize what is at stake. "Some of the scribes" began to think that Jesus's words constituted blasphemy since they saw his offer of forgiveness as usurping a role reserved for their deity (Mark 2:10). They see Jesus's words as a power move. Only in this moment—so that he can counter his doubters—does Jesus comply with the pleas of the man's friends. Jesus heals here to demonstrate his own power in front of detractors. He pulls a similar move later in Mark's story when he heals a man's "withered hand" in an act of anger because "the Pharisees" did not answer his question about healing on the sabbath (3:1–5). Jesus heals the man to show his critics—his competition—what is what. He heals the man not for the man's sake but for his own.

Jesus later performs a miracle so that he can ensure that a crowd of eager auditors around him will not disperse. Details in the narrative of Mark 6, a story known popularly in shorthand as "The Feeding of the Five Thousand," make it possible to rename the passage "Jesus Miraculously Multiplies Food in Bid to Keep Fans." When the crowd coalesces despite Jesus's quest for seclusion, he sees an opportunity. They are "sheep without a shepherd," and he steps in to herd them around himself. When his disciples, attuned to the impending mealtime, urge him to send the crowd home, Jesus obviates the need to disband them by turning two fish and five loaves into enough food for everyone.

Concerns around authority, power, and hierarchy dictate not only the context of Jesus's teaching but also its content. His much-lauded claim that the sabbath was made for humans rather than they for it culminates with Jesus asserting himself as "lord" *even* of the sabbath. He could have left it with the part that empowers people, but he instead pushes on to make a privilege-laden claim about his own dominance. Jesus further creates and reinforces hierarchy when he tells enigmatic parables and then reveals their meaning only to a select few in his inner circle (4:10–20). Even as Jesus confounds most of his auditors intentionally, he takes no responsibility for their confusion. In his famous "parable of the sower," Jesus likens listeners who do not understand to soil that cannot grow a seed. The soil is either too exposed to hungry birds, or too rocky for roots, or too thorny for a seed to thrive—but it is never the fault of the sower. Jesus does not consider that a seed might grow into a flourishing plant were the sower to cultivate, protect, nourish, and tend. He teaches crowds into confusion, and then only offers explanations when he is alone with his close circle of companions:

> With many such parables he spoke the word to them as they were able to hear it; he did not speak to them except in parables, but he explained everything in private to his disciples. (Mark 4:33–34)

The solution to Jesus's mystery is only for the chosen disciples.

Combined with the secrecy motif in Mark's gospel, Jesus's choice of all men for his inner circle of secret-worthy disciples creates a series of situations where only men are present. Women in Mark are systematically excluded from important events, spaces, and scenes. Since women were not among the Twelve, for example, women were not among those given "authority over the unclean spirits" (6:7). Women were not there to see Jesus walk on water (6:45). Since Jesus and his disciples were in the middle of a body of water, away from others, no one except the disciples on the boat had even a chance to participate. Women were not there, further, for the transfiguration. The narrator reports that "Jesus took with him Peter and James and John, and led them up a high mountain apart, by themselves" (9:2). To Jesus and Peter and James and John are then added Moses and Elijah. Men only. And then a voice marking Jesus with a masculine relational term: Son. As they come down the mountain, Jesus orders the men not to tell anyone else for now. Since "they kept the matter to themselves" (9:10), women also did not have the opportunity to hear or know what had happened even second-hand. Further, in Mark 10:32, Jesus takes the Twelve aside to explain what will happen to him in Jerusalem, privileged information given only to men. Women were not there for the Last Supper (Mark 14). Only the Twelve had places at the table. Women were not there in the Garden of Gethsemane: "He took with him [only] Peter and James and John." (14:33). Women were not there.

Only after Jesus's arrest, trial, torture, and death by crucifixion does the narrative offer any clue that women have been following Jesus: "There were also women looking on from a distance" (15:40). From a distance indeed—the women have been so distant that they have been invisible.[35] The text goes on: "Among them were Mary Magdalene, and Mary the mother of James the younger and of Joses, and Salome. These used to follow him and provided for him when he was in Galilee; and there were many other women who had come up with him to Jerusalem" (NRSV). This near-throwaway line comes as something of a shock in narrative context.[36] *There were women there? Where?* The women's labor and support were unimportant, or perhaps just so expected of them as to be literally unremarkable. Until, that is, the narrator of Jesus's story in Mark needs them. Indeed, the narrator must mention the women here if the reader is to have any context at all for who it is who is about to discover Jesus's empty tomb in the story. Readers familiar with other New Testament gospels or with Christian tradition will bring with them memories about Mary Magdalene, one of the most recognizable gospel women, but Mark does not elaborate on her.

Mark's earliest available ending (16:8) does not resolve the disparities between women and men in Mark's gospel. It closes with women who are scared and silent. Though the white-clothed young man in the tomb has instructed them to tell Jesus's disciples that he is not there but will meet them in Galilee, the women "went out and fled from the tomb, for terror and amazement had seized them, and they said nothing to anyone, for they were afraid" (16:8). These women who supported and followed Jesus during his lifetime, who have now come to provide care for his body, were not themselves provided with the knowledge or resources they would need to overcome their fear enough to follow this final instruction. Perhaps if they had been in the secret-keeping inner circle, with spots on the boat and seats at the table, they might have felt empowered rather than terrified.

In the so-called "longer ending" of Mark's gospel, Mary Magdalene is treated to a post-resurrection appearance of Jesus.[37] But the expansion of her role in the narrative does not resolve inequality in Mark. She shares the news she is tasked to share with Jesus's disciples, though readers do not encounter words from her mouth. She is summarily dismissed: "when they heard that he was alive and had been seen by her, they would not believe it" (16:11). Jesus later appears to the Eleven and chastises them for not believing. Mary is not in the room for this scene, for the moment she might have been vindicated. It is not really a vindication of Mary, though. The narrator reports that Jesus "upbraided" the Eleven "for their lack of faith and stubbornness" (16:14) but in the very next breath, he commissions them. "Go into all the world and proclaim the good news to the whole creation," he says (16:15). Mary is not included in the commission. This is not equal opportunity evangelism. Jesus gives the men who just failed, the men who are less qualified, a job that Mary had proven she could do. The men are rewarded despite incompetence. The woman is ignored. With his men sent out, Jesus ascends to heaven without talking to Mary again.

THE BIBLE BENEVOLENCE STANDARD

It only takes one hand to count the women with whom Jesus interacts before his death in Mark's gospel. Five women, all unnamed, known popularly as Simon's mother-in-law,

Jairus's daughter, the woman with the flow of blood, the Syrophoenician woman, and the woman who anoints Jesus at Bethany. Bible benevolence scripts recruit these women for starring roles, as Bible-redeemers claim that Jesus treated women equally, even radically so. Yet, in no case does Jesus's interaction with these women free them from patriarchal expectations or redirect their labor and lives toward something other than the interests of men. White evangelical Bible-redeemers work hard to make these women into beneficiaries of great beneficence. To make Jesus's treatment of these women exemplary requires inventive historical invective and a meager accounting of what women deserve. The lenses of the "good goggles" only work when combined with standards of judgment of Jesus's behavior that imply women are lucky to get, rather than entitled to, goods automatically granted to men.

A standard line in the Bible benevolence script when it comes to Jesus's treatment of women is that Jesus was egalitarian, or pro-women, or anti-patriarchal, or feminist on account of the fact that he healed women in addition to men, rather than just men. Simon's mother-in-law, the first woman to appear in the earliest gospel, is also the first woman Jesus heals. In contrast to John the baptizer, Simon, Andrew, and sons of Zebedee James and John, the unnamed woman is identified only by her relationship to a man. Jesus never addresses her. But "he came and took her by the hand and lifted her up." The fever leaves her, but she does not leave the house: "the fever left her, and she began to serve them." Her healing is the only one that results in the healed person's service to Jesus; no man in the gospel who is healed then serves.[38] The ending of the healing of Simon's mother-in-law contrasts sharply with that of two nearby stories in which Jesus heals men. In 1:21–28 Jesus performs an exorcism in a Capernaum synagogue. "They were all amazed," the narrator reports, and "at once, his fame began to spread" (1:27, 28). In 1:40–45 Jesus heals a "leper" who then disobeys Jesus's command not to tell anyone, resulting in more spread of Jesus's fame. With Simon's mother-in-law, there is no celebration. No astonishment. No wonder. Jesus healed her. And she began to serve them.

Jesus can be "non-discriminatory" when it comes to who has access to his healing power and still operate within a patriarchal social system and perpetuate a misogynistic environment where women's behavior is expected to comply with patriarchal norms. To take a modern analogy: Women in the contemporary US ostensibly have equal access to medical care. A woman can call and make an appointment with a physician or show up at an emergency room and expect to be seen by a medical professional. Women are not barred from accessing medical care. Men *and* women can be healed. But granting women access is not enough to mitigate misogyny. Studies consistently show that on the whole, women do not receive the same quality of care as do men.[39] It is more difficult, for example, for women, and especially for women of color, to get treatment for pain. Further, even if women were to receive the same quality of medical care, that would not mitigate hostility they face or roles they are expected to play within a patriarchal social system. "Equal" access to medical care does not dismantle patriarchy or erase misogyny.

The healing of Simon's mother-in-law results in her reinsertion into a hierarchical system in which women's labor supports the interests of men. Freedom from fever is not here freedom from service to men. Her healing is rather what makes it possible for her to get out of bed and resume domestic labor for the benefit of Jesus and his disciples, all men.[40] Some redeemers of this passage who are eager to recruit it as empowering to women argue that the Greek word underlying "serve" should be translated "ministered to."[41] This translation, for such readers, places her on equal footing with men because the action she takes is ministerial.[42] In this case, the Bible benevolence script, perhaps inadvertently, normalizes a notion that women should be satisfied with work traditionally associated with women, since Simon's mother-in-law does not do anything in the narrative that is not already expected of her. Indeed, while the men Jesus has recruited voluntarily leave what they are doing to follow Jesus, Simon's mother-in-law merely resumes nonvoluntary service that she was already performing in the home.[43]

The next time Jesus interacts with a woman will not be until Mark 5, with the interwoven stories of Jairus's daughter and the woman commonly known as "the woman with a flow of blood." Jesus heals two women and enacts a double standard. Jairus, a named man, leader of the synagogue, approaches Jesus and falls at his feet. Jairus is described as requesting more than once for Jesus to heal his sick daughter, but the narrator shares his appeal only once: "My little daughter is at the point of death," Jairus says. "Come and lay your hands on her, so that she may be made well, and live." Jesus responds immediately—"So he went with him." Appeal, followed by immediate action on the part of Jesus. No hesitation. No questioning. No problem.

The action of the story is interrupted when "a woman who had been suffering from hemorrhages for twelve years" enters the scene. She takes it upon herself to reason that Jesus is the only one who can make her well, having spent all her resources on ineffective physicians. She touches Jesus's cloak, and she is made well.[44] "Immediately," Mark writes with his favorite transition, "she felt in her body that she was healed." Jesus's healing power has left him without his consent, but not without his knowledge. He knows that his power has been used by someone, but he doesn't know who has used it. He could have just continued on to Jairus's house, satisfied in the knowledge that someone sick is no longer suffering. But instead he turns to investigate, to determine who it was who touched him.

The problem, from Jesus's perspective, is that there has been an un-negotiated use of his power. In the story of Jairus, another man of equivalent or higher status than Jesus has negotiated the use of Jesus's power for healing. The woman with the flow of blood has recognized that Jesus is a conduit for divine power but has ignored the need for an intermediary to negotiate her access to that power. Jesus is confused. He does not know who has used his power. His disciples are equally confused, blaming the large crowd for their own inability to mediate access to the divine healer. They pass the buck, as they often do in Mark's narrative. Then this woman, like Jairus, falls before Jesus. In contrast to Jairus's confident approach, the woman comes to Jesus "in fear and trembling." She is afraid. She is deferential. And only then is she rewarded. Only when a woman approaches him in a way that demonstrates her submission to patriarchal authority is her access to Jesus's power affirmed.

It is unclear initially in Mark's story how Jesus is going to respond to her. He appears mad. His anger is dissipated by her throwing herself before him. She does not challenge his privilege and position, and so she is not punished. Bible-redeemers praise Jesus's behavior here as revolutionary. In *Jesus Feminist*, for example, Sarah Bessey writes: "When the woman with the issue of blood reached out to touch the hem of his garment, Jesus did not respond with frustration. No, he touched her in return, praised her faith, set her free without recoiling."[45] This Bible benevolence move hinges on ascribing a double standard to Jesus, the presence of which is obscured by "good goggles." No modern interpreter now says with surprise, "Look! Jesus did not recoil at the synagogue leader!" The man asks and receives. The woman causes a scene. A man has the privilege of expecting Jesus to attend to him and his needs. A woman must fight for it—and must in the end become supplicant to justify it.

The woman's reward for compliance is reinsertion into the patriarchal social order. Jesus's first word to the woman claims her as "daughter." For Bible-redeemers, the address inspires relief. She is not alone; she is not abandoned. She, like Jairus's daughter, now has an advocate in the social order.[46] But the consequence that they overlook or ignore is that she is also no longer autonomous. A reading that sees Jesus's reaction to the woman as generous, as a positive for her, turns on a sense of relief that a woman operating unattached from men is now identified instead as in relationship to a man. A woman reading this passage would learn that autonomous operation is not the ideal. The woman's original act of assertiveness is not allowed to stand. Her autonomy was a threat, a problem to solve.

Interpreters who claim Jesus's interaction with the woman as liberative for women must not only soften Jesus's edges in the gospel narration but also disparage the woman beyond what the text demands. The Bible benevolence script frames her as more deviant, more dangerous, than does the gospel of Mark. In order to make this story work as an example of how Jesus treated women remarkably well, Bible apologists must express surprise that Jesus was not mean to this woman. In a video Bible study accompanying her book *Jesus and Women: In the First Century and Now*, published by Lifeway, self-described "biblical culturalist"[47] Kristi McLelland shares with an audience of women that what she loves about this passage is that "Jesus doesn't have a problem with a woman with an issue of blood for twelve years reaching for him." She is impressed with Jesus. "Doesn't seem to bother him in the least!" she exclaims. In the accompanying book, McLelland exhorts her reader: "Pay close attention to Jesus' reaction here. He didn't condemn. He didn't dismiss."[48] Elaine Storkey makes a similar claim when she writes that the "remarkable difference in this story" is that "she got no rebuke from Jesus, no sharp criticism."[49] Under the surface here is a notion that the woman with the flow of blood probably deserved to be treated with frustration—that Jesus would have been justified had he castigated her. He is accorded that privilege and then praised for not exercising it.

"Jesus would have had every right," McLelland goes on to assert, "to react harshly toward her and dismiss her, maybe even kill her." This gospel story illustrates that Jesus loves and affirms and appreciates women because, this logic goes, he did not murder a woman seeking his help. Interpreters are never as shocked to find Jesus, say, not swatting down butterflies, or not beating children. To make the logic work, Jesus apologists must venture reasons that it is surprising that Jesus was not mean to the woman with the flow of blood. The most common reason depends on fanciful historical reconstruction that simultaneously denigrates women. For Jesus's behavior to be remarkable, the woman has to somehow *deserve* it less. The story they fill in about her attributes her unspecified flow of blood to a particularly "womanly" flow of blood. They ascribe to her vaginal bleeding. According to this reading of the story, which goes beyond the gospel text itself, she has been menstruating for twelve years. This state, they then assert, puts the woman in a constant state of ritual impurity vis-à-vis ancient Jewish purity laws. The largest imaginative leap comes next and depends on negative Christian stereotypes about Judaism. These interpreters claim, counterfactually, that because the woman was ritually impure, she was untouchable.

The flow of blood can then become license for Jesus apologists to imagine the woman as an utter outcast from society. Storkey creatively exaggerates the woman's plight, for example, when she writes that the woman "faced no way out of this horribly restrictive cycle. Her chronic gynaecological problems, along with the attitudes of her culture, denied her enjoyment of regular close company or a normal social life."[50] McLelland gives this as a reason that touching Jesus might have been a problem: "In her cultural context, the idea of someone unclean touching a holy rabbi like Jesus would have been scandalous and risky." Readers who want to see Jesus's treatment of the woman as extraordinary, as above and beyond reasonable expectation, must give Jesus a potential reason *not* to heal the woman. When the reason they invent is that she is "unclean," readers are forced to adopt the view that the woman does not deserve treatment.

Ironically, as they make the woman less deserving, they simultaneously make her a much more sympathetic character. Employing common misunderstandings of Jewish purity law, McLelland fills out for her listeners a vivid picture of the utter despair that this woman must have felt. Her life was terrible and lonely. "In Jewish culture blood makes you ceremonially unclean," she says. And further, "this means for twelve years, most likely, culturally, no one has been able to touch her." To help the evangelical women in her audience empathize, McLelland equates the bleeding woman's loneliness with alienation from husband and kids: "She has not experienced sexual union with her husband, if she was married. She has not been able to touch her children, if she had children." On account of her alienation from husband and home, the woman "is practically dead."

The picture these interpreters fill out turns the woman into an extremely vulnerable outcast. Now that the interpreters have crafted a woman more despondent, more anguished, more alone than she is in the Bible's telling, they expect the audience to be even more impressed with Jesus that he does not berate her. They expect the audience to see Jesus not castigating her, not killing her, as singularly gallant. Jesus apologists need to make the woman's situation more dire in order to exaggerate the generosity of Jesus precisely because *what Jesus actually does in the gospel text as it is written is unsatisfying.*

The woman who did not deserve to be treated well is thus added to the woman who served men and the woman reinserted into patriarchal "protection." The next woman in the gospel is the one Jesus calls a dog.

How to Make the Bible Good when Jesus Is Not

A paraphrase of the story about the Syrophoenician woman in Mark 7:24–30 is almost enough to demonstrate the point that Jesus was exceptionally rude to her. Having sought Jesus out when he was hiding himself away from people, the woman falls at Jesus's feet pleading on behalf of her young daughter. The mother begs Jesus to cast out the unclean spirit who has entered the girl's body. Instead of help or even compassion, she gets a rejection compounded by an insult. Jesus responds, "Let the children be fed first, for it is not fair to take the children's food and throw it to the dogs."[51] The narrator has reported that she was "a gentile, a Syrophoenician by birth" as necessary background information to explain why Jesus behaves this way. Jesus's response means that he does not intend to heal the woman's daughter because the woman is ethnically other. In the course of saying "no," Jesus compares her to a dog. The Rev. Wil Gafney, a Hebrew Bible specialist, womanist scholar, and Episcopal priest, expresses poignantly the resulting tension for modern readers: "I know this is Jesus and we've been trained to read him and hear him religiously, more than religiously, divinely, incarnationally. But where I come from you cannot call a child a dog without calling her mama a dog and you cannot call a woman a dog without calling her a b—."[52]

The woman responds to Jesus's insult with "Sir, even the dogs under the table eat the children's crumbs." Her reply is frequently lauded as an excellent riposte, a witty reply that challenges Jesus. This reply is what propels Jesus to comply with her original request in the same breath that he dismisses her: "For saying that, you may go—the demon has left your daughter." What is sometimes celebrated as a brilliant comeback, though, is also an acceptance of dog status. She inhabits the demeaning position Jesus has assigned her. She must bark if she wants her daughter healed. All he had to do was say the word. But he didn't, until this begging mother further debased herself. The Syrophoenician dog will beg—and take crumbs. That is all that is on offer.

The Jesus of this scene demanded softening, or explaining, even within the New Testament itself. The gospel of Matthew re-narrates Mark's story but makes a significant change by calling the woman a Canaanite (Matt 15:21–28) instead of a Syrophoenician woman. Casual modern Bible readers might not be impressed by the difference. But what Matthew has done is change her national identity to make her belong to a long-gone people group, the legendary Enemy Number One of the Israelites. The change likely is meant to supply a better reason—any reason—for Jesus's insulting reply. Matthew further makes Jesus less of a dick by having him declare that it is the woman's "faith" that saves her daughter, rather than her self-debasing reply. Matthew's solution to Mark's problematic story is one followed by a host of modern Bible readers and Bible apologists, as they read Mark through Matthew almost automatically and therefore resolve, or miss entirely, the misogyny in Mark.[53]

An alternative way interpreters resolve the problem is to question whether it was really that bad that Jesus compares her to a dog. Bible apologist Kyle Butt, for example, argues that people routinely use dog imagery in expressions—"top dog," "bulldog," "every dog has its day"—and so Jesus's use of this language should not be offensive.[54] Butt must overlook that dog imagery is unevenly valanced and deployed when it comes to men and women. When a man is a "top dog" or "bulldog," it is a compliment. When a woman is a dog, she's being told, "down, girl."[55]

The history of New Testament scholarship reveals lively debates about whether Jesus's use of the diminutive for "dogs" makes Jesus's insult less severe. Puppies are cute, so if Jesus means little dogs inside the house, then they are all in the same household with the children. At least she is not an *outside* dog, this logic implies. But as one scholar quipped over fifty years ago, "as in English, so in other languages, to call a woman 'a little bitch' is no less abusive than to call her 'a bitch' without qualification."[56]

Most evangelical Bible-is-good-for-women apologists deploy a different strategy, though. They switch the focus from Jesus's behavior to the woman's, celebrating her as an empowered woman in the Bible. They subtly shift the goalposts. No longer does the underlying question have to do with how Jesus treats women; rather they point to a badass woman in the Bible as evidence that the Bible is pro-women. Barr, for example, cites Matthew's retelling of this story to claim this woman as an early leader because she, Barr writes, "won an argument with Jesus."[57] The woman's begging is turned into resilience, her desperation into admirable determination. When making this move, some readers even participate in Jesus's humiliating behavior and double-down on the woman's self-debasement with a pun, using the modifiers "dogged" or "doggedly."[58] The dog-woman is thus hailed as an empowering example for women.

What must be ignored is that the woman is strong and resilient and impressive not because of how Jesus treated her but *in spite of how Jesus treated her.* White evangelicals deploy a rhetorical shift to make the Bible good when Jesus is not. When Jesus can be presented as an exemplar, he is. When he cannot be an exemplar because his behavior toward a woman is not actually a positive example, interpreters shift to celebrate the woman instead. The woman's good behavior then redounds to the Bible. The Bible becomes good either way: when Jesus is the model, or when the woman is the model. When Jesus is kind to women, the Bible is good for women. When Jesus in unkind to women, the Bible is still good for women. It is a win-win rhetorical strategy. It is a rhetorical strategy, further, that displaces acclaim from a woman to whom it is due onto a man to whom it is not. The Bible benevolence script gives Jesus credit for what women do.

Good for What?

Often the stories of celebrated gospel women, though, are actually less about affirming women as people and more about rewarding women for compliance with patriarchal expectations, including the direction of their lives and labor toward supporting the interests of men. The fifth and final woman Jesus interacts with in Mark's gospel is the unnamed woman who anoints him at Bethany (14:3–9). She and her alabaster flask enter the scene as Jesus reclines to eat in the home of "Simon the leper," and she pours the valuable contents over Jesus's head. Some of the people present become indignant at what strikes them as a waste of costly ointment. "They scolded her," the narrator reports. It could have been sold and the proceeds given to those in need, they say. Jesus rebukes them. He counters by commenting that "she has performed a good service for [him]." Anticipating his impending death, he interprets her action as anointing his body for burial. He says of her, "Truly, I tell you, wherever the good news is proclaimed in the whole world, what she has done will be told in remembrance of her."

The story of the unnamed anointing woman is perhaps the most promising for interpreters who see Jesus as a special friend to women. She is not put to domestic service, as was Simon's mother-in-law. She is not afraid of Jesus after approaching him, as was the woman with the flow of blood. She does not have to beg or endure insults, as did the Syrophoenician woman. Instead, it seems, Jesus defends her and even celebrates her. To make this case, interpreters must ignore that the text says Jesus defends not her but *her service* to him. He celebrates not her but *what she has done* for him. For Jesus to demonstrate particular concern about her as a woman (or as a person), he would need to protect her from the critique of onlookers for her own sake, to say that she herself will be remembered when the gospel is proclaimed. But her name is not preserved even in this story. Jesus finds her as a person valuable only incidentally to what she is good for, what she has done for him.

The negotiation required to make this passage, and the Bible generally, into an advocate for women requires a strategic definition of *what* is good for women. To accomplish this, white evangelical Bible-redeemers claim the term "feminism" to constrain it. They define it simply as a belief that women are human. This move forms the substance and the subtitle, for example, of Bessey's book *Jesus Feminist: An Invitation to Revisit the Bible's View of Women—Exploring God's Radical Notion that Women are People, Too.* On its pages Bessey ascribes this view to Jesus as well. "Jesus thinks women are people, too," she writes.[59] It is Jesus who, she says, "made a feminist" out of her.[60] In support of her extended argument that the Bible's portrayal of Jesus and women is affirming to women, Bessey writes in *Jesus Feminist:*

The women of the gospel narrative ministered to Jesus, and they ministered with him. The lack of women among the twelve disciples isn't prescriptive or a precedent for exclusion of women any more than the choice of twelve Jewish men excludes Gentile men from leadership. We can miss the crazy beauty of it because of the lack of fanfare in Scripture. Women were simply there, part of the revolution of love, sometimes unnamed, sometimes in the background, sometimes the receiver, sometimes the giver—just like every other man in Scripture, to be engaged on their own merit in the midst of their own story.[61]

Bessey construes a lack of textual evidence as a "lack of fanfare" so that she can retrospectively include women in Jesus's story where they do not appear in the Bible.

The catchphrase "women are people, too" is identical to the title of a wave-making 1960 *Good Housekeeping* article by (in)famous feminist Betty Friedan, an article that anticipated her argument a few years later in the explosive book *The Feminine Mystique*.[62] But Bessey's appropriation of the line subtly shifts its meaning to something drastically different from what Friedan meant. When Bessey writes that "Jesus thinks women are people, too," she appears to mean that Jesus thinks women are people just as he thinks men are people. *Women* are people too.

When Friedan wrote "Women are People, Too!" she meant not that women are people just as men are people but rather that women are people in addition to being wives and mothers. For Friedan, recognizing women's humanity was not in the first place an affirmation of the equal humanity of women when compared to men but was rather a conviction that the individual, autonomous humanity of each woman is valuable in the face of pressures to conform to society's expectations of her to dedicate herself to family life. Women are *people* even as they are wives and mothers. Friedan's point was that women have hopes and dreams and needs, and they should have lives that are not identical to family lives. Friedan wrote, for example: "A woman may live half her lifetime before she has the courage to listen to that [internal, discontented] voice and know that *it is not enough to be a wife and mother, because she is a human being herself.* She can't live *through* her husband and children. They are separate selves. She has to find her own fulfillment first."[63] Not: *Women* are people too. But: Women are *people* too.

When white evangelical Christians celebrate the Bible as good because Jesus on its pages thinks women are people, they limit "feminism" and "feminist" strategically to make a definition of "pro-women" cohere with what the data about Jesus on the pages can tolerate. This move baptizes feminism into patriarchy. The claim that Jesus is pro-women because he sees women as people exists perfectly well alongside patriarchally-conditioned constraints on women's behavior and opportunities. In Mark 14, Jesus sees the woman at Bethany as human *and also* her humanity is ever-directed toward supporting the interests of men. She is remembered for the service she performed. She is a person *too*, but perhaps not a *person* too.

The idea that women are people challenges neither patriarchal social order itself nor the regulation of women as women within such an order. Women who serve men are people too. Women subjected to double standards are people too. Women whose bodies are not theirs to control are people too. An anecdote in Bessey's *Jesus Feminist* illustrates well the ease with which men's control of women's bodies can coexist with claims to women's empowerment. As she reflects on her own background, Bessey tells her readers a story they are supposed to find charming about how her parents met one another, became high school sweethearts, and later married and started a family. Her mom and dad met outside their high school, and then he did something daring. "My dad whisked her to a pub in the middle of the school day," Bessey writes, "and when she told him to take her back to school for her typing test, he grinned and said, 'No way.'" The narration continues playfully, "They fell crazy in love, the way teenagers do."[64] Built into this meet-cute is a man taking a woman somewhere and then refusing her request to be returned. Built into the telling is implicit approval, even admiration, of a man's denial of a woman's agency, to positive effect.

Good for Him!

The white evangelical Bible benevolence script regularly depends on anti-feminist, or insufficiently feminist, practices of assessing women, their sexuality, and their bodily autonomy. This is the case particularly when the gospel of John is mined for evidence that Jesus was a special ally of women. A key piece of evidence that Dan Kimball uses to show that Jesus treated women with "respect, dignity, and equality," is that "Jesus Spoke with Women, Even Scandalous Women."[65] Claiming Jesus as pro-women because Jesus spoke to women is a common line in Bible benevolence scripts concerned with misogyny.[66] Kimball's parade gospel example is the Samaritan woman at the well in John 4.

In a play on the betrothal type scene, Jesus is here depicted as meeting a woman at Jacob's well. His first words demand service from the woman. "Give me a drink," he says. (He does not say please.) The woman demurs and asks him why he, "a Jew," is asking "a woman of Samaria" for a drink. The narrator interrupts the dialogue to offer a reason for her comment, telling readers that Jews and Samaritans did not share. After a verbal back-and-forth between Jesus and the woman about some living water that Jesus claims to be able to make available, she addresses him as "lord" and then makes a request of him: "give me this water, so that I may never be thirsty or have to keep coming here to draw water." She wishes not only for her thirst to be quenched but for her labor of drawing water—the precise labor that Jesus asked her to do for him—to be relieved.

Instead of giving her the water, though, Jesus commands her to go get her husband first. It is a jarring response. Does she need a man with her to be able to receive this water that Jesus wants to give her? Jesus's question would imply so. But when she states that she has no husband, Jesus reveals that he already knew this. He knew it but said it anyway. He says, "You are right in saying, 'I have no husband,' for you have had five husbands, and the one you have now is not your husband. What you have said is true!" The woman once again calls him "lord" and adds "prophet." While this moment has often been read as her recognition of Jesus's identity, it can also be read as her verbal acknowledgment of their power differential. He is a prophet, she a profligate.

Deploying a tactic of misogynistic control over women's sexuality within patriarchy, Jesus slut-shames this woman.[67] And yet virtually all Bible benevolence laborers are impressed with Jesus for engaging with her. Kimball and others who name her a "scandalous woman" shame her simultaneously, participating in Jesus's own slut-shaming.[68] When Kimball says, "even scandalous women," he forges a distinction between "good women" and "bad women" down lines of whether they comply with a patriarchal expectation that their sexual activity be confined to heterosexual marriage. This is perhaps unsurprising given that conservative Christianity typically patrols such a boundary when it comes to sexuality. Kimball makes less of the scandalous piece, though, and more of the woman piece. The author exclaims, "Jesus not only talked with her, he spoke openly about theology and discussed God with her—a woman!" The "a woman!" here is Kimball ventriloquizing an ancient person, temporarily inhabiting an anti-woman position that expects a man *not* to talk to a woman in order to perform amazement at Jesus's perceived exceptionalism. Kimball is constructing ancient misogyny as a benchmark by which to assess Jesus's willingness to talk to women. He *must* use ancient misogyny, rather than modern, on this point because it would feel absurd today to identify "willing to talk to a woman" as a hallmark of feminism. In *Jesus Feminist*, Bessey acknowledges this necessity: "When we look at these passages or letters through the lens of our egalitarian modern culture, sure—they seem like small potatoes, probably even offensive. But in a patriarchal culture, women were never included in the teaching, encouraged to prophesy, or given dignity as participants."[69]

In this day and age, speaking to women does not a feminist make. The act of talking to a woman is not sufficient to counter misogyny. To assess whether a particular individual is a misogynist, one would have to assess not whether that person speaks to women but how he speaks to women, and why, and whether his speech enforces patriarchal norms or polices women's behavior. Women can be spoken to and also compelled to comply with patriarchal expectations. Women can be spoken to and also systematically marginalized. Women can be spoken to and also sexually assaulted. Less spectacularly: the problem that men are statistically allowed to speak longer and more authoritatively than are women, in part because women are more frequently interrupted (by men, usually),[70] cannot be solved by pointing to an example of a man, remarkable or otherwise, speaking to a woman.

Interpreters who make much of Jesus speaking to a woman are taking a cue from the text of the gospel of John itself, which says in verse 27 that Jesus's disciples "were astonished that he was speaking with a woman." While this line is usually counted as evidence that ancient rabbis did not speak to women, an alternative reading is that the disciples were astonished not because Jesus was doing something ancient rabbis did not usually do but because he was doing something *he* did not normally do. Perhaps it was because Jesus's talking to a woman was actually unusual. Decentering Jesus from a hero position makes it is easier to see the marked contrast between Jesus and the Samaritan woman's community, who embrace her.[71] The members of her community are the ones who listen to her and who welcome her speech (4:39–42).[72]

Siding with someone other than Jesus is not part of the white evangelical Bible benevolence script. The disciples' astonishment in verse 27 offers instead support for a common reading in which Jesus is understood as crossing a cultural boundary as a Jewish man speaking with a woman. Jesus is made a feminist by making him a feminist-by-contrast. Other religious Jewish men in antiquity here become, counter-factually, the misogynistic foil against which Jesus's perceived progressivism then becomes apparent.[73] The Bible benevolence script cherry-picks misogynistic passages from later Jewish sources (sometimes as late as 500 CE), ignoring counterevidence for rabbinic views toward women, and then compares them unfavorably with cherry-picked passages that sound women-friendly from first-century Christian sources, all the while ignoring misogynistic passages in the New Testament.[74] This myth, with its supporting methodology, has become so widespread that popular writers see it as axiomatic. Kimball, for example, does not betray a need to offer any evidence in support of it. This historical fantasy is such a common part of the Bible benevolence script that it has become "common knowledge."

Anti-Judaism in Christian feminism has been written on extensively.[75] What is less remarked upon, though, is that this interpretive move simultaneously compels the interpreter to denigrate women. Any reader whose interpretation depends on being surprised that Jesus spoke to the woman also depends on anti-feminist assumptions that women do not automatically deserve to be spoken to and, further, that women are receptacles of men's speech. The notion that a man speaking to a woman shows that he values her encodes a regime of masculine privilege and feminine deference. The (privileged) man is entitled to speech, and the woman is expected to be gratified to get to listen to him. The man becomes a knower, an explainer, a holder forth,[76] while the woman is expected to see her privilege as being spoken to rather than ignored. She is expected to give her attention to a man as though doing so were a gift *to her*.

When Kimball writes in (feigned?) surprise that Jesus spoke to "a woman!", he temporarily inhabits the ancient, anti-woman perspective that he has presented as normative in antiquity. His reader must also do so, in order to follow his logic. But, significantly, the temporariness of this inhabiting turns out not to be temporary at all, since Kimball does not go on to outline what a modern-day analogy would look like. He ends this section with the assertion that "There are several accounts [in the Bible] of Jesus speaking with and caring for various women, people a religious leader of his time would not associate with." A woman reading this section of his book must relinquish, whether momentarily or longer, any entitlement she feels to be a worthy conversation partner.

The short story about Jesus recounted in John 7:53–8:11 is another popular gospel resource for those who depict him as particularly concerned for women. Known by scholars as the *pericope adulturae,* it is likely not original to the gospel of John, but this makes it no less a beloved and enduring story about Jesus among Christian readers of the Bible.[77] One white evangelical Bible-redeemer points to this passage as evidence for his claim that Jesus "consistently treated women kindly and accorded them equal status with men as they found in him the solution to Israel's problems."[78] The same interpreter goes on: "the story of the woman caught in adultery but then forgiven by Jesus in John 7:53–8:11 crystallizes the kind of thing Jesus did and is consistent with his association with prostitutes (Matt. 21:28–32)."[79] The script categorizes this woman with sex workers, presumably putting them together because they are conceived as sexually deviant, perhaps lustful, women. It matters not, it seems, that "prostitutes," "adulteresses," or really any women in patriarchal social orders typically do not possess the same agency or autonomy as powerful men to control who has sexual access to their bodies. The white evangelical Bible benevolence script depicts the women of the gospels who are in need of Jesus's supposed revolution as utterly oppressed, controlled, maltreated, and limited by a misogynistic system around them—until it comes to sex. Then the women are held accountable for the choices they are believed to be making about their bodies.

The woman featured in this passage, like so many gospel women, is unnamed. But English language Bible headings call her variously "the woman caught in adultery," "the adulterous woman," "an adulteress," or a "sinful woman."[80] Centering the woman, rather than Jesus or the other men, though, might make this passage better called "The Woman Nearly Stoned." But interpreters who reckon this passage as evidence of Jesus's special care for women focus not on her experience but on her perceived sexual transgression. She rarely gets empathy when pity is available as the option considered more virtuous than judgment.

Shaming monikers for the woman adopt the narrator's judgment. The narrator indicates that "the scribes and

Pharisees" brought to Jesus "a woman who had been caught in adultery." The religious leaders force her to stand not only before Jesus but also, publicly, before a crowd of people who had gathered to hear him teach at the temple. They do this in order to test Jesus (8:6). In other words, this woman is collateral damage, at least potentially, in a contest for power among religious leaders who are men.[81] Jesus's rivals seek a reason to charge him. The content of the test boils down to whether Jesus will enforce "the law Moses commanded to stone such a woman." They've caught Jesus between a rock and a hard place, as he must decide, ostensibly, whether to toss stones in or Moses out.

Jesus will best his challengers. But only by putting this woman's life in jeopardy.[82] He does not go to her. He does not address her. Perhaps he does not even look at her. He instead bends down and mysteriously draws in the dirt. When he is done, Jesus invites them to kill her. "Let anyone among you who is without sin be the first to throw a stone at her," he taunts. Working with and extending the patriarchal constructs that have led to this situation in the first place, Jesus does not challenge the premise that she deserves stoning, only the right of the men jockeying with him for power to mete out the punishment.

To turn this story into one about Jesus's special care for women is to use an extremely low standard for what counts as advocacy. In her dramatization of this scene, McLelland asks her audience to imagine what the woman is experiencing: "How do you feel? What is running through your heart? What is running through your mind?" She envisions the woman desperately contemplating an impending death. "She's probably wondering," McLelland speculates, "if she's going to live to see the sun set that day. Or if her stoning will happen right then." Readers could, but do not, expect Jesus to protest her public shaming, to mitigate somehow the terror she must have been experiencing, to refuse to make her wonder if she will in fact be murdered right there and then. Other interpreters point out, though, that the scribes and Pharisees likely had no intention to stone her or have her killed. Otherwise their test of Jesus makes less sense as a test. They must be expecting that Jesus will say, "don't stone her," and thereby violate Mosaic law. That is the outcome that would make their trap effective. This means while this woman has been made to stand and suffer scrutiny in front of everyone, she perhaps would not have experienced a real fear of execution until *Jesus* tempts the possibility.

Readers steeped in a sin-salvation paradigm typically already know the end of the story, and so likely see cleverness behind Jesus's winning reply. Jesus has found another way. He will neither kill the woman nor abandon the law. The usual narrative is that Jesus is a savior figure, a hero who steps in and both rescues her from her accusers and forgives her of her sin. But the person Jesus actually saves here is himself. The way the story is narrated in John, it is Jesus who is the primary target, the potential victim. He is also ultimately the victor. He saves his stature, guards his own reputation— all the while gambling with this woman's life. Jesus sees his adversaries' public shaming and raises them a potential, if finally unrealized, public execution.

No one accepts Jesus's invitation to stone the woman. They walk away one by one. Then only Jesus and the woman remain. This is a moment where several white evangelical women interpreters pause to identify with the woman of John 8 facing Jesus. Bessey affirms Jesus's treatment of "the woman caught in adultery," for example, by imagining herself and her women readers in the place of the woman nearly stoned: "There aren't too many of us women who don't imagine ourselves there, exposed, used, defiant or broken—sometimes both—and humiliated."[83] As McLelland weaves her argument that this story is fundamentally about Jesus contending for the woman, she asks her audience to pause once again and imagine the woman's fear. But this time, the woman is afraid of Jesus. McLelland says: "Only her [sic] and Jesus are left face to face in this moment. In a gospel sense, this is actually the scariest moment of all for her. Because who is sinless and who can throw the stone?" The answer is Jesus. "He could," she remarks with a pause for dramatic effect, "pick up a stone and throw it at her." This is a chilling line. McLelland recognizes the peril that this woman is in. She recognizes the fear that the woman must feel amidst the danger. The woman is powerless, unable to hide. She is voiceless, unasked what she thinks about the law. This reading then asks Bible readers to be relieved, or perhaps impressed, that Jesus does not in fact kill her with rocks.

Indeed, rather than stone her, Jesus asks her two questions. They are not genuine questions, though. He does not ask, "Are you okay?" He does not ask, "What happened and how can I help?" He does not ask, "What do you need?" He does not ask, "Are you in danger?" He says, rather, "Woman, where are they? Has no one condemned you?" These are not questions about her.[84] These are in fact rhetorical questions, questions that are meant to have her view and verbalize that Jesus has won. They are questions that force her to admire what he has done.[85] The scribes and Pharisees had turned this woman into a pawn. Rather than humanize her, Jesus plays the game. And once he's won, he compels her to be the one to announce "checkmate." Rather than demonstrate recognizable care about the true victim, Jesus revels in his victory.

Jesus then points out to her that he has not stoned her—"neither do I condemn you." He dismisses her with more than a hint of blame: "Go," he says, "and sin no more." A subsection of the Bible benevolence script that presents this story as evidence of Jesus's equal treatment of men and women argues that Jesus here treats the sin of men and women equally. Bessey reads this story as "feminist" because she sees Jesus here as "level[ing] the playing field for both sin and marriage."[86] Jesus judges the scribes and Pharisees as sinful, and he judges the woman as sinful. Men = sinful; women = sinful; sinful = sinful; men = women. A closer look at the gospel text reveals that this reading must assert that unequal treatment is actually equal treatment. Jesus does not handle them, or their perceived transgressions, in the same way.[87] He gives the men the opportunity to evaluate themselves with respect to their perceived sin, each one allowed a near-private opportunity to self-assess and slip away. Jesus issues the woman, by contrast, a mandate.[88]

Freedom from public execution does not turn out to be freedom from patriarchal social organization or misogynistic regulation of women's behavior within such a system. To think with Manne's phrasing, the story ends with Jesus doing law enforcement for patriarchy. He affirms that the woman has been a bad woman by the logic of patriarchal social organization. By telling her to "sin no more," Jesus commands her to return to her role within a patriarchal order wherein she has sex only with her husband. The very category "adultery" within patriarchal social order is itself a tool of misogyny. In both antiquity and modernity, "adultery" constructed as a wrong has served a regulating function, often to ensure that the reproductive labor of a womb is dedicated only to one man. Further, in both antiquity and modernity, "adultery" is steeped in double standards by which women partners in heterosexual marriages are punished more frequently or severely than are men for extramarital sexual activity.

Jesus reinforces rather than challenges the notion that this woman is a "bad woman" by accepting her accusers' accusations as accurate descriptors of behavior deemed inappropriate.[89] A woman reading John 8 could reasonably come to its conclusion having learned that it is dangerous for her not to comply with the sexual expectations of patriarchal order. Jesus does not hate this woman, or all women. But his behavior is misogynistic nonetheless, since it serves to regulate her behavior according to patriarchal norms. By using the word "sin" to describe what she has been accused of doing, Jesus is reinforcing the patriarchal expectation that her sexual activity is tied to the interests of men.

The white evangelical Bible benevolence script admires Jesus on this point. The reaction of white evangelical women interpreters is interesting to observe in particular. Rather than stop with their sense of relief that Jesus has, in their view, saved the woman from scribes and Pharisees and stones, the Bible-redeemers praise Jesus for his final admonition of the woman. "Jesus freed the adulterous woman from condemnation," Wendy Alsup comments, "without undermining God's strong feelings on the scourge of adultery."[90] Bessey writes with a tone of satisfied awe: "And he, bless his name, restored, forgave, protected, drew a shield of grace around her with his dusty fingertip; and her accusers vanished. 'Go,' he said, 'and sin no more.'"[91] McLelland sees the resolution as, in her words, "gospel-gorgeous." She understands Jesus's "sin no more" as beautiful, even empowering. "It brings me great comfort in a strange way," she says, "that Jesus doesn't just say, 'You know what? It's just adultery . . . I mean, really, let's just all go for muffins.'"

The interpreters' comments suggest that they do not want Jesus to let the woman go without judgment or correction. The judgment of the woman is accepted as a fundamental good. These comments function to mimic, and perhaps internalize, the regulation of women's sexual activity within patriarchally-conditioned bounds. The passage as it's written does not really let them do otherwise. In fact, McLelland even uses the woman nearly stoned as paradigmatic of all women, all of whom are sinful and ashamed. She asks her all-women audience, "What's the worst thing you've ever done? The worst. . . . What's that thing that when you even *think* of it in your memory it makes you feel shame? Makes you feel embarrassed. What's that thing for you? This story speaks to that." Bible benevolence becomes an opportunity to invite women to self-shame.

The Sweat of the Script

Jesus's good reputation has been so carefully managed that it is difficult for many readers to see that a "meta-Jesus" who is especially kind to, loving toward, and concerned for women is precisely that: a construct that exceeds the textual data and requires no small degree of interpretive sweat. Jesus's behavior in Matthew and Luke cannot mitigate such a conclusion.[92] In both of those gospels, Jesus teaches material that does not appear in Mark's gospel. Scholars have noticed a pattern in which Jesus teaches in "gender pairs," meaning that he often delivers the same lesson through two different parables, one that engages traditionally male-coded activities and one that engages traditionally female-coded activities.[93] Some evangelical writers make much of the notion that Jesus *taught such that women could understand* as evidence that he was especially caring for women. What they fail to reflect on, though, is that by doing so, Jesus reifies boundaries around the realms that women are conceived to inhabit, thereby circumscribing women.[94]

Some stories distinctive to Luke, widely dubbed the gospel most concerned for women, are also difficult to reconcile with a Jesus-as-feminist model. The parables told by Jesus that are distinctive to Luke's gospel presume male normativity and an audience of men only, even when the parables feature women as characters.[95] Jesus is also, at least once, just plain insulting. Luke 11:27–28 offers a brief anecdote of Jesus interacting with an unnamed woman as he was teaching about his power to banish unclean spirits. "While he was saying this," the text reads, "a woman in the crowd raised her voice and said to him, 'Blessed is the womb that bore you and the breasts that nursed you!'"[96] This woman exclaims in admiration of Jesus, celebrating the woman whose body bore him and nourished him. Jesus does not accept the compliment. Instead, he corrects her. "But he said, 'Blessed rather are those who hear the word of God and obey it!'" Jesus's response denigrates two women simultaneously, the woman whom he corrects and his own mother—a mother who has been portrayed as nothing if not obedient to God! God has used Mary's reproductive labor to bring Jesus into the world; Jesus rejects that it was praiseworthy.

It takes a lot of work to make Jesus good for women—at least a Jesus accessible through the gospel narratives of his life that are in the Bible. The labor seems effortless to those who do it, though. There is little to support the claim that Jesus is especially good to or for women. There is scant evidence that he is interested at all in their plight within patriarchal social order. Jesus is portrayed as interested in his standing among other men. In service of that concern, he polices patriarchal borders alongside other powerful men. It is truly a remarkable feat that so many Bible interpreters who make Jesus good for women have rendered their own labor invisible. Its invisibility is part of what makes it persuasive. It feels obvious because it appears effortless.

The obviousness of Jesus's goodness is likely why secularists or other Bible critics, like the fictional *God's Not Dead* congresswoman challenging Pastor Dave, do not typically point to Jesus as part of their critique about the Bible and women.

In the movie scene, the congresswoman protesting the Bible's misogyny does not say, "Jesus didn't appreciate his mama!" or "Jesus called a woman a bitch!" or anything else about Jesus.

She turns rather to a different target, a bigger target—the apostle Paul.

Does a woman have to keep her head covered when church gatherings happen? (1 Corinthians 11:3–16)

Does a woman need to submit to her husband in everything? (Ephesians 5:24)

Does a woman need to have a baby in order to be 'saved'? (1 Timothy 2:15)

Oh, the many amazingly weird and wonderful questions the Bible raises!

—Dan Kimball, *How (Not) to Read the Bible*

THREE

Making Paul Less Bad

The Fantasies of White Evangelical Men

The apostle Paul creates a challenge for Bible redemption so apparent that not even the conservative evangelical film franchise *God's Not Dead* can avoid his comments on women. In the movie's imagined national referendum on the Bible and misogyny, the disdainful congresswoman crows to Pastor Dave: "Paul ordered women to cover up their hair, to wear a veil in the assembly. Do you think *I* need to wear a veil for *you*?"

The pastor protagonist cannot tell her to veil. That would be absurd in context. Doing so would prove her point and in turn tarnish the Bible's reputation. At the same time, Pastor Dave cannot deny that Paul's New Testament letters address what women should wear.[1] Strategically, he does not answer yes or no. With a twinkle in his eye, he expounds on the qualification he has previously offered as he makes the Bible good for women: "the Bible is one of the most pro-feminist documents in history"—"*considering the time when it was written.*" History can save the Bible from this critique. History can save the evangelical Christian in the bind between what the Bible says and what society thinks is good for women.

Pastor Dave goes on to invent a history behind Paul's words to make them more palatable. Ancient Roman men, whom he supposes all had hair fetishes, were the ones oppressing women during the time of Paul, not the apostle himself. "Single women in the Roman empire," Dave states, counterfactually, "were required by law to unveil their hair for the visual pleasure of men." Compounding the historical fantasy, he says that women who were married or widowed (and thus previously married) were exempt from such objectification. Offering a modern analogy, Pastor Dave speculates: "It would be like today if we forced a young woman to dress immodestly," which, in keeping with evangelical purity culture norms, he judges to be "totally exploitative." The "we" in this scenario goes undefined, but, for the analogy to work, it must mean heterosexual men in positions that accord them the privilege to regulate how women dress.

Paul, by contrast, was a progressive because he commended single women to cover themselves. Paul did not want to ogle women but rather to protect them. "When Paul told women to veil in the assembly," Pastor Dave says, "he was adding to the dignity of women." Paul was communicating to single women a sentiment that Dave views as empowering:

"You are every bit as good as a married woman or a widow, and you don't have to put yourself on display. At least not in here."

Pastor Dave will not tell the congresswoman to veil for him. But he *will* imply that she, as all women, should be ever cognizant of the male gaze on her body, which remains in his accounting determinative for women's dress. He suggests that Paul's commands around women's self-presentation are for their own good, all the while framing women's social status as bound up in patriarchal relationships and women's bodies fundamentally as objects of sexual desire, whether realized or not. As he makes the Bible good for women, Pastor Dave cannot change the words on the pages of his Bible. He must instead play with what "good for women" means. His answer to the charge that the Bible is misogynistic is to be misogynistic himself while branding it as a net positive for women. He repackages misogyny as a fundamental societal good because its norms protect women (from men). Dave's comments no less regulate the dress of women for the benefit of men than do those of Paul in the historical fantasy he has offered. The pastor does not consider that perhaps neither he nor Paul should be so entitled. He redeems Paul not to affirm the woman in his presence but rather to save the Bible—and, crucially, himself—from critique.

Reflecting a common Bible benevolence strategy among white evangelical Christians, Pastor Dave's Bible redemption entails a history lesson, or rather a fantasy about history. He invents a historical context for the New Testament to help him suggest that Paul did not mean what he said in a sexist way. Just like Jesus, Paul becomes pro-women by contrast—because his version of patriarchy is protective rather than exploitative, or because when his words are put in historical context he is better than the alternative, or both. In contrast to Jesus, though, Paul is a thorn in everyone's side. If Jesus was the flashpoint of change in the Bible's fundamental affirmation of women, as many Bible-redeemers argue, Paul's explicit statements about women are troublesome because they challenge a notion that Paul, and therefore the Bible, consistently advances the pro-women ethic presumed to be instituted by Jesus. While Jesus is celebrated, Paul must be exculpated. Bible-redeemers have to figure out how to bring Paul into compliance with their vision of Jesus.

The white evangelical Bible benevolence script turns on identifying, and ultimately sympathizing with, Paul's *motivations.* Histories are invented to show that Paul had good reason for writing what he did, as Bible benevolence projects seek to posit reasonable explanations for why 1 Corinthians 14:34–35 and 1 Timothy 2 command women to be silent, why 1 Corinthians 11 regulates women's hair and/or dress, and why Ephesians and Colossians commend hierarchy of husband over wife.[2] If Paul had good intentions, the reasoning goes, the Bible too can be good. History can save the Bible from this critique. History can save evangelical Christians in this bind. Yet, in the end, the goodness of the Bible is not what is ultimately at stake in exculpations of the apostle. A close reading of the Bible benevolence script suggests that Bible-redeemers save Paul to save their own reputations.

CRAZY WOMEN, CRAZY-*SOUNDING* BIBLE

First Corinthians 14:34–35 is a troublesome passage for Bible-is-good-for-women advocates. "Women should be silent in the churches," the Bible proclaims, "For they are not permitted to speak but should be subordinate, as the law also says." If they want to learn something, the text goes on, "let them ask their husbands at home. For it is shameful for a woman to speak in church." Some Bible-redeemers get around this passage's presence in Paul's corpus by hypothesizing that it is

not Pauline. Perhaps it was penned by a later scribe, interpo-
lated into a manuscript of 1 Corinthians, and then incorporated into later manuscripts of this letter.[3] This explanation,
notably, only stands to absolve the Bible of one instance of
women-silencing. It does not erase 1 Timothy 2 from anyone's
Bible. But interpreters who ascribe the silencing sentences in
1 Corinthians to Paul must figure out why it was acceptable
for him to say such things to Corinthian women, an interpretive constraint that has fired many historical imaginations
about the setting of the community to whom Paul wrote.

"There were some pretty crazy things going on in the
Corinthian church meetings," Santa Cruz megachurch
pastor Dan Kimball ventures in his book *How (Not) to
Read the Bible*.[4] The ancient Corinthian recipients of Paul's
letter, as they often do, take the blame for creating circumstances that made Paul silence women. Their church was
disordered and unruly. Their depravity created a need for
Paul's discipline. Paul, in Kimball's explanation, was writing
"to correct these abuses and guide the people to unity."[5]
This justification of Paul's motivation depends on a naive
understanding of "unity" as a transparent good, even though
appeals to unity often protect the interests of the powerful at
the expense of those with less power.[6] Unity is so desirable,
the reasoning goes, that reaching it is worth disempowering
some individuals—in this case, talkative women whose
speech is apparently contributing to the "crazy things"
happening in the Corinthian church.[7]

Kimball does not explain precisely how women being
silent would solve the problems he thinks were plaguing
the ancient Corinthian church. The only specific charge
he names is that the Corinthians were taking the Lord's
Supper inappropriately, an issue tied in no obvious way to
gender, or sex, or speaking. Capitalizing on his readers' likely
assent to a claim that the Lord's Supper *must* be executed

correctly, Kimball implies that silencing the Corinthian women must have been essential too. In so doing, he deploys a frequent strategy on the part of Bible apologists: pairing a live, contested issue with a settled one in order to resolve the former issue by association.[8] Kimball makes a similar rhetorical move by grouping slavery together with shrimp and the American pastime of football. "Stranger Things: Shrimp, Slavery, and the Skin of a Dead Pig," one chapter title reads. The two issues bookending slavery here are widely considered settled, as most mainstream gentile Christians in the US do not observe Jewish dietary laws prohibiting shellfish and pork, and further do not view the eating of shrimp (or not) or the playing of football (or not) as potential challenges to the morality of the Bible.[9]

The implied *reductio ad absurdum* argument goes: if the Bible endorses slavery, then it also prohibits football. The Bible cannot be prohibiting football (!), so the Bible cannot be endorsing slavery. Kimball's pairing a passage from Exodus 28 with slavery does analogous work. The Exodus passage depicts a commandment from God to Moses regarding priestly vestments for Moses's brother Aaron and his descendants: "You shall make for them linen undergarments to cover their naked flesh; they shall reach from the hips to the thighs; They shall be worn by Aaron and his sons when they go into the tent of meeting or when they come near the altar to minister in the holy place, so that they do not bring guilt on themselves and die" (28:42–43). Kimball playfully hyperbolizes what he expects his readers to recognize as absurdity by referring to the priests' vestments as "magical underwear."[10] It is a funny turn of phrase. By pairing a nonissue, rendered humorously, with the very real issue of slavery, Kimball distracts from the seriousness of the latter. Combining the transparently absurd with the actually problematic over and over again, Kimball describes offending biblical passages as "crazy and unsettling"[11]; "bizarre and even embarrassing"[12]; "strange and difficult to understand"[13]; "crazy and disturbing"[14]; and "bizarre and strange, even evil and harmful."[15]

When it comes to potentially troubling biblical passages about women, though, Kimball combines "amazingly weird" and "wonderful." If Bible readers ignore how individual verses fit into the whole Bible, he warns, "we will all-too-easily believe that mythical, magical unicorns are in the Bible (along with talking snakes), that churches don't let women speak or ask questions, and many other crazy and very strange and weird-sounding things."[16]

But it is not actually *crazy* to observe that women and their speech have been and still are highly regulated, especially but not exclusively in church contexts. For many women, it is neither weird nor wonderful.

In addition to minimizing the seriousness of the problem, the white evangelical Bible benevolence script makes Paul good for women by making the apostle appear moderate. He could have entirely silenced women, Bible-redeemers point out, but he did not. Bible benevolence projects like Kimball's depend on an unstated assumption that as long as Paul was not silencing *all women for all time*, then the apostle, and therefore the Bible, is not misogynistic.[17] With the terms set in this way, the only thing they need to prove is that Paul was not universally and eternally limiting women's speech. The most common reason offered in support of this argument is that Paul acknowledged some women speaking in Christian churches, as in 1 Corinthians 7. "Unless Paul is contradicting himself," Kimball writes, "he doesn't intend for women to never speak a word. It must mean something else." What cannot be true is that Paul would contradict himself.[18] Bible-redeemers constrained by a conviction of the Bible's internal consistency mobilize that expectation of consistency to make a total prohibition on women's speech inconsistent with the Bible. Because the Bible must be internally consistent, Paul cannot mean that all women for all time cannot speak in churches. For such Bible benevolence projects, that is enough to get Paul off the hook.

Histories unconsidered here include that Paul might have been targeting a group of women prophets in Corinth, whose speech he could not help but acknowledge but whose power and influence in the Christian community he sought to constrain, a project that climaxes in his attempt to silence them.[19] White evangelical Bible-redeemers not only assume Paul's perception is accurate but also presume that his perspective is the only one that matters.[20]

A semantic sleight of hand helps Kimball, like other Bible-redeemers, avoid such possible reconstructions of Paul's circumstances. He frames "misogyny" and "pro-women" as opposites. Kimball's exploration of the topic in *How (Not) to Read the Bible* falls under the section heading "Boys' Club Christianity: Is the Bible Anti-Women and Does it Promote Misogyny?" This interrogative is, in reality, a combination of two questions: "Is the Bible anti-women?" and "Does the Bible promote misogyny?" Blending these questions into one allows Kimball to recruit evidence suggesting the Bible is "pro-women" simultaneously as evidence that it does not promote misogyny, thereby making the latter easier to prove than if these questions were considered separately. Equating misogyny with anti-women sentiment is a useful way to defuse charges of misogyny by limiting its definitional scope. Equating misogyny with being "anti-women" makes it much easier to argue that the Bible is not misogynistic since one only must show evidence that Paul sometimes acknowledged that women did things like speak or even lead.

Yet Kimball's chapter title "Can't Keep a Good Woman Down" illustrates how easy it is to be "pro-women" and misogynistic at the same time. The slogan is almost certainly meant to be a rallying cry that champions women generally.

Women are pushed down but do not stay there. But in the image this slogan conjures, not all women actually rise. It is the "good" ones who prevail. If there are good women, there are bad ones. (And, it be must asked, by whose lights?) Kimball's chapter title classifies women by their "goodness," which in turn is a precondition for their success. Kimball transforms a claim that *good* women rise into evidence that all women rise, despite the fact that the expression he uses depends on the existence of *bad* women left behind. If there were no bad women, the use of "good" here would be incoherent. "Pro-women" belief, or even proclamation, functions perfectly well within a patriarchal social structure wherein women face disparities of opportunity and influence.

A perusal through the website of the church that Kimball now pastors, called Vintage Faith Church, illustrates the ease with which an authoritative man supporting the notion of women speaking in church can coexist with male-dominant authority, traditional gender stereotypes, and fewer opportunities for women. The church offers a men's ministry and a women's ministry with different mission statements. The men's ministry includes outward engagement through "service" in the context of leadership and public-facing efforts, while the women's ministry includes neither and is framed as insular.[21] Photos of the men's ministry depict men pushing a giant tire on a beach, roasting hot dogs on a fire in front of an American flag, and sitting on hay bales in a rustic barn. Photos of the women's ministry show women standing in a clothing-filled thrift shop and gathered in a polished sanctuary with a nice refreshment spread of coffee, fresh fruit, and lemonade. A flyer depicting a '50s style kitchen advertises "Soul Kitchen: A Ministry for Women." The church is governed by a leadership council, currently comprised of five men and one woman. The woman on the council bears the title "Director of Family Ministries (Kids and Youth)." She is a director, not a minister, and the parentheses limit her scope of influence to include only people who are not adult men. The disparities continue in the leadership positions beyond the council as well. Men govern such domains as theology; discipleship; adult ministry; creative arts; teaching; facilities; and finances; while women are in charge of staff; office management; operations; and ministries aimed at women, families, youth, and kids. "Good" women rise—but only so far.

Yet Kimball's exculpation of Paul focuses not on the present but on the past. Paul needed to silence the Corinthian women for the good of the Corinthian church—and doing so was not out of the ordinary in Paul's time. In writing 1 Corinthians 14:34–35, Paul was in good company in antiquity, since "temporary silencing was normal in [Paul's] culture." Perhaps it was because Paul wanted the women to learn before they spoke,[22] or because women were seated separately from the men and for reasons unknown were "shouting across the room" to ask their husbands questions.[23] It matters not if a scenario is a precise illustration of misogynistic disciplining—as in the learning-before-teaching example. This possibility presumes that women must be trained, by men, in order to become acceptable as teachers. It matters not, further, if a scenario is logistically implausible. Kimball does not explain, for example, why only married women would be yelling across the room, or why those women comfortable shouting across the room, each to her own husband, would not feel just as confident shouting their questions to the speaker instead.

Ironically, Kimball does not need to offer one convincing explanation to make Paul's words explicable. The existence of a range of possibilities for a historical scenario that demanded Paul's silencing of women works to make Paul's words feel more explicable, even as a thorough understanding of the historical scenario remains inaccessible. Its inaccessibility is masked by confidence. "To the women back then," Kimball asserts, Paul's command "would have made sense." It matters not, it seems, if Paul's command does not make sense (to women) today. All that can be known for sure is that Paul could not have been silencing women for all time or asking them "to submit like servants or people of lesser value," because if he had, it would, in Kimball's words, "invalidate and contradict everything else we see in his writings as well as the trajectory of Scripture as a whole."[24]

Yet one other possible explanation that Kimball offers for Paul's words in 1 Corinthians 14 requires investigating something else in his writings—the other scriptural silencing passage, 1 Timothy 2:11–12. This troublesome excerpt reads, "Let a woman learn in silence with full submission. I do not permit a woman to teach or to have authority over a man; she is to keep silent." In Bible benevolence projects, this is where the history often gets especially creative. This is where the history gets *sexy*.

BAD WOMEN, WORSE HISTORY

Ephesian women are the ones who command attention when Bible-redeemers turn to 1 and 2 Timothy, since Paul's addressee Timothy is supposed to reside in ancient Ephesus. Kimball imagines what must have been happening in the Ephesian context to explain the Bible's second silencing passage. "Much like the letter to the Corinthians," he writes, "the church in Ephesus had significant problems."[25] The problems were the result of the prevailing religion in Ephesus at the time, he claims—specifically, a goddess primarily worshipped by women. In Ephesus, Artemis "posed a serious challenge to the new church."[26] And women coming to the church from her cult are the root of the church's problems. With a robust historical imagination and no invocations of evidence,

Kimball envisions for readers what these women might have been like, what kinds of assumptions and practices they might have been bringing along with them into the church. The incoherence of Kimball's subsequent characterization of the Artemis cult is masked by shock appeal. He claims that the "Temple of Artemis" was "an all-female religion with castrated men serving as priests." An astute reader might wonder how an evangelical writer like Kimball could understand a group as "all-female" if it includes men. Unless one thinks of a penis-bearer without balls as female, which is unlikely within conservative evangelicalism, the statement as written is impossible. Significantly, though, it serves a rhetorical purpose. The description of the cult in this way characterizes the Ephesian women as adjacent to nonconformity, and particularly a type of nonconformity that a modern, conforming evangelical man might find disconcerting or even threatening.[27]

Anxiety about desexualization next becomes indulgence in oversexualization. Artemis, Kimball asserts, was "a fertility cult where worship involved sexual rites, including prostitution, practices that would shock people today."[28] The claim that there was cult prostitution at the Artemis temple in ancient Ephesus is entirely fictional.[29] Yet the myth is ubiquitous enough that Kimball need not cite any evidence for it. Entertaining and unpacking the premise, however, shows further how confounding Kimball's reconstruction of the Artemis cult is. Given his description of the Artemis cult participants as "all-female," a likely presumption that temple prostitution involves heterosexual exchanges, and the invocation of fertility (which usually comes with a desire for pregnancy), it is unclear who is presumed to be coming to the temple to procure service from prostitutes, who are presumably women. The castrated priests? Women seeking to become pregnant? It ultimately does not matter. Prostitution serves here to complete a trifecta of shocking (to evangelicals) sex stuff that could threaten normative gender distinctions and circumscribed sexual activity—"emasculated" men, women misappropriating their wombs, and women selling sex for money.

For evangelicals for whom cisgenderism, heterosexuality, and monogamy are normative, these provocative claims tantalize enough to sound true and scandalize enough to discourage scrutiny. "Some women in Ephesus," Kimball suggests, "were now part of the new faith, part of the worship gatherings of this new church" to whose leader Paul writes in 1 Timothy. By portraying the women in the Christian community as having come to the church from a cultural context of sexual deviance, Kimball renders Paul's silencing of them more agreeable to readers who are primed to see such deviance as dangerous.

Kimball's rhetorical accomplishment here illustrates one of the most common solutions to the perceived problem of Paul's misogyny. If interpreters can "recover" an ancient background or circumstances in which Paul was writing that are believed to mitigate the trouble of the troubling passages, his words can be made more palatable to modern ears. Part of what gives this strategy its power of persuasion is that the apologists who deploy it present their task not as innovating or constructing so much as retrieving something lost. The project is presented as one aimed at recovery. But these Bible apologists are in fact constructing rather than excavating. They are *producing* something: a "context" within which to situate Paul that will explain his behavior. What Kimball produces is a picture of dangerous women surrounded by sexual deviance. Implied is that these women deserved Paul's silencing.

Significantly, a standard feature of the contexts that Bible-redeemers manufacture is that they are pornographic—fantastically and productively so. *Fantastically* in the sense that they indulge in fantasy, both sexual and historical. Sex, sexiness, and sexuality are introduced in places where they are not originally in view, as historical "facts" are invented entirely through creative (and, some might say, inaccurate) interpretations of ancient literature. The pornographic renderings are *productive* because they function to communicate what behavior on the part of women is acceptable and what behavior warrants their silencing. Bible-redeemers' depictions of women, whether they recognize it or not, sift women into categories of *good* and *bad*. The striking irony is that interpretations presented as anti-misogynistic are actually, to recall Kate Manne's definition of misogyny, doing the police work of patriarchy.

This Bible rehabilitation technique is therefore not only pornographic but, to coin a term, *pornodoxic*. Interpreters who deploy this strategy engage in *pornodoxy*, the regulation of right belief and practice while imagining sex, sexiness, or sexual desire. Pornodoxic readings of Paul invent dangerous, sexy women in the course of explaining potentially troubling Bible passages about women, all the while engaging in the regulation of women's bodies and behavior.[30]

Pornodoxy

A figure within white evangelical biblical interpretation with an outsize influence on other Bible rehabilitators in this vein is Scot McKnight, who writes a popular evangelical blog called "Jesus Creed" currently hosted by *Christianity Today* and who serves as Professor of New Testament at Northern Baptist Theological Seminary in Lisle, Illinois.[31] McKnight is the author of numerous Bible commentaries and other books about the Bible, including *The Blue Parakeet: Rethinking How*

You Read the Bible, published by Zondervan in 2008 with a second edition released in 2018. In this book, McKnight creates an ancient context for Paul that helps him argue a case that the Bible does not, in fact, silence women. Examining the Bible's ancient historical context was transformative for McKnight's position toward women's participation in church leadership. He reports in the book that he did not always support the full participation of women in church ministry leadership. He pauses his argument to apologize for not having spoken up sooner on behalf of women he respected who were disallowed from leadership positions:

> Before I go on, I must confess I believe I (and my colleagues) failed our female students at Trinity, that we should have engaged this debate 'tooth and claw,' and that had we done so the Evangelical Free Church as well as that seminary may have been a much more liberating institution than it is today. I want to confess to the many female students that we (and I) were wrong and I'm asking you to forgive us (and me).[32]

The Blue Parakeet is McKnight's belated intervention in the debate, his move from apathy to advocacy. Yet when it comes down to naming what it is that changed his mind, McKnight does not point principally to the women but rather to the Bible—the very texts he had been studying and teaching about for years.[33] More specifically, the Bible's ancient context impressed itself upon McKnight. "My change was gradual," he writes, "and what most changed it was the study of the New Testament and the realization that I believed the New Testament—all of it—*emerged from and therefore was shaped by* the first-century Jewish and Greco-Roman culture, including what it said about women."[34] Examining the Bible's originating ancient historical context became the key that unlocked the door. Close attention to the historical reconstructions offered in *The Blue Parakeet* reveals that they rely on historical invention. The key only fits a lock of McKnight's own design.

In order to "contextualize" Paul's words in the letters to Timothy, McKnight develops a global claim about the sort of women on the scene in Roman antiquity. He writes that there was an "aggressive, confrontational public presence on the part of women during the very time Paul was writing these letters."[35] McKnight goes on to list a series of characteristics of these women and to illustrate the traits with literary or archaeological evidence from outside the Bible.

One way this problematic "public presence" manifested was, McKnight suggests, in sexy dress tied to sexual behavior. "First," he begins, "the new Roman woman was expressing her newfound freedoms in *immodest, sexually provocative, and extravagant dress.*"[36] Without explaining why he associates "extravagant" dress with sexual provocation, he goes on to suggest that these women's sluttiness was of a kind even the pagans do not tolerate: "Rome was not terribly conservative but these women were flouting even the limits of the Romans."[37] The extrabiblical piece of evidence that McKnight summons to illustrate the "fact" that such women were present in ancient Ephesus—the purported setting behind Paul's letter to Timothy—comes from an ancient novel by Xenophon called "An Ephesian Tale." McKnight pulls from this ancient novel a *femme fatale*. Her name is Anthia, and he pictures her doing a striptease in church.

A *FEMME FATALE*

McKnight offers a scenario in which an extravagantly dressed Ephesian woman engages in sexually provocative behavior by, in his words, "baring her body to a man in a worship service."

The passage from Xenophon's novel that McKnight quotes to illustrate Anthia's behavior reads:

> And so when the procession was over, the whole crowd went into the temple for the sacrifice, and the files broke up; men and women and girls and boys came together. Then they saw each other, and Anthia was captivated by Habrocomes, while Love got the better of Habrocomes. He kept looking at the girl and in spite of himself could not take his eyes off her. Love held him fast and pressed home his attack. And Anthia too was in a bad way, as she let his appearance sink in, with rapt attention and eyes wide open; and already she paid no attention to modesty: what she said was for Habrocomes to hear, and she revealed what she could of her body for Habrocomes to see. And he was captivated at the sight and was a prisoner of the god (1.3).[38]

"Seduction in the middle of a worship service," McKnight writes of this passage.[39] "That's what Xenophon described in this novel," he claims, "and that is why Paul says what he says about women in the church services at Ephesus."[40] Anthia becomes for McKnight a shocking, extreme example of what women should not do, of what Paul wants women not to do. She is the reason Paul had to say what he did in 1 Timothy 2, when he writes that "the women should dress themselves in moderate clothing with reverence and self-control, not with their hair braided or with gold, pearls, or expensive clothes, but with good works, as is proper for women who profess reverence for God" (9–10). McKnight introduces sexiness into the scene by invoking Anthia.

This reading requires a leap of logic that goes unacknowledged. It makes make-believe real. Anthia is a character from a work of fiction (written, not incidentally, by a man). To use a moment from Xenophon's novel as evidence for what real women were doing in antiquity would be analogous to a modern movie-goer watching *The Wedding Planner* (2001) and concluding that two decades ago it was widespread practice for women to plan weddings for a living only to ensnare and wed the betrothed man out from under the original bride. No reasonable viewer would leave a screening of this film in a panic over wedding planners becoming man-stealers in the real world. McKnight's reading takes a woman created in a man's imagination and turns her into a real ancient woman. It then takes that imaginary real woman's behavior and generalizes it to become the behavior of *lots* of real women. Imaginary woman = real woman = lots of real women. Imaginary sexy seductress = real sexy seductress = lots of real sexy seductresses. Lots of real sexy seductresses = why Paul instructed women to be quiet in 1 Timothy. The implied argument is that readers today should not hold Paul so accountable for his words about women because his words were understandable given the actual or potential behavior of the real women acting like Anthia. They gave him no choice.

In addition to a logical leap, this reading requires a great deal of interpretive license. McKnight's reading of Anthia does not capture how *Anthia the character* is actually portrayed in Xenophon's novel. Important details of the novel's plot that do not appear in the passage McKnight excerpts militate against interpreting Anthia as the *femme fatale* McKnight makes her out to be. That is, her sluttiness is not only condemned in this pornodoxic reading; it is invented. A full reading of Xenophon's novel reveals that what McKnight calls a "love affair, a glorious one" between the two protagonists is in fact a courtship and marriage.[41]

The moment in the novel that McKnight represents as a seduction scene at a worship service is better described as a meet-cute at a public town festival, a fated encounter that will lead to a wedding. This scene is a stock part of the ancient romance genre in which a man and a woman fall madly in love at first sight—only to be separated and eventually find their way to be together. This is exactly what happens with Anthia and Habrocomes. Further, in Xenophon's "Ephesian Tale," a legitimate question could be raised about the degree of agency that Anthia has in the romance at all, for the meet-cute has not come about by natural means. The god Eros (translated "Love" in the excerpt McKnight quotes) is pulling strings behind the scenes as a sort of power play. Feeling insufficiently appreciated by Habrocomes, Eros grabs his "full armory of love potions and set out against" him. His plan is to make the man fall in love.

After they meet at the festival, at the bidding of Eros, Anthia and Habrocomes part from one another lovestruck. As time goes on and they are not together, lovestruck becomes lovesick. The protagonists are distraught, and they both become physically ill from longing each for the other. Because neither has confessed their love to anyone, their parents do not know how to help them. When Anthia and Habrocomes's bodies reach the point of near-death, their respective fathers appeal, as a last resort, to the oracle of Apollo for help. As a result of the enigmatic prophecy returned to them, the parents decide to marry Anthia and Habrocomes, hoping to placate the god. The pair is, of course, overjoyed. They are married and only then ravish one another. They make dramatic oaths to one another to remain sexually faithful. The rest of the novel narrates their successful follow-through, even in the face of numerous temptations sent their way. At the end of the story, readers are assured, the pair "lived happily ever after."

McKnight's portrayal of the setting of the couple's initial meeting as "a worship service" makes the moment feel more scandalizing to modern readers than it likely would if readers were given more of the novel. What is depicted in the story is not a worship service. It is, rather, a public festival. The townspeople and visitors alike have gathered in Ephesus for a mile-long procession to the temple of Artemis. As are the other girls, Anthia is dressed as Artemis, a virginal huntress.[42] McKnight cites only one line about Anthia's hair to represent her as immodestly dressed. But the full text describes Anthia this way:

> Her hair was golden—a little of it plaited, but most hanging loose and blowing in the wind. Her eyes were quick; she had the bright glance of a young girl, and yet the austere look of a virgin. She wore a purple tunic down to the knee, fastened with a girdle and falling loose over her arms, with a fawnskin over it, a quiver attached, and arrows for weapons; she carried javelins and was followed by dogs.

McKnight's word "seduction" to describe Anthia's behavior conjures images of a sexually experienced woman baring her breasts in order to ensnare an unsuspecting sexual partner. But the text does not describe her this way at all. When it really comes down to it, Anthia is a *fourteen-year-old girl wearing a lot of clothing in a public setting.* She very likely would have trouble baring very much of her body. Her tunic is long and under an animal skin. Her sleeves are flowy and obstructed by hunting equipment. Her parents are there. Everyone's parents are there. The whole town is there.

McKnight's interpretation of Anthia's behavior as innovative in its lurid nature also strains the evidence. Xenophon's novel is not in fact presenting "new" behavior on the part of women or a woman. The religious practices the characters are engaged in are not the subject of the story but rather a background against which the action of the novel can take place, which means that the religious behavior of the characters should be considered routine and unremarkable rather than exceptional or scandalous.[43] The text gives every indication, further, that Anthia is complying with, rather than flouting, Roman expectations of her behavior. By this point in the story, the narrator has already told readers that "it was the custom at this festival to find husbands for the girls and wives for the young men." In other words, Anthia is doing exactly what is expected of her—she is finding a husband. Further, in the novel Anthia does not have sex with Habrocomes until they are married, even in the face of deep desire beforehand, and she goes on to refuse to have sex with anyone but Habrocomes in their post-nuptial adventures. Not only is she complying with Roman expectations of her behavior but she could easily be described as an appealing model for modern evangelical Christians who decry premarital or extramarital sex.

When read in the context of the whole of Xenophon's novel, Anthia is more virgin than vixen, flirty without being fast—and only that with the man she will later marry, to whom she will stay faithful forever, and with whom she will live happily ever after. McKnight's pornodoxic reading of Anthia turns a lovesick fourteen-year-old girl who flirts across a crowded festival with her future husband, to whom she later becomes an ever-faithful wife, into a *femme fatale*. When put next to 1 Timothy, this depiction of Anthia is supposed to provide a rationale for Paul's words, to explain the apostle's motivations as a way of defending what he said, not only about modest dress but also about speech. The very next sentence in 1 Timothy 2 is Paul's command for women to be silent. *Oh, that's the type of woman Paul was silencing. That makes sense. She really should not have been doing that.* It is acceptable to silence certain kinds of women, the argument implies. In the fleshing out of the kind of woman whose behavior needs policing, this inventive reading of Xenophon generates a "bad woman" who needs correcting. McKnight makes her up so Paul can shut her up. And then everyone can feel good about it.

FROM SEX TO SPEECH AND BACK AGAIN

McKnight pairs Anthia the seductress with an unnamed woman who talks too much. His second invented woman is one who speaks, particularly in a space where speech is deemed a prerogative of men. The "new Roman woman," McKnight writes, "was noted for *snatching the podium for public addresses and teaching.*"[44] The word choice of "snatching" here implies a speech economy in which the podium is properly reserved for men; it is his to lose and hers to (inappropriately) take. The perceived threat has transitioned from seduction to usurpation. McKnight's extrabiblical support for this claim comes from a section of ancient text called *Satire 6* written by Juvenal. McKnight states that the words he presents from Juvenal are "words that describe something like what Paul was concerned about." The passage in question reads:

> But most intolerable of all is the woman who as soon as she has sat down to dinner commends Virgil, pardons the dying Dido, and pits the poets against each other, putting Virgil in the one scale and Homer in the other. The grammarians make way before her; the rhetoricians give in; the whole crowd is silenced: no lawyer, no auctioneer will get a word in, no, nor any other woman; so torrential is her speech that you would think that all the pots and bells were being clashed together . . . She lays down definitions, and discourses on morals, like a philosopher.[45]

The loquacious woman is, like McKnight's version of Anthia, ripped from a larger work whose attributes are hidden from view in McKnight's argument.

A closer look at *Satire 6* reveals the creativity required to make this passage serve as evidence that Paul's Ephesian women were snatching podiums. The first invention becomes apparent from a reading of only the lines McKnight quotes: there is no podium in this scene, nor public address. The arena is instead the dinner table, where an educated woman speaks and the narrator is annoyed that she speaks so much and out of place. Like Xenophon's Anthia, further, the loquacious woman is a fictional character. She is not a real woman, which makes it difficult to make a case methodologically that the behavior of the woman in Juvenal's satire matches the behavior of real women. It is even more of a stretch to claim that such behavior matches that of real women in Ephesus, since, unlike Xenophon's novel, Juvenal's work has no explicit connections to Ephesus.

One must also ignore the genre of Juvenal's work to claim this woman as representative of real women. It is the nature of satires to exaggerate for effect. To make this passage work as evidence for McKnight's argument is also to assume that the narrator can be equated with a real person, the author. Yet in *Satire 6*, Juvenal has created what classics scholars call a *persona*, an adopted character. The narrator's speech must be analyzed differently than if the piece were a treatise penned by an author representing his own perspective at each turn. When *Satire 6* is read in its entirety, it becomes clear that the narrator has one goal: to convince his friend, named Postumus, not to get married.[46] He pulls out all the stops, though Postumus is ultimately unpersuaded. It is to such an end that the narrator consistently hyperbolizes, universalizes, and then rails against "bad" behavior of all wives. The point is that no woman at all is worth being married to. All wives, according to the narrator, are adulteresses. As a specific example, the narrator describes the wife of Claudius, who sneaked out each night to prostitute herself at a brothel. Once there, "she graciously received all comers, asking from each his fee." The narrator indicates that she stayed the longest, went the hardest, and even then was sad to have to leave. She returned "exhausted but unsatisfied."

Yet, the narrator continues, when it comes to women, "their sins of lust are the least of all their sins." A man cannot marry for money, he argues, because a woman with a dowry cannot be trusted. She is too independent. A man cannot marry for beauty because the beauty will fade—but in the meantime she will have bled the man dry by taking and taking. She is too dependent. Even a "perfect" wife—one who complies with every expectation of appearance, behavior, and pedigree—is not desirable. To the woman who is the most beautiful and chaste and wealthy and well-bred and brilliant, the narrator objects: "yet who could endure a wife that possessed all perfections?" She will be intolerably haughty, he reasons. "And who was ever so enamoured as not to shrink from the woman whom he praises to the skies," he asks, "and to hate her for seven hours out of every twelve?"

The list of indictments goes on. The satire's narrator asserts that a married man will never be at peace as long as his mother-in-law is alive. He claims that "there never was a case in court in which the quarrel was not started by a woman." He suggests that women are so unfaithful that even if a man locks his wife up at home she cannot be trusted because she will have sex with the men guarding her in exchange for their silence about her extramarital escapades. Women who are musical cannot be trusted, but it is better, he says, "that your wife should be musical than that she should be rushing boldly about the entire city, attending men's meetings, talking with unflinching face and hard breasts to Generals in their military cloaks, with her husband looking on!" Insufferable, too, is the woman who whips her neighbors because their dog barks too loudly at night. Then comes the section of material about the talkative woman that McKnight quotes—the "most intolerable of all," the educated woman who speaks at dinner. The narrator goes on to exclaim that he hates it when women learnedly research language, when they understand everything they read, and when they use a quote the narrator has never heard of. "Let husbands at least be permitted to make slips in grammar!" he implores angrily.

Over the course of his speech, the *Satire's* narrator gets increasingly enraged. As a result of his desperation to make any argument that will work, he engages in hyperbole and even downright misrepresentation of women's behaviors.[47] By the end, he is incoherent. He angrily attacks wives for being "calm and calculating" even as he sees them as lacking self-control.[48] As one classics scholar has observed, "it is evident that the only person out of control here is the speaker himself."[49]

The point of the satire's narrator is that no wife can ever be good enough. That is why, the narrator argues, his friend should not get married. McKnight pulls out one hypothetical woman from this hyperbolized diatribe without regard to the satire's aim or other contents. If Paul were to use this satire as a metric of Roman expectations worth imitating, he would also need to tell the women in Ephesus to stop tormenting their neighbors over noisy dogs and to stop having sex with the guards placed at their bedroom doors. In fact, if Paul were to use this satire as a metric of Roman expectations worth imitating, he would also have to enjoin the men in his audience to eschew women and marriage altogether and to sleep with boys instead. Indeed, the *Satire's* narrator asks his buddy how he can possibly marry a woman when it would be "much better to take some boy-bedfellow, who would never wrangle with you o' nights, never ask presents of you when in bed, and never complain that you took your ease and were indifferent to his solicitations!"

McKnight selectively quotes *Satire 6*, ignores its genre, and assumes its fictional characters represent real people in antiquity—all in order to show that Paul had good reason to regulate women's speech in 1 Timothy. The Bible is made good through bad readings of non-biblical texts.

Having moved from Anthia to the outrageous wife—from sex to speech—McKnight returns once more to sex, directing attention to Artemis as he rounds out his context for Paul's words about women.

A Really Weird Fertility Cult

The Bible can also be made good through good readings of bad historical texts, as long as the reader reproduces the ancient authors' fears of potential transgressive women. This strategy is what ultimately animates McKnight's depiction of the women in Ephesus who venerated Artemis. Like Kimball, McKnight characterizes the Artemis cult as "a religious fertility cult" with castrated men as priests, but rather than invoke prostitution, he decries women's purported refusal of marriage and, especially, maternity. With detail likely to be both alluring and alienating to modern evangelical readers, McKnight describes veneration of Artemis in this way:

> This worship cult not only favored the freedom of women in public religion but it also surrounded these worshipers with eunuch (castrated male) priests. Part of their worship was the elimination of normal sexual relations; these women despised marriage and child-bearing and child-rearing. Furthermore, this fertility cult extended their sexual and gender freedoms into open practices of abortion and contraception.[50]

Unlike in Kimball's reconstruction, the main problem here is not inappropriate sex but rather not having appropriate sex and then accepting its potential consequences of pregnancy and childbirth. Yet, "weird sex stuff" gets piled together again, combined in this case with "gender freedoms," a phrase undefined but that presumably means refusal of traditional roles assigned to women as mothers.

Significantly, these women are also inventions—inventions of ancient authors whose anxieties around women modern authors can replicate when it serves their interests to do so. McKnight does not offer ancient evidence for his description of the cult of Artemis and its practices; he instead includes a footnote referencing works of two modern scholars, also evangelical men, who read ancient Roman written sources about abortion naively.[51] Classics scholars have shown that the claims of ancient authors who wrote that women aborted children are not reportage but rather part of a "moral discourse in which women, particularly elite women, serve a symbolic purpose."[52] Literary references to abortion in the writings of Seneca, for example, the parade (but paltry) evidence offered in one book that McKnight cites "appear to be based on gossip or moralising fantasy rather than circumstantial knowledge of an established practice."[53] As classicist and ancient historian Susanne Dixon writes, "the historical value of such claims is moot."[54] Pointing out that real women, for a variety of reasons, would not have confided in men like Seneca if indeed they had had abortions,[55] she goes on: "These literary references, though taken for centuries as evidence of the moral decline of Roman society, are useless as historical information. Rather, they express masculine fears about secret female practices."[56]

For Bible benevolence projects, though, history does not have to be useful as historical information. History only has to be useful for Bible redemption. And imagining transgressive women is useful for such a project when one accepts the premise that their transgressions are what makes Paul's regulation good. McKnight constructs an ancient context for Paul's writings through inventions of women who are inappropriately sexually provocative, inappropriately talkative, and inappropriately refusing patriarchal use of their reproductive capacities. In so doing, McKnight interchanges women's speaking with women's sexual expression. He melds together women who take something conceived as not rightly theirs to take—platforms for speech—with women who give or withhold something conceived as not rightly theirs to give or withhold—their bodies. For evangelical Bible readers, this combination is likely to function similarly to Kimball's pairing of a settled issue with an uncomfortable one. Evangelical Christians for the most part agree that sex is rightly reserved for marriage, and that pregnancy, a potential result of such sex, is a righteous goal. Tying together sex— the regulation of which evangelicals regard as fundamentally good—and speech, then, turns regulation of sex into a reason to control women's speech.

BIBLICAL PORNODOXY

McKnight's pornodoxic historical reconstructions lead him to oversexualize Christian women as he reads the biblical text. That is, his logic exaggerates or whole cloth invents sexual promiscuity or gendered deviance on the part of women, who all turn out to be fictional—including the promiscuous women in Paul's community. McKnight quotes Paul:

> As for younger widows, do not put them on such a [widow] list. For when their *sensual desires* overcome their dedication to Christ, they want to marry. Thus they bring judgment on themselves, because they

have broken their first pledge [of faith in Christ].
(emphasis added).

Informed by the evidence he has constructed, McKnight
interprets:

> The language Paul uses for these women is noteworthy:
> he is describing a widow who has developed a promis-
> cuous, sexual lifestyle and who is thus abandoning the
> faith. These are not ordinary Christian young widows;
> these widows are a group of young women with a well-
> known reputation of public sexuality. This sounds very
> much like the new Roman woman.[57]

There is no evidence from 1 Timothy that the women in
Paul's community were violating sexual expectations. What
McKnight says the text says is not what the text says. It
is not even close to what the text says, except that both
1 Timothy and McKnight are thinking about women and sex
and whether women having sex is good or bad.

The biblical text says that the young widows are experiencing sexual desire and on account of that desire want
to get married. Marriage is the context in which they can
have authorized sex. McKnight turns this into young widows
having sex promiscuously, accusing them of having sex
outside of marriage.[58] Implied in his logic is that women who
experience sexual desire are having illicit sex. Women who
experience sexual desire while not married to a man must
be sluts. But for 1 Timothy, the women's sexual desire is a
problem not because it causes them to live promiscuously but
because it makes them want to get married. First Timothy is
not concerned that these women are sexually promiscuous but
that, as women who had already been widowed and vowed
to remain celibate, they are now breaking their vow to God.

The argument here is one that assumes that young people are quick to change their minds because of their sexual desires, in contrast to older women (1 Tim 5:9) who are presumed to be no longer flighty due to sexual urges.

The women in view in 1 Timothy 5:9–11 are channeling their sexual desire toward sex in a marriage. This is precisely what Paul wants them to do: if a young woman finds herself widowed, she should get married again. Otherwise, she will ultimately embarrass the group (5:13–14) by becoming a busybody and gossip. By putting herself under the authority of a man, her wayward womanly nature will be kept in check. Paul's concern is that they don't make and then break a sacred vow in the process. Contra McKnight, the widows seeking remarriage are in complete compliance with patriarchal expectations of their sexual activity (if not Paul's ideals of vow maintenance). They are choosing, in Paul's words, to marry rather than burn (1 Cor 7:9). These women are sluts only by McKnight's accounting, not by Paul's.

Yet 1 Timothy is still doing patriarchal police work. "When Paul asks women to be silent in 1 Timothy 2, he is not talking about ordinary Christian women," McKnight writes. Rather, Paul is targeting "a specific group of women," namely "some untrained, morally loose, young widows who, because they are theologically uninformed, are teaching unorthodox ideas."[59] For McKnight, Paul's policing is framed as beneficial because McKnight approves of Paul's motivations. Paul is engaging in misogyny when he regulates women by patriarchally-conditioned expectations of their behavior. Though Bible-redeemers do not state the fact so baldly, this is a premise that no evangelical Bible interpreter can get around without violating evangelical biblicism by, say, excising chapters and verses from their Bibles. Because they cannot argue that Paul was not regulating women, they are left with arguing that Paul's regulation was good. One way to make such regulation good is to make the women being regulated bad. Paul's policing is benevolent because the women were not complying with accepted norms. The Good Book is good because it turns bad women into good women.

In making such an argument, Bible defenders join Paul in doing the police work of patriarchy. Bible-redeemers are satisfied that Paul was not misogynistic if he can be understood as silencing only certain women at certain times in certain spaces for certain ends. Silencing women is not misogynistic *if* certain conditions are met. It is okay, the logic goes, to tell women to shut up if:

1. They are whores or might be whores.
2. They are assertive.
3. Their speech is distracting from one's goals.
4. Their speech is making one less respectable to the wider culture.

To make Paul good for women today, Bible-redeemers must supply circumstances of silencing that exceed the text, conditions for the silencing that Paul does not himself provide.

Without explicit guidance from Paul, Bible-redeemers themselves are the ones who articulate what sort of women are silenced and under what conditions. By rejecting a flat reading of the silencing passages, these evangelical interpreters introduce a regime of control over women's behavior that stands to elicit more compliance from women than if they saw in Paul's words a universal silencing. A total ban on women's speech would likely lead, perhaps even require, women today to reject the silencing passages entirely, and perhaps Paul and the Bible too. Total silence is not reasonable as a matter of pragmatism, if not ethics. Offering contours to Paul's silencing creates a system of reward and punishment for women wherein silencing is a stick and speech a carrot.

Women who comply with expectations of dress, conduct, and content of speech are the ones allowed to express themselves. As Bible-redeemers make Paul more benevolent, they make misogyny more feasible. This is a win-win for white evangelical Bible-redeemers who are privileged men, since they can enforce Paul's misogyny while presenting themselves too as benevolent, and their own desires as good for women.

It is simultaneously a lose-lose for women, since it makes no difference what women actually do. Though pornodoxic rhetorical projects rely on invocations of sex, sexiness, and concerns for sexual deviance, they are not ultimately about sex itself. They are, rather, about the *appearance* of sex, a suspicion of sex—a fear on the part of a man or men about the *potential* that a woman or women could engage in sexual activity that dominant men do not authorize. This is in part why it does not matter for the success of McKnight's argument whether fantasies about Anthia, the talkative woman, the venerators of Artemis, or the Christian women in Ephesus are tethered to reality. The reality that matters is merely what men perceive.

"Respectability" and Reputation Management

The privileging of what men see is fundamental to a different, or perhaps further, way that Bible-redeemers attempt to make Paul explicable and therefore acceptable. Empathizing with the apostle, they impute to him a goal they believe justifies the misogyny. Paul, in this common accounting, was ultimately addressing how the appearance and behavior of Christian women might impact the potential appeal of Christianity to an outside audience. McKnight writes, for example, that Paul was concerned "about the reputation of the gospel and the respectability of Christian women for fear they might be associated with the offensive side of such behaviors."[60] The Bible can be rendered good, then, so long as Paul's misogyny is deemed to be in service of a higher purpose, the accomplishment of which is viewed as the utmost priority: the advance of "the gospel."

Respectability is a common discourse for Bible benevolence projects to invoke in exculpations of Paul. Paul wanted the early Christians to be respectable, Bible-redeemers reason, which is what explains how he could say things that by today's prevailing standards are difficult to reckon with. He wanted the church to evangelize effectively and to do what it took to gain more adherents. He therefore wanted women to cohere with proper Roman expectations for women—for the sake of the gospel. The respectability-for-popularity argument animates white evangelical Bible-redeemer Philip Payne's benevolence project, particularly when it comes to 1 Corinthians 11, where Paul regulates women's appearance during specific religious activities.[61]

The apostle writes in 1 Corinthians 11 that "any woman who prays or prophesies with her head unveiled [or uncovered] shames her head—it is one and the same thing as having her head shaved." Paul mandates that women cover their heads while praying or prophesying. Interpreters, including translators, disagree about what precisely Paul wanted the women to cover their heads with, whether a veil made of fabric or their own long hair done up neatly on their heads. In either case, Paul certainly did not want women to have shaved heads. It is clear that the apostle was at least *that* interested in the Corinthian women's coiffure. No answer to the question of whether Paul wanted veils or pinned-up hair can enable either Paul or his redeemers to transcend the misogynistic monitoring of women's appearance. The very terms of the debate already ascribe to the apostle the entitlement to determine what women should look like when they pray or prophesy. This feature of the debate, then, must be concealed in the-Bible-is-anti-misogyny arguments.

Payne argues fervently that Paul meant long hair done up, not veiling, and that this conclusion shows that the Bible is pro-women.[62] Payne regards his conclusion about Paul's meaning to be the better option for women, though the reasons why are not articulated. It is certainly better for Bible redemption within white evangelical Christianity in the US, though, given that veiling is a foreign-feeling specter likely to be seen as inherently oppressive (as in the *God's Not Dead* movie scene). For Payne, it is good news for women that Paul wanted women to have long hair put up on their heads rather than veils.

A similar inattention to misogyny already built into the debate attends Payne's redemption of Paul when it comes to the logic animating the apostle's mandate. First Corinthians 11 can sustain multiple interpretations of the *reason* that Paul wanted the women to cover their heads—including one that views the apostle as helping women avoid sexual penetration by angels.[63] While traditionalist complementarians tend to embrace the notion that Paul was enjoining a material symbol of a woman's subordination to man,[64] Payne and other self-described egalitarians prefer a reading that sees Paul as accommodating Roman expectations of modest dress and deportment. Payne assumes that this, too, is good for women, presumably because it is better for women than the complementarian alternative.

Payne is satisfied with the idea that the Bible is good, including for women, if he can show that Paul meant long hair done up (versus veiling) and was motivated by a bid for respectability (versus subordination for some other reason). In this argument, Paul's motivation was to ensure that Christian women and men cohered with what Payne in turn endeavors to show were Roman expectations around proper gendered appearance. Rhetoric of respectability and adherence to custom suffuses his interpretation of the evidence he gathers. "There is abundant evidence," he writes, "that it was customary for women to wear their long hair up neatly on their heads in Corinth as throughout the ancient Roman and Hellenistic world of that time."[65] Payne invokes extant Roman statuary portraits as he claims that "invariably, respectable women had their hair done up."[66] "It only makes sense," he suggests, imputing his own perspective to ancient women, "that the women being portrayed wanted their statues to depict them in a respectable light." Paul, in Payne's view, had a good motivation because he wanted the appearance of Christian women to line up with Roman expectations for good Roman women.

Language of respectability further marks Payne's presentation of how Jewish women were supposed to wear their hair in antiquity. "Within Jewish culture," he claims, "all respectable women wore their hair done up in public."[67] Within Jewish culture it was "shameful," he goes on, "for a woman to have hair hanging down loose in public."[68] Paul did not want the Corinthian women to be found indecent by such a standard, particularly because, Payne says, "hair unbound was the sign of the accused adulteress."[69] The "accused" part of the phrase "accused adulteress" reveals that, as in the Numbers 5 passage that Payne invokes, it does not materially matter whether the women are complying with the patriarchal designation of their bodies as exclusively for their husbands' sexual access.[70] The accusation is what must be avoided.

What is at stake in Payne's accounting of Paul, ultimately, is what onlookers *think* the Corinthian women are doing with their bodies when it comes to sex. Even if (or even though) they were not having sex with partners who were not their husbands, they cannot let their hair down because doing so would endanger the reputation of the Christian community and, particularly, of the women's husbands. Payne asserts that "the Corinthian women had a moral obligation to exercise control over their heads by not letting their hair down, since that symbolized sexual looseness."[71] Payne draws comparisons to the cult of Dionysus, which he believes to be potentially influencing the Corinthians. He speculates that the Corinthian women might have wanted to let their hair down because they were influenced by practices common to the cult of Dionysus, which encouraged ecstatic experience and emphasized freedom. "Dionysiac practice," he writes, "reinforced the symbolism of hair let down loose: sexual looseness and repudiation of marital commitment to sexual fidelity."[72] A woman letting her hair down would have been "embarrassing, if not an affront" to members of the Corinthian church, but more significantly would have failed to protect a designated man's reputation. "It would be particularly disgraceful to her husband," Payne intuits, "since it symbolized her repudiation of sexual fidelity to her husband."[73]

A woman's husband is deemed entitled to admiration by outsiders, and her appearance must be modified to ensure he gets the respect he is presumed to deserve—all the while using her manner of dress as a means of conveying to the world her compliance with patriarchal demands. Women are thus expected to communicate to a viewing public, via their hairstyle, compliance with patriarchal norms around sex, for the sake of their husbands' reputations.[74] Christian interpreters who sympathize with Paul's motivation here because they see the apostle as pulling out all the stops to help the ancient Christian community win the respect of Romans are assenting to the idea that a man's regulation of women's dress and speech in compliance with patriarchal norms is desirable as long as it serves a higher purpose.

Their arguments rely on an implicit, though ultimately incoherent, alliance of what is good for "the gospel" with what is good for women. Significantly, the respectability-for-popularity argument can only work if "the gospel" is interchangeable with the opinions, aesthetics, and interests of dominant men in a patriarchal social order. Respectability in these projects is always represented as a transparent good. Yet to be "respectable" to a culture is to reflect the values of the powerful—those who define, benefit from, and demand "respect." These are the people who have enough status that they can define "respectable" in such a way that it works to their benefit and helps them maintain power, a fact well illustrated by the history of "respectability" discourse as a tool wielded by privileged white Americans to patrol Black men and women.[75]

The respectability-for-popularity argument presumes a particular type of person as the target whom Paul wanted to attract: the hegemonic. The argument only works if Paul's primary concern was to appease and attract powerful men who were setting the agenda for women's appropriate behavior. A "respectable" woman is a woman who coheres with the expectations of patriarchy. This reasoning disempowers women and others whose behavior must be modified to appeal to the powerful. If one were to imagine a community attempting to attract the oppressed, the powerless, the marginalized, one would not demand that community members be "respectable" to Roman elites. The fact that today—at least in places where public opinion reckons human enslavement a moral evil—the same logic can only be *very* uncomfortably applied to Paul's endorsements of slavery underscores that the conform-to-attract argument protects the power of the powerful, whose aesthetics and expectations become normative.[76] As the gospel advances, so do the interests of dominant men in the Christian community.

Paul, within a discourse of respectability, assents to prevailing norms that view a woman's manner of modest dress as conveying her sexual fidelity to one man and that deem dressing immodestly to be wrong because it sends the message that she is available to men when, by the norms of patriarchy, she should not be. The Paul of these Bible-redeemers accepts rather than contests the notion that the way a woman dresses is supposed to make her legible to men and that her speech must be carefully managed so as not to usurp the privilege of privileged men. This Paul joins the Romans he desires to attract in conceiving of women's bodies as inherently sexual and women's speech as earned. He joins the Romans, further, in rendering the purpose of women's bodily presentation as communicating to men the women's sexual (un)availability, which itself is determined by patriarchal norms around sex and marriage. By affirming Paul, Bible-redeemers replicate these views of women. "Most men would agree," Payne writes as he explicates Paul, "that of all creation, woman is the most beautiful."[77]

A woman reading any of these Christian interpreters' apologetics might reasonably internalize that her body is for men to see, to assess, and to potentially access—depending on the men's assessment. There is a double compliance expected of women, then. Pragmatically, they must dress in a certain way, avoiding adornment or adorning themselves the right way. Intellectually, they must buy into a system of patriarchal regulation of their bodies, avoiding affirmation of their agency and desire. A woman's body becomes not only an object of surveillance by privileged men but also an object of inspection—inspection that treats her body as a sexual commodity and her sexuality as something that, if harnessed, can be leveraged to support a "greater" cause that advances the interests of the inspectors.

White evangelical Bible benevolence projects that claim the Bible as good because it is empowering to women must presume that these views of women are empowering to women. Paul's misogyny must be made good for women through creative rhetorical work. With respect to

1 Corinthians 11, Payne suggests that Paul had a "thorny problem" to solve because the apostle was fundamentally a gender egalitarian who also perceived a need for reputation management.[78] "How could women demonstrate Christian liberty and equality in Christ," he imagines Paul asking himself, "without bringing offense to the gospel?"[79] The answer, Payne suggests, is that Paul does so "by honoring women as fully human even though this clashed with cultural conventions, and [affirming] prophecy by women if done with modest deportment (1 Cor 11:4–5)."[80]

Both the question and the answer Payne formulates for Paul engage in strategic semantics to make the Bible benevolent. Each presents fundamental goods available to women because of Christ, which are then immediately followed by a caveat. In the question, the goods are liberty and equality. In the answer, the goods are, on the one hand, being recognized as human and, on the other, being allowed to prophesy. Though Payne does not acknowledge that the caveats present constraints, they are indeed limitations. The question's built-in limitation is that women cannot exercise liberty and equality as they see fit—they can do so only when it does not threaten to damage the community's (and their husbands') good reputation. The answer's built-in limitation is that women, who are humans, cannot prophesy in any way they see fit—they can only do so when it coheres with patriarchally determined norms around how women should comport themselves. Pragmatically, each limitation makes the goods offered to women worth less or disappear altogether. This is especially the case when it comes to precisely the value Payne most wants to attribute to Paul—egalitarianism.

Payne's use of the terms "liberty" and "equality" as though they are functionally synonyms masks the inequality that is inevitable in this system. His language, together with confidence, hides the fact that the scenario Payne envisions makes it logistically, if not logically, impossible for women to be equal to men, unless patriarchal social order were already eliminated outside of Christian participation. Liberty and equality are in fact of fundamentally different characters. Liberty is relative. It can exist on a sliding scale. Women can be more or less liberated. Equality, though, is absolute. Equality does not come in degrees. One cannot be more equal or less equal and still be equal. Equality, unlike liberty, is a zero-sum game. As soon as there is a disparity of equality, the result is inequality. Putting any kind of limitation on equality makes it cease to exist. This fundamental difficulty for the argument is harder to see, however, because Payne builds in a version of Pastor Dave's "considering the time when it was written" benevolence strategy. He praises Paul for seeing women as humans even though doing so "clashed with cultural conventions."[81] The Bible is conceived to be fundamentally good because the goods Paul offered women— even if limited—were good by comparison to those offered by others during the historical time period in which Paul was writing.

When it serves their argument for Paul to be bucking cultural conventions, Bible-redeemers contrast the apostle with the surrounding culture to present him as progressive for his time. When the evidence regarding what Paul did or said cannot possibly be said to be bucking cultural conventions, they characterize him as intentionally fitting in with the surrounding culture for the purpose of respectability. With such an interpretive paradigm, white evangelical writers can make any piece of data support a Bible benevolence project by moving strategically between a "progressive-for-their-time" depiction and a "fitting-in-for-a-higher-purpose" explanation. The alternation functionally eliminates the very possibility of counterevidence. It is a win-win strategy to recruit Paul to their side because when either option is available, no piece of data is unexplainable.

This combination of strategies is an ingenious way to meet the demands of the evidence that actually exists in the Bible, which is most naturally interpreted historically in support of a conclusion that Paul can be located comfortably within the range of points of view and acceptable behaviors available to men in antiquity when it came to women. He is the-same-but-sometimes-different in precisely the way that other men were similar to and yet sometimes different from one another in antiquity. White evangelical Bible-redeemers need for Paul to be special enough in his context that they can depict him as affirming women—but not so special that his affirmation of women damages the Christian community's reputation in the eyes of the prevailing (patriarchal) society. This is a kind of specialness guaranteed not to make any real challenge to the status quo.

This strategy also plays out with respect to Jesus. In the same Bible benevolence project, for example, Payne argues that Jesus was transformative in his treatment of women but that there were constraints on women in Jesus's ministry because cultural expectations in his historical context limited what Jesus could do and still maintain "respectability." Payne explains the lack of women in the inner circle of Jesus's Twelve by envisioning that Jesus followed an ancient version of the "Billy Graham rule," the famous evangelist's practice of refusing to be alone with a woman who was not his wife, even for a ride in a car or elevator.[82] Payne writes that the absence of women in Jesus's leadership team was due to "practical issues." The issues have to do with notions of propriety and respectability:

It is one thing for a number of women to be mentioned as following Jesus from time to time in his preaching in the towns . . . but traveling full time for three years with late night meetings such as at the Garden of Gethsemane and spending periods of time in the wilderness are quite another thing. Strong cultural objections and moral suspicions would undoubtedly be raised not only about Jesus, but also about the men whom he chose to be with him. Married women could hardly leave their families for such a long period, and single women would have been even more suspicious. To have chosen women disciples would have raised legitimate suspicion undermining the gospel.[83]

Payne goes on to say that slaves should also not be barred from ministry just because Jesus did not include slaves in the Twelve: "The church should no more exclude women from its leadership simply because none of the Twelve were women than it should other social groups since they were not among the Twelve, including Gentiles, slaves, and freed slaves." "Why exclude based on silence?" he asks.[84]

Close attention to this train of thought emphasizes that liberty and equality are not in fact synonyms and, further, that neither one guarantees the other. "Slaves who became church leaders," Payne writes, "exemplify the equal standing of slaves in the church."[85] That enslaved persons can be imagined as somehow "equal" while simultaneously enslaved goes to show that making someone "equal" in the church does not require dismantling systems of oppression. Making someone equal, or thinking of someone as equal, does not necessitate liberty. The sentiment "let slaves be ministers" is very different from a charge not to enslave people at all. So also "let women be ministers" is different from a charge to release them from patriarchal regulation. Liberating someone from particular constraints does not mean that they are therefore equal.

Discourse of "respectability," particularly when presented as an uninterrogated value, distracts from the fact that limitations are limitations. It disguises constraints. Respectability is thus a way not only to make the Bible's hierarchical social structures benevolent by hiding the hierarchy but also a mechanism to ensure that the status and privileges of dominant men in the social hierarchy are not undermined. History can save the Bible from critique—but only if it is invented or strategically deployed. History can save the evangelical Christian in a bind between what the Bible says and what society thinks is good for women—but only through obfuscations that make them appear to coincide.

Ultimately, white evangelical Bible-redeemers who make this argument do so in order that they themselves will not bring offense to "the gospel" in a time and place in which explicit or obvious misogyny is not socially acceptable. They perceive that it is not "respectable" to outsiders in their own context to be a misogynist.[86] The resulting apologetic is not really about women. It is also not *really* about the Bible. Bible benevolence projects advanced by privileged, influential white evangelical men often defend in the end not women, not even the Bible itself, but rather the reputation of the apologists' biblicism. The Bible's misogyny must be merely apparent, not actual, so that they can adopt the Bible as a moral guide and not be misogynists. The Bible only *seems* to be misogynistic, they seek to prove. They can ascribe to its authority, then, without risking falling out of step with prevailing social norms in the US that deem sexism and misogyny outdated, undesirable, or unethical. Their own reputation is bound up with the Bible's reputation.

SAFE WOMEN, DANGEROUS BIBLE

In *How (Not) to Read the Bible*, Dan Kimball begins his discussion of the Bible and misogyny with his own experience as a man encountering uncomfortable verses about women in the Bible. He narrates how he came to grapple in the first place with biblical passages that prohibit women from speaking in churches. The way that Kimball tells the story is revealing.

Kimball documents his successive experience in two evangelical churches, one in England and one in the US, that he observes had contrasting stances on women in the church. It was only when he took on a leadership role in the US church and was compelled to read aloud the biblical "silencing passages" in the presence of women that he realized these verses were in the Bible and needed wrestling with.

Of his London church of about twenty elderly members, Kimball writes: "They began teaching me about Jesus. The pastor and his wife were in their eighties, and although the pastor was the leader of the church, when I asked questions his wife was always incredibly helpful. She knew the Bible really well and taught me a lot." In fact, many of the elderly women "had a lot of Bible knowledge" and were welcoming of his questions. As a result, he writes, "I had many Sunday lunchtime theology discussions with them in the basement of this church, eating sandwiches that they brought to feed me." Kimball then moves to tell a story of how he visited a US church, where upon his very first encounter he became conscious of the gender disparities on the church bulletin and in the worship service itself. "I would guess that half the people in this church were female," he observed, "but from an outside perspective there was no doubt this was a male led church." The pastors, elders, and teachers of adult education classes were all men, while one woman was listed as church secretary and another as "director" of women's ministry, a sematic subterfuge that avoids giving a woman the title of "minister" even if she is performing labor that is functionally parallel.

Based on the fact that Kimball's description of this second church occurs as an opening to his argument that the Bible is pro-women, one might expect that his next move would have been to find a different church, one that was more in line with his own convictions. But Kimball writes next about what happened as he "got involved in the life of that specific church." By his accounting, his experience in the initial London church caused him to value the contributions of women. But when he came to a US church that obviously excluded women from the highest positions of power, his previous experience did not dissuade him from getting involved. Rather than sounding alarm bells for him, the inequity worked in his favor. He noticed that women were functionally ministering "behind the scenes," without titles. "But the women were highly respected," he writes, "so I didn't think too much about the topic" at the time.

One might wonder why his experience in the first church did not encourage him to interrogate the gender disparities in the second church. Close attention to how he writes about the women in the London church shows that those women, while influential for him, were safe. They were operating within patriarchal expectations and cohered with patriarchal norms. He tames the pastor's wife's knowledge of the Bible by describing her principally not with an adjective like "impressive" or "inspiring" or "imposing" but with the word "helpful." Her Bible knowledge and teaching were valued insofar as they *helped him.* He paints a picture of the London women as nurturers, offering goods to him traditionally associated with feminine labor. Their labor and their knowledge are valued as far as they were directed for his benefit. The women nourished him with food they had prepared. This was no potluck wherein he was expected to contribute equally, or even at all. He receives from women as givers—of time, of answers, of sandwiches.

Kimball narrates that he did not think much about why women in the second church were not given equal access to power or leadership titles, until, he says, "the day I had a very awkward and uncomfortable Bible study session that I will never forget." While serving as a ministry leader for young adults, he led an in-home small group meeting.[87] The topic one night was women in the church, and he had been given a handout from the church leadership with Bible verses supporting their stance. He and his young adults decided to look up these Bible verses and read them. A woman read aloud to the group 1 Timothy 2:11—"a woman should learn in quietness and full submission. I do not permit a woman to teach or assume authority over a man; she must be quiet."

Kimball reports being haunted by this moment: "I still remember the uncomfortable feeling that began spreading around the room. There was an awkward pause and the female college student asked a question and made direct eye contact with me, looking puzzled." Before he could respond, he writes, someone else in the room read 1 Corinthians 14:34–35, compounding the befuddlement. "It felt quite surreal and jarring," he recounts, "to hear these Bible verses being read out loud and then having all eyes fixed on me." It was especially uncomfortable, he shares, because of the *sort* of women in this group—"several female college students studying economics and computer science, and another getting a PhD in microbiology." Educated women in fields traditionally dominated by men are onlookers he stands to be ashamed in front of. He reports that he "sat there thinking 'Oh God, oh God, oh God, what do I say?'" before demurring and saying he would ask the church pastors later. "I wanted to hide behind the couch and wait until they all left," he discloses. But he couldn't. He was, in that moment, "embarrassed that these verses were in the Bible."

In this story, Kimball became a Christian, got through two churches, and became a leader of ministry in one of them before he had to ask questions about the Bible and women. It was his own embarrassment in a context wherein he would otherwise be due admiration that sparked his interest in investigating the troubling passages. His quest to resolve the disturbing questions that the silencing-women passages raised is framed as a quest to avoid discomfort on his part. It was to restore his confidence—to get him out from behind the couch.

Kimball's book does not appreciate that for Christian women seeking to resolve these questions, the matter is much more existential than awkward. "If you are a thinking Christian in today's world or someone who is considering Christianity," he writes in a direct address to his readers, "I don't believe you have a choice—you must explore these verses." He directs his reader to consider "what [they] would have said to those women." Later in the chapter, he comments that "it can be awkward to talk about Bible verses that—at face value—seem to demean and devalue women." Each of these sentences presumes an audience of men, those who share Kimball's privilege of neglecting the silencing passages because they themselves would not be subject to being silenced by them. "Maybe you are like me," he suggests, "and [you have] never really thought much about those verses, but that is no longer an option."

The reason he offers that it is not an option to ignore them is *not* because he desires Christians not to use these biblical verses to oppress or limit women. It is because, rather, he wants to equip his reader to avoid embarrassment. "Verses like these are now shared across the internet," he observes, "and if you don't have a response when asked about them, you need to get one." Kimball's language together with his implied audience suggests that his advocacy here is not for women but rather for the respectability of the Bible and his own reputation as a Christian seeking moral authority.[88] Kimball's book, like other such Bible benevolence projects, is not fundamentally an advocacy resource for women who find themselves resisting oppression in contexts where the Bible is treated authoritatively. Kimball's book is an explainer to help those privileged enough not to face oppression resist being seen as oppressors for following the Bible. His Bible benevolence is about his own respectability and that of others who see the Bible as universally authoritative and unconditionally benevolent.

Who Must Paul Be Made Good For?

At the same time, Kimball refuses to be governed himself by demands for respectability within the Christian community. He does not want to be regulated by what Paul, or anyone else, says about how he should dress or wear his hair. When it comes to his own self-expression and autonomy, ancient Roman history is irrelevant. Paul's motivations are irrelevant. Even the Bible itself is irrelevant.

In a book entitled *Adventures in Churchland: Finding Jesus in the Mess of Organized Religion*, published prior to his Bible benevolence book, Kimball dedicates a chapter to recounting pain he experienced when a church pastor advised him to cut his hair and to dress in pleated khakis once he assumed a leadership role in the church. He found the experience humiliating, stifling, and wrong. It did not feel right, not at all.

Kimball was nervous but excited, he shares, to take on a role helping with the church youth group. That is, until his enthusiasm was met with a type of supervision he did not expect in the pastor's office one day. "Okay there are some things you'll need to do if you're going to work with youth here," Kimball recalls the pastor saying. Smiling, the pastor went on: "First, you really need to get a haircut." Kimball reports being stunned into silence by this comment—and then again when the pastor slid a twenty-dollar bill his way. "Here. This haircut is on me."

Kimball's hair, he writes, was styled into a pompadour in honor of his favorite '50s musicians. He really liked his hair the way it was. It was meaningful to him. "I had never thought," Kimball narrates with palpable anguish, "that I'd be asked to cut my hair to serve in a ministry of the church." The church pastor went on to inform the stunned Kimball that he had already heard some complaints about his appearance from concerned parents in the church. Kimball describes his reaction in terms of a near-existential crisis:

> As he was saying all of this, it was as if everything in my body, mind, and soul was aching. I felt horribly embarrassed, wondering how many others in the church also felt this way about my appearance. I was already sensitive to the fact that my background as a punk and rockabilly musician might be seen as a negative. Being a fairly new Christian, I was devastated. I assumed that because the church and this pastor felt this way about my hairstyle, God felt that way too. I felt foolish, ashamed that my hair could be displeasing to God, since I badly wanted to be doing what God wanted me to do.[89]

After hair came clothes. The pastor, the story goes, next suggested that Kimball take a black Sharpie marker to the "flamboyant" yellow stitching on his shoes. He invited him to his home to dress him in "appropriate" clothing for ministry. "I felt embarrassed and judged and pretty terrible," Kimball says. He left the pastor's office "head down" and "heart crushed."

Kimball got his hair cut, even as he was tormented by the task. He went to the pastor's house and reluctantly tried on the pastor's conservative clothing, including golf shirts and, to his horror, "puffy" pleated pants. Kimball recalls his traumatic theodicy brought on by the experience: "As I was trying on all of these clothes, looking at myself in the mirror in disbelief, I thought, Oh God, is this really how you want me to dress? God, is this really what you want me to do? . . . Oh dear God, do I really have to wear these puffy pants?"

No, he later decided. God did not require him to wear puffy pants or Sharpied shoes or shorn locks. And, further, the regulation of his dress and hairstyle was misguided. He reckons it, even as he expresses compassion toward the well-meaning pastor, a form of harm that humiliated him personally and is also detrimental to the church's mission. The regulation was judgment, he later decided; and judgment is not Jesus-like, he argues. Kimball hated the haircut and the golf shirts and the pleated pants—he winds up donating the clothing to Goodwill and growing his pompadour back for good—but what he is polemicizing against in the end is not the specifics of the dress code but the fact of its existence and enforcement. Significantly, he sees it as unbiblical.

Yet it is not a close reading of the Bible that led Kimball to decide the regulation of his hair and dress was not biblical. It was, rather, a personal and private experience of deity, one that confirmed what he already wanted to think. As he was driving away from the pastor's house in his '66 Mustang, Kimball reports, he suddenly "felt this incredible wave of emotion" as he was expressing his deep hurt to God in prayer. "In the midst of my praying, embarrassment, and confusion, I experienced a physical sense of calm and confidence," he writes. And then:

> I can't quite explain it, but it felt like someone had turned on the heater in the car and the coldness had suddenly become warmth. I had a strong sense of

peace realizing that God wasn't primarily concerned
about my hair or my clothing. Deep in my gut, I knew
that Jesus did not really care all that much about my
appearance.

This story represents for him "the first time [he] realized that
in Churchland, some Christians' expectations are based not
on the Bible but on personal preferences." "There is not a
single verse in the Bible," he claims, "that says how a youth
worker should dress or style their hair." If Kimball had asked
that church pastor for his biblical warrant, however, the pastor
might have pointed him to 1 Corinthians 11:14–15a, where
the apostle writes, "Does not nature itself teach you that,
if a man wears long hair, it is dishonoring to him, but if a
woman has long hair, it is her glory?" It does not materially
matter for Kimball whether there is a Bible verse that regulates hair, though. He wears a pompadour because a personal
religious experience convinced him God does not care about
his appearance.

A similar degree of autonomy is not likely to be granted
to evangelical women. Their religious experiences are not as
likely to be taken seriously as revelatory or authoritative, even
in their own lives. And yet white evangelical men are not the
only ones advancing Bible benevolence projects focused on
the Bible's goodness for women. Their Bible redemption does
not tell the whole story.

What happens when Bible-redeemers are women, who
are themselves subject to misogyny? What happens when
Bible-redeemers are precisely the ones who are governed by,
or at the very least potentially governed by, Paul's constraints
on women? While white evangelical men, just like Pastor
Dave, save the Bible to save themselves from disrepute and
to protect and lay claims to dominance, white evangelical
women interested in making the Bible benevolent are in a

fundamentally different position. As they wrestle the Bible into the Good Book, they, too, lay particular claims to status but must simultaneously wrestle with the fact that if they do not comply with what is expected of them, they might be silenced, sexualized, or subject to abuse. History might be able to save the Bible from critique, but it cannot save all evangelical women from the bind between what the Bible says and what they often intuit is good for themselves. Their Bible benevolence projects cannot save them from misogyny. But they do them anyway.

FOUR

Making Paul Less Bad, Again

The Complicity of White Evangelical Women

Good old Reverend Dave is not the only contender *God's Not Dead: We the People* sends from Arkansas to DC to protect the Bible's reputation on the national stage. When a hostile liberal congressman suggests during the congressional hearing that Bible-based homeschooling might be "anti-rational and anti-science," a young white mother named Taylor Hays speaks up. "Belief in the Bible isn't anti-science," she asserts with an unexpected level of confidence. Until now, she has been meek, mousy, and a bit mysterious. Her moment to demonstrate courage becomes the viewers' chance to find out her story, to understand why her opinion matters. To everyone's surprise, she is not merely a working-class restaurant manager struggling to make ends meet. She has an advanced degree in aerospace engineering. She previously worked for NASA! She only took on a less demanding job because her military husband was killed, and she needed to make a change to care more adequately for her son. With her credentials newly apparent, Taylor proceeds to defend the Bible from its detractor. But her argument does not address the contents of the Bible at all. She reports that the first food or drink consumed on the moon was communion, that the book of Genesis has been read in space, and that her son knows that "Jesus" is not an acceptable answer to chemistry questions. Her reasoning will appear strained to outsiders, but for the intended viewers of this film the speech inspires confidence, principally through affect, that biblicist Christians can be smart too.

The crescendo of Taylor's speech takes a surprising turn. She demands that the now-abashed congressman no longer address her as "Ms. Hays" but instead call her "Mrs. Hays"—out of respect to her marriage and her husband's memory. This request marks the second moment of anxiety in the film around feminine honorifics. Earlier, when a social services representative inspecting the Arkansas church co-op introduces herself as Ms. Dowd, one of the homeschooled Christian kids immediately asks whether it stands for "Mrs." or "Miss." Dowd, confused, replied that it is not short for anything. A parent then intervenes to explain that the little girl was "just asking if you're single or married so she might address you properly" (as if this were a perfectly typical thing to do). Ms. Dowd's contempt-filled answer is meant to make her look ridiculous. "I identify as self-partnered" is a line played for laughs.

The Bible is not sexist—and, at the same time, fidelity to it is tested by whether women desire to be addressed according to their relationship to men.

BIBLICAL WHORES

For some white evangelicals, the explanation for why Paul's writings in the Bible are good for women is simple. Paul's letters are biblical; Paul's letters mandate patriarchy. Patriarchy is therefore biblical, and because the Bible is good, patriarchy must be too. This is a standard position of traditionalists, or so-called complementarians, who insist on men's headship in homes and/or limit to men leadership roles in churches or beyond. Many prominent writers who espouse this position are themselves powerful men who benefit materially from widespread compliance with their position. Evangelical women have long negotiated explicit constraints on their activities and realms of power, even as they creatively carve out for themselves precarious positions of influence.[1] Alongside men who deploy Paul's corpus to defend and maintain their own power are white evangelical women who labor, under patriarchal surveillance and within patriarchal constraints, to present patriarchy as biblically and benevolently normative.

One such woman is Wendy Alsup, former women's ministry leader at Mars Hill Church in Seattle, Washington. She is the author of several books, including *Is the Bible Good for Women?*, in which she adopts a biblical-and-benevolent position toward Paul's statements on women. Alsup served at Mars Hill under megachurch pastor Mark Driscoll, whose name is now nearly synonymous with misogyny, even within many evangelical Christian circles. Driscoll's transgressions became the subject of the popular *Christianity Today* podcast "The Rise and Fall of Mars Hill," a *Serial*-esque depiction of the pastor's rise to power, his controversial celebrity, and a plunge into disrepute.[2] Driscoll's militant brand of Christian masculinity, forged in part through brash commentary about sex both from the pulpit and through book publishing, was originally part of his appeal to his evangelical Christian churchgoers.[3] Driscoll's "real-talk" insisted that "real men" wanted (heterosexual) sex, and that women should service their husbands. In a now-notorious sermon, he interpreted 1 Peter 3:1, which tells wives to submit to their husbands "so that even if some do not obey the word, they may be won without a word by the conduct of their wives" (ESV) as a biblical command for women to get their husbands to church by wordlessly giving them oral sex.[4] Women in his world should literally be on their knees. But Driscoll's authoritarian leadership and views of women have now garnered scrutiny and outrage as some evangelicals seek to distance themselves from what they now view as transparent sexism and misogyny.

On her blog "Theology for Women," Alsup evinces a deep ambivalence toward Driscoll, who came to label her a "contentious woman."[5] This "down, girl" insult, with language lifted right from the Bible (e.g. Prov 21:9, 19), apparently served as a regular tactic in Driscoll's repertoire, keeping women in line and protecting his authority. "Mark Driscoll had a low bar for labeling a questioning woman as contentious," Alsup shares.[6] She goes on to say that she "didn't have the emotional confidence to bear up under such a label." Had he called her this name "in the early years," she "would have believed him."[7] In an earlier post, Alsup acknowledged that she was afraid of critiquing Mars Hill Church. "I personally have feared speaking at times," she writes, "because of [the risk of being dismissed as 'bitter'] and the shame of being possibly labeled a gossip or, worse yet, a contentious woman."[8] Driscoll's tactic worked.

But Alsup originally fit Driscoll's expectations for women. In 2008 Driscoll used Alsup as a model of how he believed women should behave. "We have worked very hard so that the women who teach here are like Wendy Alsup, who I really love and appreciate and respect," he commented. The compliment punctuates a teaching session treating "spiritual warfare" in which Driscoll describes "female manipulation" as satanic. Alsup is the only clear exception to Driscoll's otherwise disparaging portrayal of women as gossipers and busybodies, using language straight from Paul (1 Tim 5:11–15). She is acceptable, in part, because she teaches "under the authority of [her] husband, Jesus, and the elders." Driscoll likens identifying good women for leadership to "juggling knives."[9] He paints a vivid picture of "the wrong women":

> You put the wrong women in charge of women's ministry—the drama queen, the gossip mama—all of a sudden all the women come together, tell her everything, she becomes the pseudo-elder, quasi-matriarch. She's got the dirt on everybody. And sometimes the women all get together to just rip on their husbands in the name of prayer requests. Happens all the time. Happens all the time.[10]

The target of his critique shifts seamlessly between, on the one hand, specific types of women of whom he disapproves and, on the other, women generally. His complaint is not exclusively that the wrong woman is a leaky information repository; his language of "pseudo-elder" and "quasi-matriarch" betrays anxiety that such a woman has also accumulated too much power. Driscoll goes on to lament that it is "the wrong women" who aspire to leadership. But Alsup, he says, "is not like that." The right woman, he suggests, is "the humble woman, who isn't fighting to be the center of drama, control, and power; who doesn't have to be up front; she's usually the one who is most capable and qualified." The best women are not usurpers of privileges that are held to belong properly to men, women who do not threaten patriarchal authority and who cohere with patriarchal expectations of their deportment.

Soon after Driscoll publicly stepped down from leadership at Mars Hill, amidst an internal investigation into his leadership practices, Alsup penned a reflection entitled "Blessings and Cursing."[11] As she critiques Driscoll's failure to address the people he had harmed, Alsup also expresses love and admiration for him. "I also experienced legitimate one-on-one pastoral care of myself and my family in my early years at Mars Hill directly from Mark and his wife," she writes. She names one particularly memorable sermon, which happened to be about women. "I'll never forget his 'Ho, Ho, Ho, Merry Christmas' sermon, about the whores in Jesus' lineage." The sermon presumably treated Tamar, Rahab, Ruth, and/or Bathsheba, Old Testament characters who are listed in the gospel of Matthew in the genealogy of Jesus (1:1–17). Alsup acknowledges that the punning sermon title is intentionally provocative, a "classic Mark Driscoll move." Yet while "ho" may be Driscoll's term, Alsup's lack of punctuation around *whores* means she is participating in the name-calling. Even as she maintains that this sermon was "not misogynistic," she laments its execution in a space where women had been previously subjected to Driscoll's disparagement of women.

It was in this context that Alsup wrote her Bible benevolence project, *Is the Bible Good for Women?* Driscoll is nowhere explicitly addressed in Alsup's book. But post-publication writing reveals that Alsup's intervention was intended to rescue the Bible, to defend its goodness specifically from critics of Driscoll who simultaneously, and erroneously in her view, challenged evangelical biblicism. Alsup reports that she wrote *Is the Bible Good for Women?* because of a specific woman: late blogger and best-selling author Rachel Held Evans, a figure whom the *New York Times* dubbed the "voice of the wandering evangelical" upon her untimely death at thirty-seven years old in 2019.[12] She had wandered too far, in Alsup's judgment. Evans critiqued Driscoll and masculinist Christianity, and simultaneously developed a competing biblicism that many progressive evangelicals and other Christians found liberating, as the white evangelical establishment viewed her as a dangerous woman challenging biblical (and their own) authority.[13]

In a reflection on Evans's death, Alsup writes that her questioning was warranted. Her critiques of Driscoll were welcome. But, Alsup says, Evans went too far by doubting the relevance, authority, and clarity of the Bible, particularly around issues of sex and gender.[14] For Alsup, the authority of the Bible must be separated from authoritarian leaders' misdeeds. She seeks to disentangle the Good Book from (a) man's mistakes and misuse.

Is the Bible good for women? Alsup's book title poses a yes-or-no question. Her answer cannot be "no." But if the answer were a straightforward "yes," there would be no need for a book-length resolution. A close reading of her work reveals that her answer is actually "yes, but only if . . ." Yes, but only if, for example, readers read it with a certain set of presumptions and a willingness to accept hard conclusions. The Bible must be good; the Bible must mean what it says; the Bible spells out desires of God for how people should live today. As Alsup's book goes on, her grappling with *what the Bible says* leads her ultimately to reach an answer to her title question that many advocates for women would find difficult to accept. A paraphrase: Yes, but only if women suffer.

WHAT DOES "GOOD" REALLY MEAN, ANYWAY?

Alsup begins *Is the Bible Good for Women?* by inviting her reader to share her assumptions about the Bible. She outlines what she sees as the Bible's "frankly audacious" self-referential claims about its origin, authority, and intentions.[15] These claims coincide with assertions of evangelical biblicism: the whole Bible (2 Tim 3:16–17) is a divinely-derived (2 Pet 1:2–21) practical guide for human life (Ps 119:105).[16] Alsup's approach depends on a hermeneutic of trust. This includes from the outset a trust in the goodness of the

Good Book—even if, and when, it might not feel good. She conscripts even hesitant readers in by compelling them—by virtue of reading her words on the page—to ask for divine help to perceive good in the face of doubt:

> If you are not confident in either Jesus or the Bible, it may feel unsettling to engage God in prayer to understand Scripture. Nevertheless, doing so is helpful at the start of this study: *God, open our eyes to see wonderful things in and through the Bible, even for those of us who are not yet sure what we believe about You or Your Scripture.*[17]

Alsup here requests her reader to do something that she knows might be disconcerting. But any negative feelings are not to be trusted because, she implies, they are a result of the reader not yet being able to see rightly, to perceive well. It might take an act of God for some people to see the good.

Alsup's answer to her title question "Is the Bible good for women?" is predetermined by her biblicist commitments. The answer must already be "yes" because of the nature of what the Bible is. If one thinks otherwise, the problem is not with the Bible but with the interpreter who does not share God's definition of *good*. Eighty-five pages in, Alsup makes this explicit. "I submit to you that the Bible is very good for women, but we have to be precise in how we define *good*," she writes.[18] Alsup makes a distinction between "communal good" and "individual good." Sometimes it is necessary for an individual to sacrifice what is (or seems) good for them in service of something good for a group. Alsup's language of "the best kind of good," "God's version of good," and "ultimate good" implicitly acknowledges that it is not universally or obviously apparent how some ideas or passages from the Bible are good for women. It is possible in her schema, further, for a good not to be perceived as good for people during their lifetimes:

> God's goodness is very good, and it is very good on earth, but there is a clear element of it that includes dying to self that we might become alive to God and experience it. Through death to self, we find flourishing life. The good that God wants us to seek is counter-intuitive—a good with a long view of life on earth and eternity future.[19]

Practically, evangelical Christians following Alsup's paradigm have at their disposal a can't-lose strategy. If something is universally and obviously good for people, it requires no explanation. If something expected to be good turns out to be bad, it can be explained by positing that it *will be* good after people have died. Part of the can't-lose aspect of this strategy is that no evidence can possibly exist that would challenge its veracity. It cannot be disproven. It depends on the existence of a system of reward and punishment that by its nature cannot be shown to exist since it is only "provable" once someone is dead, and dead people cannot report back. The impossibility of testing or challenging its reality encourages people to continue following instructions even if they are painful and their results are bad. The bad is temporary, the reasoning goes, because it is in service of a longer good that will only be realized upon death.

When it comes to specific interpretations of the Bible, Alsup moves from easiest-to-explain passages to the most difficult, culminating in prescriptive New Testament passages that, in her words, "feel difficult for twenty-first-century women."[20] (Feelings, though, cannot be trusted.) The difficult-feeling Pauline passages are the household code in Ephesians 5, the silencing and salvation-through-childbirth verses in 1 Timothy 2, and the regulation of women's dress and speech in 1 Corinthians.[21] These passages are in fact so difficult that Alsup begins the chapter that treats them with a disclaimer that she might not be able to explain them satisfactorily. Alsup has already prepared her reader to entertain this possibility with her insistence that sometimes goods are eternal rather than presently transparent. She writes, "Note that we will not resolve all questions in the New Testament pertaining to women. I can't imagine that is possible this side of heaven!"

This rhetorical move equips readers to buy into Alsup's confidence of the Bible's goodness even if they cannot accept Alsup's interpretations of the specific verses under consideration. She goes on:

> Even questions that I am able to answer for myself I may not answer for you. I am convinced that the Holy Spirit is able to correctly apply Scripture in the hearts of individual believers. I will hand out thoughts and suggestions in this chapter, and I will share my personal convictions. But in the end, I will leave you to wrestle with the Spirit in your own study of the Word to draw your personal conclusions and private applications.[22]

Alsup here shifts from her earlier focus on valuing community at the expense of the individual to prioritizing the individual. Such a move reflects evangelical notions of the priesthood-of-the-believer as a framework for interpretation. At the same time, it insulates Alsup from potential critique by deferring any authority the reader might have ascribed to her. Such demurral exemplifies the humility and deference expected of women within traditional evangelical gender performance. Driscoll, presumably, would approve.

HURTS SO GOOD

Alsup requires of any readers who are suspicious of the effects of patriarchy on women to adjust what they see as beneficial to the welfare of women. Because "good" must be defined by eternal standards and sometimes means individuals suffer for the sake of the community, suffering in the present is not a sign that the Bible's instructions are bad for people. "To be consistent with Scripture," Alsup writes, "we have to face a 'lose your life to find it' kind of good."[23] She does not consider in this book that such a schema necessarily serves to disenfranchise women, and potentially subject them to abuse, since this principle cannot be equally applied to men and women in a patriarchal social order. Women are much more likely to be the ones expected to endure suffering. And women have less available to sacrifice before there is nothing left.

In the Bible benevolence script, when it comes to the New Testament, women's pain must be concealed entirely, embraced as normative, or camouflaged as something else. Concealment, acceptance, and rebranding combine in interesting ways in Alsup's treatment of 1 Timothy 2. In this second of Paul's silencing passages, in which he also regulates women's dress and limits their authority, the apostle offers an interpretation of Genesis 1–3 that culminates in a surprising statement about the mechanism through which women "will be saved." That mechanism is childbirth, which, in the Genesis story, God intentionally makes painful for women as a punishment for Eve's transgression. For Paul, the reason to prohibit women from having "authority over a man" and to enjoin them to "keep silent" is bound up in the Garden of Eden:

For Adam was formed first, then Eve, and Adam was not deceived, but the woman was deceived and became a transgressor. Yet she will be saved through childbearing, provided they continue in faith and love and holiness, with self-control. (1 Timothy 2:13–15)

Evangelicals are divided over whether this passage prohibits women from leadership positions over men. Alsup is part of the more conservative contingent who reserve top leadership roles for men. Her project must be in part, then, to explain why *that* is good for women.

Alsup explores what Paul might have meant by "teach or exercise authority" by looking to examples of activities that women are represented as doing in the Bible. Deborah was a judge of Israel. Junias was "outstanding among the apostles" (Rom 16:7). Priscilla, in Alsup's words, "discipled men *in cohort with her husband*" (drawing on Acts 18:26; italics added).[24] Phoebe was a deacon, or servant (Rom 16:1). Based on passages in the Bible where women did things, Alsup concludes that 1 Timothy 2 cannot be limiting women from "informally" teaching men, serving in civil leadership capacities, or speaking in church settings in any capacity.[25] Rather, she argues, what Paul is doing is reserving the top of the church authority structure for men. Alsup states this limitation, which will disappoint some women readers who view this conclusion as disempowering, at the end of a sentence whose structure and verb choice downplay the fact that patriarchal social structure is a construct and further remove agency, and therefore fault, from its enforcers. "There are distinctions in the church," she writes, "particularly relating to the spiritually authoritative role of elder, or overseer, which Paul reserved for men."

When Alsup explicitly addresses the question driving her inquiry, printed in bold letters—"Is this passage good for women?"—the next word is not "yes." In fact, Alsup does not come out and say "yes." Instead, her answer hedges:

> We are called again to consider our definition of *good* here, for many would not see goodness in limiting women from the office of elder in a church or from teaching with spiritual authority in corporate worship. But if we value the distinctions of gender as part of image bearing as much as we do the overlap, we are equipped to consider that maybe God has something good to communicate to us even through such a limitation.

This is not a bold affirmation. Her answer must be "yes"—but she does not say it directly. The initial sentence sets the terms on which the biblical material can be good for women: it is a "good" that hurts. The question Alsup is actually addressing with this answer is not "Is this passage good for women?" but rather something along the lines of "Can this passage possibly be thought of as good for women?" Alsup's rhetoric is tentative, perhaps even reluctant. Readers may merely *consider* that *maybe* there is something good here. To reach a place of such consideration, readers need to be *equipped*—language that implicitly acknowledges that this passage can only be commendable under a certain set of preconditions. One must trust that it is good because one has already decided that the Bible is the Good Book.

A pre-commitment to (re)defining "good" based on what one finds in the Bible is one reason that Alsup is able to entertain biblical interpretations that would strike many today as ethically problematic, perhaps even ludicrous. Combined with a relative disregard for the experience of women in the here-and-now, this pre-commitment leads Alsup to make an uncomfortable suggestion about how exactly a patriarchal social order can be good for women. When dealing with Paul's statement in 1 Timothy 2 that "the woman" will be "saved through childbearing," Alsup writes that one straightforward reading is that Paul was correctly observing a fact. Women have historically been saved—*from physical annihilation*—through childbearing. She writes, "even at the most brutal points of history, when physical strength and stamina were most valued, women and children were still protected." The paragraph goes on:

> Why? Because humanity couldn't go on without them. In a world that has oppressed women at every turn in history, in every culture, womankind has been consistently saved from annihilation through her ability to bear children. This is the thing that fundamentally sets a women's body apart from a man's, and it is powerful. It is crude to suggest, but men could be completely wiped from the earth, and as long as one jar of semen was preserved, humankind would go on. But not so with women.[26]

Not being murdered is the bar for "good for women." Here "good" means merely staying alive at the mercy of men, and only then to bear babies.

Alsup offers this explanation as merely one possible way to make sense of the troubling "saved through childbearing" verse. While it is not ultimately her favorite option, she offers it as an acceptable one nonetheless. Here women are conceived to exist in a world of men, where men are entitled to determine who lives and who dies. The criterion for deciding who lives assumes that men assert sexual access to women's bodies and, presumably, control over their reproductive capacities. This interpretation of the "saved through childbearing" verse also presumes a definition of women that is based on reproductive potential or success, mirroring some very early biblical language that interchanges "women" and "wombs" (Judg 5:30). This world of men is a place where women are allowed to exist, by the choice of men, for the use of women's bodies by men in the service of their own interests.

Not All (Wo)men

Alsup's preferred accounting for the "saved through childbearing" passage is a classic explanation in which Paul means specifically one woman's childbearing: that of Mary, the mother of Jesus. Reifying sexist categorizations of women as either sinners/temptresses or saints/mothers, this notion purports that it was a woman's role in the birth of Jesus that reverses women's shame that resulted from Eve's sin. Alsup prefers an interpretation of 1 Timothy 2 that restricts the childbearing to one woman, Mary. The implication is that this is more palatable to women readers than a scenario in which they, too, have to bear children to be saved.

This interpretive move mirrors the strategy many evangelicals use to exculpate Paul from misogyny charges wherein they limit the number of women Paul had in view in the silencing passages. For Alsup, interpreting 1 Timothy 2 as mandating man-over-woman hierarchy without silencing *all women* in the church is the key to "unlocking" 1 Corinthians 14. Paul did not mean all women in all times and places—a conclusion that Alsup shares with egalitarian coreligionists. As a conservative complementarian, though, Alsup connects the regulation of speech to a mandate that women should submit to designated men (a mandate found, for example, in the household code passages in Ephesians and Colossians). "The speaking in question," Alsup comments of 1 Corinthians 14, "was the opposite of submission."[27] Women may speak, then, as long as doing so falls inside the bounds of deferral to a designated patriarch or patriarchs.

Alsup endeavors to identify Paul's intended patriarchs as her argument continues. Such designation is a necessary step in the exculpation of Paul whenever one reads his mandates as enforcing patriarchy, since when the Bible and patriarchy are intertwined, they are evaluated together. Alsup must address the potential objection that sometimes patriarchal social order is not transparently good for everyone. Her tactic is to limit the scope of submission by identifying certain men to whom women are expected to submit. She goes to great lengths to argue that a woman is to submit only to her husband, which Alsup then uses as a model for affirming women's submission to men in church leadership. "Many cultures worldwide (including some Christian churches) practice universal male dominance: the idea that woman in general needs to follow man in general," she writes disapprovingly. For Alsup, this is not right. A woman is "a crown to her husband, and her husband only," she writes, drawing on Paul's language in 1 Corinthians 11:3. Woman should submit to no other master. The reason Alsup offers is not because the universal dominance of men is oppressive or puts women at risk. Instead, she argues, it is not right because universal submission of women distracts from or threatens the special submission that a woman owes her own husband. Paul's purpose was to "protect the sanctity of the husband-and-wife union from the projection of other male authority over a wife, particularly in the context of female slaves and their masters who used them sexually."[28]

Some might object, Alsup realizes, that this limitation of scope is not itself empowering to women. "For many," she writes, "any suggestion of a husband having authority over his wife is problematic." Some might object, too, that in a modern context wherein enslavement is less a live possibility, submission-as-protection is no longer necessary. This is where Alsup must shift the terms to defend the Bible by defending not Paul but patriarchy itself. She claims that "the problems we see in modern culture that have also infiltrated the church are not primarily from husbands who have learned to love, care, and sacrifice for their wives as Christ's example teaches." This sentence, with the word choice "infiltrated," reveals that Alsup conceives of harmful patriarchy as something concocted originally outside of Christianity that then corrupted an originally good Christian patriarchy.

Good Christian patriarchy is made good, in her logic, by its fidelity to the Bible. Alsup writes that the Bible contains "pretty strong guidelines" for the appropriate behavior of men. The guidelines are not exactly specific, though. Alsup invokes Paul's command to men in Ephesians 5 to love their wives as Christ loves the church. The Bible here becomes its own standard of judgment. What results is a Bible benevolence loop into which any piece of evidence or potential objection can be inserted to reach the same conclusion. The Bible is good. Because the Bible is good and mandates patriarchy, patriarchy is good. When patriarchy is not good, that is because it is not biblical. Patriarchy is good when it follows the Bible—because the Bible is good. The Bible is insulated from charges of complicity in misogyny, since harms against women are attributed to something external to the Bible, which itself can only be recognized by looking to the Bible rather than considering the consequences to women. The Bible is good. And women suffer.

Patriarchy in Peril?

Alsup's Bible benevolence project reveals that when patriarchy is biblical, patriarchy must be defended alongside the Bible. Just as the Bible's goodness is delicate, so also is patriarchal social order, whose norms demand consistent enforcement for it to work well. Reading Alsup's Bible benevolence project alongside her biographical writing highlights this point. Subsequent books and articles from Alsup reveal that after writing *Is the Bible Good for Women?* she experienced a painful divorce from her husband. The agony of the divorce was compounded by difficult financial fallout, sudden solo parenthood, a cross-country move, and finally a cancer diagnosis.[29] Alsup's divorce simultaneously alienated her from evangelical legibility. It moved her outside the comfortable bounds of normal patriarchal social order. In an article published by *The Gospel Coalition*, Alsup shared that her "journey as a divorced woman in conservative religious culture" included "awkward conversations and weird looks." She went on: "I've experienced insensitive comments and even isolation as others in the church didn't quite know what to do with a newly divorced woman in their midst."[30]

Divorced women do not fit neatly in a patriarchal social order, especially in conservative evangelical contexts where heteronormativity, marriage, and monogamy are presumed as natural. Divorced women can be regarded with suspicion in such circles because they stand as counter-evidence to the notion that patriarchy always works. The very existence of divorced women suggests that patriarchal social order can break down. If marriage is an institution that supports patriarchal social order, divorced women constitute challenges to patriarchy even if they themselves see patriarchy as desirable or normative. Divorced women are reminders of the potential vulnerability of patriarchy, the endless requirement to enforce its norms in order for it to function smoothly. Books that argue for the benevolence of patriarchy in the face of potential objections are part of that maintenance project.

Neither Driscoll nor divorce convinced Alsup that the Bible or its patriarchy is flawed. In fact, her recovery process included her reinsertion into biblical patriarchy. Alsup reports joining a new church after having moved from Seattle to her family's farm in South Carolina. "As a divorced woman," she writes, "I was careful in the church I joined."[31] The care she took was not principally about avoiding awkward conversations or other markers of alienation that divorce can cause. It was about selecting the right men. "I chose my church cautiously," she says, "knowing the pastors in my church, along with my dad, would have a role of influence, even authority, in my life that I needed and wanted."

As Alsup comes to wrestle in print with her own heart-rending suffering, the Bible is made good for her through a different, though not inconsistent, means. The Bible becomes good not principally through apologetic defense of its patriarchal mandates but rather through use of its words and reckoning of its contents as resources for comfort amidst suffering. Alsup celebrates the Bible as an access point to a supernatural help and a set of literary and theological supplies that enable her to hope for a better (eternal) future in a painful present. Strikingly, such a reckoning fits well with how Alsup articulates in *Is the Bible Good for Women?* a possibility of what "good" means—perhaps unrecognizable in the present, potentially ever-deferred. "In truth," she writes in the conclusion, "I cannot imagine someone finding the Bible good if that person doesn't believe in a God whose eternal purposes give meaning to its hard stories."[32]

In 2021 Alsup publicly re-upped and defended anew her biblical interpretation and affirmation of patriarchal social order in response to a challenge issued by a popular book published that year: Beth Allison Barr's *The Making of Biblical Womanhood: How the Subjugation of Women Became Gospel Truth.*[33] In the end, it all comes down to Paul. "My disagreement with Barr (like most folks who disagree on such matters)," Alsup writes, "comes with Barr's analysis of the writings of Paul in Scripture."[34] Same Bible, same goal, different Paul.

How to Make Paul Want to #EndChristianPatriarchy

Beth Allison Barr's *The Making of Biblical Womanhood* is a sensation. It would be difficult to exaggerate the reach of this book and the controversy it has caused in Christian circles following its release in 2021. The book has even made its way beyond traditional religious outlets, attracting the attention of the *New Yorker*[35] and National Public Radio's "Morning Edition."[36] Attuned to the prevalence of sexual harassment and abuse of women in Christian institutions and beyond, Barr, a Baptist pastor's wife[37] and professor of medieval history at Baylor University, seeks to disentangle the Good Book from the harms of patriarchy. Like Alsup, Barr sees bad patriarchy as something generated outside of Christianity that inappropriately makes its way in. But for Barr, all patriarchy is bad patriarchy. If patriarchy is not benevolent, it also is not biblical. Barr regards evangelical refusal of leadership positions to women as an oppressive result of patriarchy and a misapplication of the Bible's true message. #EndChristianPatriarchy is Barr's signature Twitter hashtag.

"Rather than patriarchy being God-ordained," Barr writes, "history suggests that patriarchy has a human origin: civilization itself."[38] Christian patriarchy is not the result of faithful Bible interpretation but of the church bending to external societal pressures. In *The Making of Biblical Womanhood*, Barr historicizes modern evangelical insistence on women's subordination as a product of sociocultural factors and institutional changes through the centuries, tracing how such movements as the Reformation, the Enlightenment, and the Industrial Revolution placed constraints on opportunities for women. Barr blames Christian misogyny on fallible people who misuse the Bible, against God's and the Bible's own intentions. They have misused Paul in particular, she claims. "Christians in the past may have used Paul to exclude women from leadership," she observes, "but this doesn't mean that the subjugation of women is biblical."[39]

Defending the Bible from criticism is not Barr's primary stated goal, but the grand thesis of *The Making of Biblical Womanhood* cannot be accurate if the Bible can be held to account for the ills she is fighting against. If she traces subjugation of women all the way back through the centuries and finds that it is mandated by the Bible, then such subjugation turns out to be gospel truth after all. Barr has created a history project in the service of advocacy that hinges on Bible benevolence.

Since for Barr Christianity rightly practiced and the Bible rightly read are anti-patriarchal, she must figure out how to present Paul's patriarchal mandates as anti-patriarchal, as only *apparently* patriarchally normative. "What if Biblical Womanhood Doesn't Come from Paul?" she asks her readers to consider in one chapter title. In Barr's view, patriarchal readings have missed Paul's, and as a result the Bible's, true meaning. "What if evangelicals have been understanding Paul through the lens of modern culture," she asks, "instead of the way Paul intended to be understood?"[40]

Before doing textual analysis, Barr prepares her evangelical readers with assurances that her interpretive schema can coexist with accepted tenets of white evangelical Bible reading. With a nod to Reformation-inflected biblical interpretation, Barr characterizes the traditionalist interpretation of Paul as a corruption. Her preferred, anti-patriarchal readings are rather the most natural and biblically faithful, she suggests: "What if, instead of a 'plain and natural' reading, [traditional evangelical] interpretation of Paul—and subsequent exclusion of women from leadership roles—results from succumbing to the attitudes and patterns of thinking around us?"[41] Evangelical readers are invited to consider the possibility that patriarchy is imported into the biblical text from the outside without being asked to give up on the Bible.

The Bible Benevolence Loop

Barr argues that when Paul, as part of the Bible, sounds patriarchal, that is because Paul was writing in a context where patriarchy was normative. But such patriarchy is always, in Barr's paradigm, introduced from the outside. This creates a win-win interpretive schema that forms a Bible benevolence loop into which any piece of data can be inserted and explained: The Bible is good. Patriarchy is bad and therefore unbiblical. It comes from the outside. When Paul sounds patriarchal, which is to be expected given his ancient Roman context, that is because he is reflecting the fallen world's patriarchy around him. When Paul can be reckoned as anti-patriarchal, that reflects the Bible's true intent—because patriarchy is bad and the Bible is good. Close examination of Barr's treatment of the silencing passage in 1 Corinthians 14 shows how her schema functions as a loop.

Barr suggests that "a better understanding of Roman history can change how we interpret" the silencing passage in 1 Corinthians.[42] Barr then recounts this story: In the third century BCE, Rome passed the Oppian Law, legislation that limited luxuries and expenditures for women in an effort to tighten the empire's belts following a devastating military defeat. Decades later, once Rome prevailed and the crisis passed, (elite) Roman women gathered publicly in the streets to demand that the constraints on them be lifted. Barr quotes a speech from a consul named Cato the Elder in which he argues for the law constraining women to be upheld. Cato's speech, created for him by the writer Livy in book 34 of his *History*, provides evidence of ancient Roman misogyny.[43] Cato complains about "female fury," and then recounts a moment from his recent past in which he encountered "a band of women" in public. He retrospectively castigates them with these words: "What kind of behavior is this? Running around in public, blocking streets, and speaking to other women's husbands! Could you not have asked your own husbands the same thing at home?" (34.2). Barr recognizes that this part of Cato's misogynistic rant sounds strikingly similar to a line in 1 Corinthians: "If there is anything they desire to know, let them ask their husbands at home."[44] She attributes this similarity to "echoes" that "ended up in the New Testament."[45] "Paul's words" Barr writes, "are drawing from his Roman context."

Then Barr presents an argument that "Paul's words" are not in fact Paul's words. They are instead the "faulty understanding" of the Corinthians Paul was addressing. Paul was quoting them in order to refute them. This suggestion follows a common line of New Testament scholarship that sees Paul as quoting so-called "Corinthian slogans" in various places in his Corinthian letter for the purpose of correcting the position he quotes.[46] Barr poses the question, "What if Paul was so concerned that Christians in Corinth were imposing their own cultural restrictions on women that he called them on it?" Barr points to a modern English translation as evidence that this is what Paul meant: "The Revised Standard Version (RSV) lends support," she writes, "to the idea that this is what Paul was doing."[47] This is a puzzling claim, methodologically speaking. Modern English translations cannot provide *support* for a judgment on what Paul *meant* in antiquity. Translations are, by their very nature, already interpretations. Modern translations represent modern judgments on ancient meanings. A more accurate phrasing of the relationship of the RSV's translation to Paul's intention would be: the RSV translators interpret Paul's meaning in antiquity a certain way and render it that way in modern English. Barr may think that the RSV translators accurately represent what Paul meant in antiquity, but the translation itself is not evidence in support of her interpretation. Rhetorically, what the methodologically clumsy sentence does for Barr's exculpation of Paul is to ground it in an authority higher than herself—there is a Bible out there that agrees with her.

Though Barr's exculpation of Paul depends on attributing the words of the problematic silencing passage to the Christian men in Corinth rather than to Paul, her creative historical method also allows her to exculpate Christianity. She does so by driving a wedge between Christians and Romans. She writes, for example, that in 1 Corinthians 14, Paul "quoted the bad practice, which Corinthian men were trying to drag from the Roman world into their Christian world, and then he countered it."[48] Barr constructs two worlds—a Roman world and a Christian world—that can either overlap or not but always remain distinct. By doing this, Barr functionally exculpates Christianity from blame for oppression of women, since she represents the practice of silencing women as something external, something Roman, something that can be part of Christian practice only as a deviation from the norm. She here participates in an apologetic strategy that depends on a retrospective theological organizing of Christians into categories of good or bad, normative or deviant, godly or worldly, orthodox or heretical. Barr's theological organization puts patriarchy on the latter side of these binaries. "The early church," she writes in the introduction to the book, "was trying to make sense of its place in both a Jewish and Roman world, and much of those worlds bled through into the church's stories."[49] What this rhetorical move then allows her to do is attribute to Paul what she likes and to everyone else what does not fit her narrative or ethical framework.[50]

She protects the Bible from patriarchy, and therefore critique, by alternating between the assertions that, on the one hand, Paul was reflecting Roman patriarchy and, on the other, Paul was fighting Roman patriarchy. In either case, Roman patriarchy can be counted as ever-external to Paul and therefore the Bible. In this rhetorical project, extrabiblical ancient literature is claimed either as context or contrast, depending on which is more beneficial to making the Bible benevolent. Paul is exceptional—except when he is not. The Bible is exceptional—except when it is not.

Good Enough

Strategic comparison is integral to the task. Following a popular trend in Bible benevolence projects, Barr manufactures Paul's goodness by contrasting his words with those of other ancient figures to make Paul look good in comparison. Paul might initially seem bad, but the Romans were *really bad*. If Paul is good by contrast, then he is good enough. To work for Bible redemption, such comparisons must rely on selective data collection along with strategic presentation and interpretation of that data. Ultimately, Barr's argument only works when she exercises the interpretive controls of Christian exceptionalism and biblical exceptionalism, the views that Christians are better than all other people and the Bible is better than all other literature. Bible-redeemers like Barr must see Paul as special—special specifically and exclusively in ways that benefit their argument.

There is more to Livy's *History* than Barr tells when she compares Cato's words to those in 1 Corinthians. While Cato's is the only speech Barr mentions, it is not the only speech in the source text. Livy's *History* depicts a second

speech, a competing speech. This one is delivered by a man
named Lucius Valerius, one of the tribunes of the people,
who argues *in favor of* repealing the law constraining Roman
women (34.5–7). Livy presents Cato's position as only one
position in the debate, which he considers a small matter (*res
parva* [34.1]), and further as an example of a view held by an
ultra-conservative political faction. Livy's Valerius pokes fun
at Cato's misogyny when he accuses his opponent of using
up "more words on criticizing married women than he has on
rebutting our proposal" (34.5).[51] If Paul is aligned with Cato,
whose words Barr sees echoed in 1 Corinthians 14, then he is
aligned with the most conservative position that even other
ancient Roman men could see as anti-women. Barr's preferred
reading, though, which sees Paul as quoting the silencing
command in order to counter it, would see Paul aligned rather
with Valerius—the one who counters Cato's conservatism.
Mentioning *this* comparison, however, would undermine the
ability to cast Paul as outside of Roman patriarchy.

All of these men are, in fact, inside of Roman patriarchy.
Even Valerius, whom Livy presents as defending the Roman
women who gathered and spoke in the street, disparages
women with stereotypes and argues in favor of the authority
of men over women. He says, for example, "never can the
subservience of women be removed while their kinsmen still
live—and yet they themselves hate the independence they
are granted by the loss of husbands or fathers."[52] Reading
the data without biblical exceptionalism means seeing Paul
as thoroughly part of, rather than potentially apart from,
his ancient Roman context of patriarchal normativity in
which privileged men debated with one another about how
best to regulate women, including when it came to women's
speech. Reading more of Livy's *History* shows that Paul fit
well within a spectrum of ancient Roman misogynistic regulation of women.

Barr's Bible benevolence project deploys a similar strategy for exculpating Paul when it comes to the household codes in Colossians and Ephesians. She chooses a convenient piece of ancient *comparanda* and then frames it strategically to make Paul look progressive by contrast. The process mirrors comparisons in Jesus benevolence projects in which other actors in antiquity are stereotyped and vilified to make Jesus good by making him better. Barr exploits perceived contrasts to argue creatively that the words on the page of the Bible do not mean what they say. Barr offers at-times ingenious counter-readings to the words on the page—so ingenious that attention to the biblical passages themselves is a prerequisite for apprehending her Bible benevolence moves.

THE WORDS ON THE PAGE

The household codes in Colossians and Ephesians are troubling for any Bible booster who presents as anti-patriarchal. In the Colossians code (3:18–4:1), Paul tells wives to submit to (ESV) or to be subject to (NRSVUE) their husbands, and instructs husbands to love their wives and not treat them harshly. He tells children to obey their parents and fathers not to provoke their children. Paul tells enslaved persons to obey their masters.[53] He commands masters to treat their slaves justly and fairly since they also "have a Master in heaven."

The Ephesian household code (5:22–33) is similar, sometimes identical, wordier without being more pragmatically specific:

> Wives, be subject to your husbands as to the Lord, for the husband is the head of the wife just as Christ is the head of the church, his body, and is himself its Savior. Just as the church is subject to Christ, so also wives ought to be, in everything, to their husbands.

Husbands, love your wives, just as Christ loved the church and gave himself up for her in order to make her holy by cleansing her with the washing of water by the word, so as to present the church to himself in splendor, without a spot or wrinkle or anything of the kind, so that she may be holy and without blemish. In the same way, husbands should love their wives as their own bodies. He who loves his wife loves himself. For no one ever hates his own flesh, but he nourishes and tenderly cares for it, just as Christ does for the church, because we are members of his body. "For this reason a man will leave his father and mother and be joined to his wife, and the two will become one flesh." This is a great mystery, but I am speaking about Christ and the church. Each of you, however, should love his wife as himself, and a wife should respect [or fear] her husband (NRSVUE).

As in the Colossians code, next come instructions to the other two hierarchical pairs in the household, children-fathers and slaves-masters. Paul tells children to obey their parents, and counsels fathers to bring up children the right way. He then addresses enslaved persons, advising them to be obedient to their "earthly masters," and to treat them with the same respect [or fear] they accord to Christ. They are to do this "not with a slavery performed merely for looks, to please people, but as slaves of Christ" (a distinction made also in Colossians). Enslaved persons are told in Ephesians to work as slaves "with enthusiasm, as for the Lord [or Master] and not for humans." In other words, they are to do enslaved labor eagerly, like they are doing it for the deity rather than the householders who benefit from their enslaved labor. Masters are to "do the same" and "stop threatening" their slaves. They are all subject, Paul says, to the same Master in heaven. Both sets of household codes ground human hierarchies in a conception of all humans as enslaved to God as ultimate Master.

On the face of it, these passages mandate hierarchical organization of husband over wife, endowing the free patriarch with power as master of his household and grounding this hierarchy in an analogous power differential between God and humans. Barr and others who see an anti-patriarchal intent here are not content with the face of it. Paul was not advancing Roman patriarchy in this passage. He was actually resisting it. "Rather than including the household codes to dictate how Christians should follow the gender hierarchy of the Roman Empire," Barr poses, "what if Paul was teaching Christians to live differently within their Roman context?"[54] She asks, further: "Rather than New Testament 'texts of terror' for women, what if the household codes can be read as resistance narratives to Roman patriarchy?"

Paul and the Limits of White Feminism

The paradigmatic ancient *comparandum* that Barr excavates as a standard by which to judge Paul and find him progressive is Aristotle. Drawing on others,[55] she argues that comparing Paul's household codes in Colossians and Ephesians to the comments of Aristotle on household management reveals that Paul's aim was not to normalize Roman patriarchal hierarchies but to challenge them. In particular, she capitalizes on what she perceives to be a significant grammatical difference. Paul addressed the underlings, and Aristotle did not. The Pauline household codes, she says, "address all the people in the house church—men, women, children, and slaves."[56]

"Everyone," Barr writes approvingly, "is included in the conversation."[57] This reasoning about Paul is similar to that of Bible-redeemers who argue that Jesus's speaking to women was remarkable and demonstrated his affirmation of women. It reproduces, further, the assumption that a man speaking to a woman makes him anti-misogynist. Like the Jesus-included-everyone apologetic, this Paul-included-everyone argument exploits the very act of speaking rather than considering either the content of the speech or its effects. Barr writes affirmingly that the biblical households codes "offer each member of the shared community—knit together by their faith in Christ—the right to hear and act for themselves."[58] Testing this claim out on the master-slave addressees shows its impossibility, and further that it is more problematic than promising when it comes to ethics of liberation. Few would argue that a powerful, free man speaking to an enslaved person is an act of empowering a slave, particularly when the content of the free man's speech is telling the enslaved person to obey their master as if he were God. That cannot be reasonably understood as an invitation to participate in decision-making, and certainly not in decision-making that would erode the existing power differential. Unless one inhabits the position of the slaver benefiting from the labor of enslaved persons, it is difficult to imagine how the words addressing slaves in Colossians and Ephesians could offer enslaved persons any wiggle room to act with autonomy. Barr writes that Paul was not "imposing Roman patriarchy on Christians" but was rather "using a Jesus remix to tell Christians how the gospel set them free."[59] (Except for slaves.)

The Bible benevolence argument that sees Paul's direct address as empowering depends on a fantasy that one of the power differentials in the codes—that of gender—can be successfully extricated from the others. This fantasy is one that is likely imaginable only to women with economic status and racial privileges accorded by whiteness.[60] As she exculpates Paul, Barr invokes Clarice Martin, a womanist New Testament scholar who critiques from the inside what

she describes as the modern Black church's uneven application of Paul's codes. The husband-wife hierarchy is celebrated and enforced, while the master-slave hierarchy is
rejected. Martin observes that Black women are the ones
thereby left in oppression. Barr presents her argument about
Paul as consistent with Martin's intersectional advocacy. But
the Aristotle-Paul comparison in Barr's argument *depends
on ignoring and normalizing the real plight of enslaved persons
in the household.* This method of disentangling the Bible
from patriarchy involves disentangling gender from other
relationships of power, a long-utilized and much-critiqued
rhetorical tactic that has historically protected the interests
of white women in the US at the expense of those of Black
people, and especially of Black women.[61]

The necessity for Barr's reading of Paul to portray gender
as potentially existing outside of other dynamics of power
and oppression (even though it cannot) surfaces again when
she rehearses a common egalitarian apologetic argument that
depends not on comparison to extrabiblical literary sources
but on strategic literary organization of the Pauline text in
Ephesians. White evangelical egalitarians attempt to mitigate the hierarchies mandated in Ephesians 5:22–6:9 by
suggesting that Paul's real governing intent can be found in
a clause at the very end of the sentence preceding the code.
The whole sentence reads:

> Do not get drunk with wine, for that is debauchery,
> but be filled with the Spirit, as you sing psalms and
> hymns and spiritual songs to one another, singing
> and making melody to the Lord in your hearts, giving
> thanks to God the Father at all times and for every-
> thing in the name of our Lord Jesus Christ, *being sub-
> ject to one another out of reverence for Christ.* (Ephesians
> 5:18–21 NRSVUE; italics added)

If this final part of the sentence is rendered instead "be subject to one another out of reverence for Christ" and is printed together with, rather than apart from, the beginning of the household code, egalitarian hopefuls can find textual support in the Bible itself that Paul wanted marriage to be about mutual submission, rather than a one-way hierarchical submission.[62] For Barr, this demonstrates that Paul thought women equal to men:

> Yes, wives are to submit, but so are husbands. Instead of underscoring the inferiority of women, Ephesians 5 underscores the equality of women—they are called to submit in verse 22, just like their husbands are called to submit in verse 21.[63]

Barr's assertion fails to reckon with structures of power between (dominant) men and (privileged) women. Even if Ephesians 5:21 is successfully invoked to frame the codes within a governing sentiment of "mutual submission," the rest of the code goes on to define and describe "mutual submission" in ways that place unequal advantages on (dominant) men and disadvantages on (even privileged) women. Women must negotiate patriarchal power, for example, while men merely exercise it. Power is not in reality evenly distributed; the unevenness becomes obfuscated by the use of the word "mutual." What Barr wants to be true about the husband-wife pair, further, cannot be true about any of the other pairs. Fathers and children cannot mutually command and obey, for example. Presumably evangelicals would be uncomfortable with a dynamic that expects God to mutually submit to humans. The hierarchy of the relationship that the other relationships are modeled on in Paul's code *must* be hierarchical. Paul tells wives to submit to their husbands because "the husband is the head of the wife just as Christ is the head of the church." In their submission to their husbands, wives are to imitate the church's submission to Jesus. Evangelical readers persuaded that mutual submission is the governing trope must hold in mind a (theo)logical tension wherein Paul is upsetting one hierarchy—the husband/wife—while enforcing an analogous one—Christ/church.

But the most problematic analogy for this argument is the master-slave hierarchy. By definition, slaves and masters cannot mutually submit. Imagining that enslaved persons' obedience to their slavers could even possibly be one side of a mutually submissive, mutually beneficial, mutually empowering relationship is to give enslaved men and women agency falsely, to expect whatever agency they are granted to be directed toward the benefit of their slavers. Barr claims that reading verse 21 as Paul's thesis statement to which the rest of the codes should be subjected "changes everything."[64] But it must be asked: *For whom?* In truth, it can only change everything for women whose gender is the only stratum of their potential oppression, not for women who are subject to any additional factors that compound oppression, including but not limited to class, race, sexuality, sex assigned at birth, and marital status.

Biblical Exceptionalism is Magic

In addition to eliding ethical issues and ignoring intersections of power relations, celebrating Paul for addressing women, sons, and slaves when Aristotle does not depends on a little grammatical misdirection. Aristotle's discussion of household management does not engage in direct address. There are no imperatives. Aristotle presents the pairings husband/wife, father/children, master/slave in the *Politics* descriptively, as this discussion takes its place in a larger systematic treatment of the nature of the state and its constituent parts, of which the household is one.

The choice of Aristotle as historical *comparandum* for Paul, further, requires a strategic collapsing of centuries. Aristotle is a Greek philosopher from the fourth century BCE. He is an uneasy, if not entirely inaccurate, representative of Roman patriarchy during the first century CE, the time of Paul. Aristotle lived and wrote over three hundred years before Paul, and over four hundred years before some New Testament texts were composed—about the same amount of time that passed between Mozart and the Beatles. Comparing Paul to Aristotle and finding that Paul was resisting patriarchy is not unlike comparing the Beatles's tunes to Mozart's as a way of arguing that the Beatles were resisting rather than participating in music.

Without biblical exceptionalism driving the selection and interpretation of ancient texts, Paul's words map out differently on the ancient landscape than they do in Barr's accounting. Without biblical exceptionalism, Paul is another privileged man in antiquity enjoining patriarchal social order. Comparison to other ancient household codes would likely lead historians working without a commitment to biblical exceptionalism to conclude that Christians institutionalized Roman patriarchy in their communities. In fact, Paul's household codes can also be read as more stringent by comparison because they introduce surveillance by a deity as an enforcing mechanism. The Pauline grounding of the social order man-wife, father-children, lord-slave, in the relationship of deity to humanity in this case, cements the patriarchal social order into the cosmos. In the New Testament texts, this social order is not merely a human construction organized for the benefit of the state. It is, rather, a natural outflow of how God relates to humans. The Christian social order of the New Testament household codes is therefore, at least in theory, less malleable than other Roman patriarchal social constructions, since Paul's order is fixed even beyond nature—in a deity accountable to no other.[65] Many Bible-redeemers who present Paul's direct address of ancient subordinates as evidence of solidarity with them further find it meaningful that the Colossians and Ephesians codes address the ancient subordinate of each pair first, before the husband/father/master. White evangelical gender egalitarians see in this order of address a clue that Paul prioritized, valued, and uplifted women. It is a clue that Paul was resisting their oppression under Roman patriarchy. But without biblical exceptionalism, the order of address can be read as supporting the opposite conclusion. The order of address in this reading enhances misogynistic policing of women's behavior, since it institutes a reward system that encourages compliance on the part of women (whether they are free/married or enslaved). Paul's injunction to the husband is given only after he tells his wife to submit.[66] In this order, the wife's receipt of good treatment is predicated on her obedience. The husband's love is expected in a context in which the wife is already submitting to him. She is addressed first, he second. She obeys, and then he loves. So also with enslaved men and women, who in the biblical codes are enjoined to obey their masters before their masters are enjoined to wield their power benevolently. The order of address is rewarding wives and enslaved persons for compliance with expectations.

Many engaged in creative negotiations to absolve Paul from enforcing patriarchy in the household codes point out that Paul's instruction to the husbands in these codes limits the men by telling them not to treat their wives harshly (Colossians) and to love them as they love their own bodies (Ephesians). Yet, as complementarian interpreters realize, this reading is completely compatible with the conclusion that Paul is enforcing hierarchy. Reading without a commitment to biblical exceptionalism means considering the more probable scenario that the biblical author was not resisting patriarchal social order but rather helping Christians make patriarchy work well. Reading the Pauline household codes without biblical exceptionalism means considering the more likely historical probability that the biblical author was more similar to than different from other ancient men who wrote about household organization and management. Other ancient writers who produced household codes like those in Colossians and Ephesians enjoined the man in charge to treat his subordinates well. Philo, a Jewish writer born in the late first century BCE, for example, wrote that wives should serve their husbands but in "a servitude not imposed by violent ill-treatment but promoting obedience in all things" (*Hypothetica* 7.3).[67] Plutarch, a Greek philosopher of the second century CE, makes a similar argument: "And control ought to be exercised by the man over the woman, not as the owner has control of a piece of property, but, as the soul controls the body, by entering into her feelings and being knit to her through goodwill" (*Moralia* 31 [142e]).[68] This is good advice for the householding free man to maintain his power. Good treatment of subordinates does not make them less subordinate. Rather, it creates circumstances in which subordinates are more likely to accept rather than resist their subordination. Without biblical exceptionalism, the comparisons suggest that the Pauline codes were refining, not rejecting, patriarchy.

If the biblical household codes are read as pragmatic instructions refining patriarchy, a paraphrase would go: "Wives, submit to your husbands. Husbands, help them submit by being nice to them. *They can submit better and comply more easily if you love them.* Children, obey your parents. Fathers, don't make them angry. *They'll be more likely to obey if you do not provoke them.* Slaves, obey your masters. Masters, treat them fairly. *They'll be more likely to comply this way.*" Rather than a mitigated patriarchy, this is a better patriarchy—a well-oiled patriarchy that can run smoothly, avoiding potential hiccups in function. The codes are not about *whether* the paterfamilias wields power, but *how* he should wield it. Without biblical exceptionalism as hermeneutic determiner, comparing the biblical household codes to those of other ancient writers reveals, at most, the existence of dueling patriarchies. The limitations on slaver-patriarchs' power become in this reading not proscriptions intended to protect the wellbeing of wives, children, or slaves but rather good advice intended to help the paterfamilias maintain his power, perhaps ultimately in service of the state. To argue that Paul was therefore anti-patriarchal requires equating *refinement* with *subversion* when such projects in reality work in opposite directions.

Saving Paul by Silencing Women

One reason enforcement measures were likely necessary in the first place is that some subordinates did not—and do not—comply. In support of her case that Paul was not patriarchal, Barr writes about an ancient Roman known as Pliny the Younger, who complained about Christians for subverting Roman norms of masculinity.[69] "One more piece of evidence that convinces me that the household codes should be read as resistance narratives to Roman patriarchy," Barr explains, "is how early Christians were perceived by the Roman world: as 'gender deviants.'"[70] This mobilization of evidence rests on two fanciful historical assumptions: first, that all ancient Christians were obediently following the biblical household codes, and second, that following the biblical household codes would make Christians look deviant.

"Christianity was repugnant to Pliny because it didn't follow the Roman household codes," Barr writes, "not because it followed them."[71] If Christians were flouting Roman standards of patriarchy, it is much more likely from a historical standpoint devoid of biblical exceptionalism that the New Testament household codes were written to contain such flouting rather than to instigate it. The codes were likely directed precisely at the sort of Christians that Pliny complains about. To make the Bible benevolent within the constraints of white evangelical biblicism, Barr asserts that the existence of noncompliance provides evidence for what the biblical author meant. Yet what (other) Christians were actually doing in antiquity is irrelevant for determining what the author of the Pauline household codes meant. A modern analogy demonstrates the creative thinking embedded here: the CDC recommended that Americans get vaccinated against COVID-19, but many Americans did not get vaccinated against COVID-19; therefore, the CDC *actually* meant "don't get vaccinated." What people do in response to guidance or rules does not change the intention of the guidance.

Barr needs to change Paul's intention, which in turn obscures the reality that there existed diversity in ancient Christianity regarding gender norms and constructions. She needs to do so because her biblicism demands that she bring Paul's intention in line with her desired application of the biblical text. She cannot understand the resistors to Roman patriarchal norms simultaneously as resistors of Paul or of the codes ascribed to him, because Paul and his codes are in the Bible. Barr's Bible benevolence project, then, makes the prescriptive words of a powerful man cohere with bits of evidence that some people, who did not write the Bible, did not follow that authority. Paul-was-anti-patriarchal interpreters like Barr mobilize noncompliant women (and others) to support their case, transforming Paul-resistors into evidence that Paul is good. This constitutes a win-win interpretive strategy in Paul redemption projects analogous to that of Jesus-redeemers who give Jesus credit for what women in the gospels did. Paul becomes a hero based not on what he did but on what other people did despite him.

This form of *herasure*, to reappropriate Kate Manne's helpful term, is likewise at work in Barr's organization of reasons supporting her title question, "What if Biblical Womanhood Doesn't Come from Paul?"[72] The progression of headings in this chapter recruits both Paul's intent and women's behavior, eliding them in the process:

> *Because We Can Read Paul Differently.*
>
> *Because Paul's Purpose Wasn't to Emphasize Wifely Submission.*
>
> *Because Paul's Purpose Wasn't to Emphasize Male Authority.*
>
> *Because Paul Didn't Tell Women to Be Silent.*
>
> *Because Paul's Biblical Women Don't Follow Biblical Womanhood.*

This list is instructive for what it reveals about *who* is ascribed authority. Three out of the five of these are deconstructive, explicitly countering and working to undermine tenets of the traditional reading of Paul, by purporting to get to what Paul himself was not doing and did not say. They are about what Paul really meant and therefore ascribe authority to Paul. Interestingly, these exegetical and historical reasons that center Paul and his intentions are bookended by reasons that place agency elsewhere: the readers ("we") and "Paul's Biblical Women." But since white evangelical biblicism prioritizes what Paul meant, Barr must bring Paul into line with her anti-patriarchal motivations through means other than relying on her own experience of the world.[73]

A Good Woman

White evangelical biblicism of the sort Barr utilizes does not allow her to prioritize her own experience. To grasp for authority, she must instead present her project as if it were dispassionate history. She has done so over and over again in response to critics post-publication, invoking her expertise as a historian and marketing her book as cohering with strict academic standards. "My experience is part of my book," she commented on social media, "but historical evidence is what makes my argument."[74] She writes in the book itself: "It was historical evidence that showed me how biblical womanhood was constructed—brick by brick, century by century."[75] Barr frequently invokes footnotes as evidence of solid historical scholarship,[76] once even composing a tongue-in-cheek "Friday Haiku":

for the male blogger

doubtful of my history

the footnotes will help[77]

Barr's defenses show the great degree to which she is subject to misogynistic regulation and critique as a woman in public. She is not automatically accorded the privilege of expertise. She must counter men who dismiss her as emotional, a common misogynistic trope. She must perform her academic credentials. She must show that she is complying with accepted norms.

The credentialing she performs does not allow her to escape white heteropatriarchal normativity. Her insistence on dispassionate history reproduces the very epistemologies that animate, advance, and protect such patriarchal power. Defending her book by insisting that it relies only on historical evidence and research is at the same time accepting a norm that assumes her experiences as a woman do not, and cannot, contribute to acceptable ways of knowing.[78] Feminist critics, womanist critics, and others have long criticized the fantasy that history is a dispassionate, scientific enterprise, and have demonstrated that presenting it as such only authorizes those already in power (usually elite, white, heterosexual cisgender men).[79]

When Barr is critiqued for the accuracy of her book, she most often defends herself by asserting her expert status as a historian. When she is critiqued for the orthodoxy of her book, she code-switches: then she is (also) a pastor's wife. In Barr's Baptist circles, academia is a relatively "safe" space in which she can be an expert. Her status as a professor by itself does not threaten (white) heteropatriarchy, in part because it is possible for a person to be a professor and not simultaneously a religious leader, and in part because academia, like most public realms, is a space in which misogynistic regulation of women is the norm. Yet as Barr also advertises frequently, she is not only a professor. She is also married to a Baptist pastor (who is a man).[80] She bakes cookies.[81] She bore and raises children.[82] She does domestic labor. "Talk about showing my reality as a professor & pastor's wife!", one social media post exclaimed.[83] This narration accompanies a photograph of an old date book opened, she shares, to the week before she had her second child. The Tuesday to-do list reads, "clean house, pizza, work on lectures." Professional compliance is not the only type that Barr must, and endeavors to, demonstrate. She also performs compliance with many patriarchal expectations of her behavior as a woman, showing that her work as a professor does not mean she is not also a good wife and mother by the lights of patriarchy. That she is specifically a pastor's wife (note: not partner) means she can simultaneously leverage such compliance as evidence of her compliance *as a woman* within Christian practice and biblicism.

Barr cannot transcend misogyny. Or end patriarchy. At best what *The Making of Biblical Womanhood* does is precisely what the version of Paul that she constructs and celebrates is doing: not fighting patriarchy but mitigating it. At worst the book does the opposite of what Barr intends to do by making women feel more comfortable within a patriarchal social order, as she offers false hope, building a convincing illusion that belief in women's access to leadership roles in the church combined with belief in marriage as a partnership signals the end of Christian patriarchy. Rather than end (white) Christian patriarchy, her Bible benevolence project makes it more feasible because *The Making of Biblical Womanhood* makes white evangelical biblicism feel better. To return to Alsup's question: *Is the Bible Good for Women?* Yes, *but only if* . . . they are "good" women.

FIVE

The Cost of Bible Benevolence

The Harms of White Evangelical Power

The goodness of the Good Book is precarious, ever in need of renewal and revision. The perpetual nature of Bible benevolence results in part from the nature of the Bible itself. The Bible is simultaneously a collection of ancient texts and a modern construct. Its contents originated in antiquity, in diverse geographical settings, resulting in a vast chronological and cultural distance between the people who composed and compiled the literature that became biblical, on the one hand, and the people in the US who scripturalize this literature to make sense of their lives in modernity, on the other.[1] Making ancient texts speak to contemporary society is a process not merely of translation but of transformation. The materials must be made to speak anew to changing circumstances that the biblical writers in their time and place could not have even imagined. Contemporary interpreters must figure out what a text written *then and there* could mean for *here and now* when *here and now* is so different from *then and there*. Even so, the past is hard to reconstruct, and its reconstruction can never escape presentist concerns.

While the Bible's contents originated in antiquity, the Bible is not really an ancient book. The Bible is a modern construct. The Bible read by modern white evangelicals in the US developed in concert with capitalism, Western imperialism, and white supremacy.[2] As they endeavor to make this Bible universally benevolent, white evangelical Bible redemption projects advance capitalist and imperialist logics alongside white normativity. Though there are many ways in which the Bible has been conscripted into modern capitalist imperialism, a common one is Bible apologists' serial and loud insistence that the Bible is "the best-selling book of all time." When Steve and Jackie Green, white evangelical owners of the Hobby Lobby chain of craft stores, penned a defense of the Bible, they invoked its bestseller status: "For two thousand years, the Bible has been both the bestselling book and the most translated book in the world, year after year after year. No other book comes close to the Bible's impact and influence in transforming individuals, strengthening families, shaping nations, and determining human history."[3] "Bestseller" rhetoric in Bible benevolence projects like that of the Greens allows white evangelicals to claim the Good Book as "good" in the sense of "desirable," and then use marketplace demand as evidence for the Bible's goodness.[4] Purchases reveal the will of the people. Good sales numbers constitute evidence of a product's goodness. In this capitalist marketplace logic, if it is good for profits, it is good for people.

The rhetoric of the Bible as bestseller and therefore good interchanges two definitions of *good*. Marketplace success becomes evidence of moral suitability. This discourse also hides that both the Bible and its goodness are continually manufactured, materially and rhetorically. Printed Bibles require publishing houses, text critics, editors, translators, illustrators, authors of paratextual material, and advertisers. Bible societies must generate money to make new translations and then publish and distribute them. Bibles have to be advertised as goods that people should want or that they absolutely cannot live without. At the same time, a steady flow of books and blogs, sound bites and sermons works to market the *concept* of the Good Book—the Bible that is a cultural icon, the Bible that transcends materiality.[5]

But try as anyone might, they cannot control the text. Bible benevolence work is necessary because people sometimes do harmful things with the backing of their Bibles. Some people who read, venerate, and love the Good Book are bad— even if they don't know it, even if they don't mean to be. The Pastoral epistles praise disciplined slavers and obedient slaves as good, grounding an ethics that white Christians in the US thought was good, until they didn't. The fact that *goodness* is a contested category and the *now* keeps changing means the Bible's benevolence requires constant upkeep. Goodness is not fixed or timeless. Social mores and sensibilities evolve over time, and are never universal even if public opinion crystalizes into general consensus. Hairstyles come in and out of fashion. Harms become newly named.

For this reason, Bible benevolence scripts frequently insulate the Bible from blame for not keeping up with an evolving notion of *good* by using a variation of the sin-as-a-sorting device strategy. They organize people into those who use the Bible and those who abuse it. They forge a distinction between *use*, on the one hand, and *misuse* or *abuse*, on the other. White evangelical Bible boosters Michael McAfee and Lauren Green McAfee rehearse this strategy in their book *Not What You Think: Why the Bible Might Be Nothing We Expected Yet Everything We Need*, their attempt to persuade fellow millennials not to dismiss the Bible:

> We readily admit that indefensible acts have occurred in the name of the Christian religion, not to mention the Bible itself. Men and women have often misused the text of Scripture for their own gain. This is

inexcusably wrong. Instead we want to look at the Bible for what it says, and it never condones the violation of human dignity.[6]

This handy Bible benevolence strategy is a common one because it allows its deployers to remove blame from the Bible and themselves in one fell stroke. It's not the Bible that is out of step with the good but those who misuse it. Dan Kimball's version separates himself and the Bible from even contemporary Bible readers he believes have it wrong:

> There have been—and still are—some churches and Christians who misuse the text to create misogyny in God's name. But when you study the Scriptures and seek to understand them in their cultural context, it's clear that the Bible is not against women, but an advocate for women.[7]

Jerry Pattengale's Bible-reputation-management book encodes this rhetoric in the very title—*Is the Bible at Fault? How the Bible Has Been Misused to Justify Evil, Suffering, and Bizarre Behavior.*[8] The Crusaders, the Ku Klux Klan, and snake-handlers have all in turn handled the Bible wrongly. He suggests that such "misuses" of the Bible would never have happened if only readers had read the Bible "responsibly."[9] There is no fault in the Bible, only in its sinful interpreters, who, in each case, are other people.

In a time in the US when white evangelicals enjoy outsized political influence and decision-making privileges that affect the whole nation, despite their shrinking demographics, white evangelical Bible benevolence labor is one means they use to protect their power in a country with a diverse religious landscape that is nevertheless saturated with Christian normativity. Putting the prefix *mis-* on the word *use* automatically makes a normative assumption about how the Bible is supposed to be used. The only way something can be misused is if its proper use is established by something external to it, like an instruction manual, and someone uses it outside those bounds or for some other purpose. Since there is no universal manual for how to read the Bible, "misuse" is in reality a polemical term for "uses I do not condone." When white evangelical Bible-redeemers write a Bible benevolence script, they are writing an instruction manual to save themselves from critique. *Sure, it sounds like our Bible says some really terrible things, but that's just because you're not reading it right. Let me teach you the rules.* For white evangelicals, making the Bible into the Good Book is a practice of self-authorization.[10] White evangelical Bible benevolence is good at making white evangelicals feel good about themselves.

White evangelical Bible benevolence, with its blinkered obsession with saving the Bible, is fundamentally animated by an unchecked optimism that the Bible cannot be anything but universally beneficial. For white evangelicals, God can be both merciful and just, both three and one, both invisible and incarnate—but the Bible can't be both good and bad.

Not for lack of imagination, ingenuity, or confidence, though. White evangelical Bible benevolence relies on exercising a robust imagination when it comes to ancient history, creative engagement with widely accepted rules of logic, and the brashness to insist that they have satisfactorily answered critiques. Contents of the Bible are either prescriptive or descriptive, the script suggests. Which disjunctive from this pair is applied to a specific Bible verse or passage is based on which is more effective for making the Bible line up with modern expectations of what should be in a Good Book. The rape of the Levite's concubine in the book of Judges is framed as descriptive, for example. It's a story, not a command. Bible readers are not supposed to read this text prescriptively, the script suggests, and conclude "thou shalt rape."

When it comes to the gospels, however, Bible benevolence hinges on reading descriptive material about Jesus prescriptively. That is, the gospels are read in such a way as to turn stories about what Jesus did into material that prescribes normative behavior. This move is necessary because Jesus's actual prescriptions—his explicit commands—are insufficiently precise or just plain insufficient for making the Bible good for everyone. The Jesus of the gospels did not say, "do not enslave people" or "thou shalt not make women do unequal amounts of domestic labor." Interpreters who see Jesus as fighting inequality must in this case mine stories to find the prescription they need.

The script's strategic deployment of this *either/or* is even clearer when it comes to the Pauline corpus. The uncomfortable silencing passages are literally prescriptive—until Bible-redeemers get their hands on them. Then, they cannot be prescriptive, the logic goes, because in other places Paul acknowledges that women talked. Paul's description of reality in this case becomes a tool to subvert the literal imperative in the text. Bible-redeemers neutralize the troubling commands by claiming they could not be prescriptive if people did not follow them. The logics of those engaged in the project of saving the Bible from itself often rely on holding sets of contradictions together while insisting the Bible is consistent, with itself and with modern mores.

The refusal of white evangelicals to assess the Bible as both good and bad is not a result of refusing the notion that competing, even paradoxical, ideas can be held at the same time. White evangelical Bible benevolence depends on seeing Jesus as simultaneously metatextual and accessible *sola scriptura*. Paul is both typical and unique, special and not. Early Christians were fitting in and revolutionary at the same time, called to be respectable and simultaneously deviant. Women are both deserving and not, there and not, equal and not. They are simultaneously victims and vixens. Women are dogs, and women are people too.

Humans, by and large, are good at living in the space afforded by contradictions when doing so means they get to hold on to something they value. The white evangelical Bible benevolence business is designed to protect the dominance of those who dominate, and reward those who comply with them. Its script polices people by the norms of white heteropatriarchy while advertising it as good for them. In reality, these arguments stand to be most persuasive, or perhaps persuasive at all, to those who benefit from enforcing those very norms. The white evangelical Bible benevolence script sanctifies whiteness by presuming the innocence of the text, by hiding white subjectivity, and by trusting authority unconditionally. The stakes and consequences of their Bible benevolence come into clearer focus with the right questions posed to their fantasies, their ingenuities, and their responses to charges of harm. What is unimaginable, and why? What is *not worth* being creative about achieving? By what standard is goodness measured? What do they find satisfying, and expect everyone else to as well? Who can be sacrificed? Whose pain is ignored, denied, or even rendered necessary?

The white evangelical Bible benevolence script scripturalizes misogyny—not because white evangelicals get the Bible wrong but because they get misogyny wrong. For many Bible apologists, a return to the patriarchy of the 1950s is what is good for women. Only through feminine submission will both women and men find the good life that eludes so many in the inhospitable terrain of modern capitalism. For those who attempt to save the Bible from patriarchy, rescuing the Bible means leaving behind the women who, presumably, should also be rescued by an anti-patriarchal

Bible. The business of white evangelical Bible benevolence as currently practiced—despite any stated good intentions on the part of its practitioners—cannot empower, free, or rescue women because what it most wants to sell is the power of the Bible. What it most wants to protect is the safety of the Bible. Solutions cannot fix problems the problem-solvers do not see. Good intentions will never be sufficient to make the Book good.

Notes

Chapter 1

1 NRSVUE translation. See also Exodus 23:20–33; 34:11–16; Numbers 33:50–56; Deuteronomy 7:16–26; 20:1–20.

2 Scholars point out that literary clues in Joshua, as well as the alternate narration of the conquest in the book of Judges, show that such a total destruction was never carried out. In fact, it is possible from a historical point of view that no external conquest of this sort took place at all. But this does not get around the fact that it is in the Bible as it is. Saying it did not happen does not get it out of anyone's Bible, a point made superbly by Robert Allen Warrior, "A Native American Perspective: Canaanites, Cowboys, and Indians," in *Voices from the Margin. Interpreting the Bible in the Third World*, ed. R. S. Sugirtharajah (Maryknoll, NY: Orbis, 2006), 287–95.

3 One silly song in the *VeggieTales* canon depicts the protagonists as "pirates who don't do anything," while another catchy tune captures Larry the Cucumber's existential quest to find his, ultimately useless, hairbrush. Neither is obviously related to the Bible.

4 This biblical story together with others that narrate violence against women have been famously named "texts of terror" by Phyllis Trible (*Texts of Terror: Literary-Feminist Readings of Biblical Narratives* [Philadelphia: Fortress, 1984]).

5 On this trope and its consequences, see especially the pioneering work of Renita J. Weems in *Battered Love: Marriage, Sex, and Violence in the Hebrew Prophets* (Minneapolis: Fortress Press, 1995). See further Jennifer Wright Knust, *Unprotected Texts: The Bible's Surprising Contradictions about Sex and Desire* (New York: HarperOne, 2012), 113–52; Rhiannon Graybill, *Texts after Terror: Rape, Sexual Violence, and the Hebrew Bible* (New York: Oxford University Press, 2021).

6 Sarah Emanuel, "When Women of the Bible Say #MeToo," *Feminist Studies in Religion* (blog), January 26, 2018, https://www.fsrinc.org/women-of-the-bible-say-metoo/; Stephen Young, "Revelation Naturalizes Sexual

Violence and Readers Erase It: Unveiling the Son of God's Rape of Jezebel," in *Sex, Violence, and Early Christian Texts*, ed. Christy Cobb and Eric Vanden Eykel (Lanham, MD: Lexington Books, 2022), 239–59.

7   Allen Dwight Callahan, *The Talking Book: African Americans and the Bible* (New Haven, CT: Yale University Press, 2006), 1–48. On the formative use of the Exodus narrative by African American Bible interpreters, see further Rhondda Robinson Thomas, *Claiming Exodus: A Cultural History of Afro-Atlantic Identity, 1774–1903* (Waco, TX: Baylor University Press, 2013).

8   Howard Thurman, *Jesus and the Disinherited* (Boston: Beacon Press: 1996), 30–31; see also Cavan Concannon, *Profaning Paul* (Chicago: University of Chicago Press, 2021).

9   Emerson B. Powery and Rodney S. Sadler, Jr., *The Genesis of Liberation: Biblical Interpretation in the Antebellum Narratives of the Enslaved* (Louisville, KY: Westminster John Knox Press, 2016).

10   Callahan, *The Talking Book*, 21–26.

11   Callahan, *The Talking Book*, 21–26. See J. Albert Harrill, "The Use of the New Testament in the American Slave Controversy: A Case History in the Hermeneutical Tension between Biblical Criticism and Christian Moral Debate," *Religion and American Culture: A Journal of Interpretation* 10, no. 2 (2000), 149–86, for a survey and analysis of the hermeneutic struggles and creativities of white abolitionist and anti-slavery writers.

12   Callahan, *The Talking Book*, 39–40.

13   Claudia Setzer, "The Bible and the Legacy of First Wave Feminism," in *The Bible in American Life*, ed. Philip Goff, Arthur E. Farnsley II, and Peter J. Thuesen (New York: Oxford University Press, 2017), 183–91. Setzer provides a flexible taxonomy, helpfully organizing these figures according to whether they see "the Bible as ally, the Bible as enemy, or the Bible as bystander" (though, as she points out, the categories can coexist and people can shift between them). See also Claudia Setzer, "Slavery, Women's Rights, and the Beginnings of Feminist Biblical Interpretation in the Nineteenth Century," *Postscripts* 5, no. 2 (2009), 145–69.

14   "Woman's Rights Convention," Akron, OH, May 28, 1851. *New York Tribune* 6 June 1851: 7; cited in Suzanne P. Fitch and Roseann Mandziuk, *Sojourner Truth as Orator: Wit, Story, and Song* (Westport, CT: Greenwood Press, 1997), 141.

15   Fitch and Mandziuk, *Sojourner Truth as Orator*, 77.

16   Setzer, "The Bible and the Legacy of First Wave Feminism," 187–88.

17   Elizabeth Cady Stanton, *The Woman's Bible: A Classic Feminist Perspective* (Mineaola, NY: Dover Publications, 2002), 11–12.

18   David Plotz, *Good Book: The Bizarre, Hilarious, Disturbing, Marvelous and Inspiring Things I Learned When I Read Every Single Word of the Bible* (Harper, 2009), 20.

19   See, for example, Christopher Hitchens, *God is Not Great: How Religion Poisons Everything* (Toronto: McClelland & Stewart, 2007); and Richard Dawkins, *The God Delusion* (London: Bantam Press, 2006).

20   Bart D. Ehrman, *God's Problem: How the Bible Fails to Answer Our Most Important Question—Why We Suffer* (New York: HarperOne, 2009).

21   On the necessity of attending to how texts are made scriptural variously and repeatedly, see Vincent Wimbush, *White Men's Magic: Scripturalization as Slavery* (New York: Oxford University Press, 2012). On the continual remaking of the Bible, see Timothy Beal, "Reception History and Beyond: Toward the Cultural History of Scriptures," *Biblical Interpretation* 19 (2011), 357–72.

22   Sometimes actual businesses are in the Bible benevolence business as well. Hobby Lobby is a prime example. On the Bible boosterism of the Green family, the white evangelical owners of Hobby Lobby, see Candida R. Moss and Joel S. Baden, *Bible Nation: The United States of Hobby Lobby* (Princeton: Princeton University Press, 2017).

23   Recent years have seen an explosion of scholarly analyses of white evangelical Protestantism in the US, with attention focused on the topical constellation of race, gender, and nationalism. Sociologists and historians of religion have published significant studies with both university presses and trade presses. In the *New York Times* bestseller *Jesus and John Wayne* (2020), for example, US historian Kristin Kobes Du Mez chronicles the past seventy-five years of white evangelical entanglements with distinctively American notions of masculinity, venturing an explanation for how it came to be that evangelical Christians overwhelmingly supported Donald Trump for the presidency in 2016. Sociologists Andrew Whitehead and Samuel L. Perry, on the other hand, used surveys and other metrics in their study *Taking America Back for God* (2020) to trace the imbrication of white Christian nationalism in US political and religious fabric. Analysis of race takes center stage in *White Evangelical Racism: The Politics of Morality in America* (2021), written by historian of American religion Anthea Butler, and in sociologist Robert P. Jones's *White Too Long: The Legacy of White Supremacy in American Christianity* (2020). Both include surveys of white evangelicalism in the past century, with an emphasis on the longstanding effects of white supremacy in American Christianity. See further Sarah Posner, *Unholy: Why White*

Evangelicals Worship at the Altar of Donald Trump (New York: Random House, 2020); John Fea, *Believe Me: The Evangelical Road to Trump* (Grand Rapids, MI: Eerdmans, 2018); Bradley Onishi, *Preparing for War: The Extremist History of White Christian Nationalism—And What Comes Next* (Minneapolis: Broadleaf Books, 2023). I entered the conversation in Jill Hicks-Keeton and Cavan Concannon, *Does Scripture Speak for Itself? The Museum of the Bible and the Politics of Interpretation* (Cambridge: Cambridge University Press, 2022), in which Concannon and I outline the contours of what we call the "white evangelical Bible" as produced by the Museum of the Bible, an evangelical Christian institution near the national mall in Washington, DC. One chapter treats the MOTB's production of this Bible as fundamentally good. On this topic, see also Margaret M. Mitchell, "'It's Complicated.' 'No, It's Not.': The Museum of the Bible, Problems and Solutions," in *The Museum of the Bible: A Critical Introduction,* ed. Jill Hicks-Keeton and Cavan Concannon (Lanham, MD: Lexington/Fortress Academic), 3–36. For more on what is meant by "white evangelicalism," see Hicks-Keeton and Concannon, *Does Scripture Speak for Itself?*, 15–42. I take the same institutional approach in the present work.

24   See, for example, J. Russell Hawkins, *The Bible Told Them So: How Southern Evangelicals Fought to Preserve White Supremacy* (New York: Oxford University Press, 2021); Jesse Curtis, *The Myth of Colorblind Christians: Evangelicals and White Supremacy in the Civil Rights Era* (New York: New York University Press, 2021); Jemar Tisby, *The Color of Compromise: The Truth about the American Church's Complicity in Racism* (Grand Rapids, MI: Zondervan, 2020). White evangelicals tend to give their heroes drastic makeovers to downplay their racism and put them on the right side of history. See Michael G. Long, *Billy Graham and the Beloved Community: America's Evangelist and the Dream of Martin Luther King, Jr.* (Cham, Switzerland: Palgrave Macmillan, 2006); and Butler, *White Evangelical Racism* (Chapel Hill: University of North Carolina Press, 2021), 42–55.

25   See Daniel Vaca, *Evangelicals Incorporated: Books and the Business of Religion in America* (Cambridge: Harvard University Press, 2019).

26   Many of the ideas presented in such arguments preexist these authors' work. They are so common by now, though, that the authors rarely cite previously existing sources, except for one another in some cases.

27   By using the word "script," I do not mean to imply that any of the writers whose work I analyze is merely parroting others or performing (and therefore not earnest), though I also do not mean to suggest that these writers invented the ideas. "Script" is here a convenient shorthand to refer to the

common set of arguments that white evangelicals use, regardless of whether they originated them. There exist, of course, deviations from the script.

28 Dan Kimball, *How (Not) to Read the Bible: Making Sense of the Anti-Women, Anti-Science, Pro-Violence, Pro-Slavery and Other Crazy-Sounding Parts of Scripture* (Grand Rapids, MI: Zondervan, 2020), 275–76.

29 Copan, *Is God a Moral Monster? Making Sense of the Old Testament God* (Grand Rapids, MI: Baker Books, 2011), 169.

30 Copan, *Is God a Moral Monster?*, 169–70.

31 Copan, *Is God a Moral Monster?*, 169.

32 Kimball, *How (Not) to Read the Bible*, 276.

33 Copan, *Is God a Moral Monster?*, 163.

34 Kimball, *How (Not) to Read the Bible*, 276.

35 See, for example, Clay Jones, "We Don't Hate Sin So We Don't Understand What Happened to the Canaanites: An Addendum to 'Divine Genocide' Arguments," *Philosophia Christi* 11, no. 1 (2009): 53.

36 Copan, *Is God a Moral Monster?*, 160. Copan's articulation is attended by rhetoric of Western supremacy: "Despite many gains over the centuries in the areas of human rights and religious liberty, due to the positive influence of biblical ideals in America and other Western nations, Westerners have their own share of decadence . . . " (160). So also Jones, "We Don't Hate Sin," 68–72.

37 Kimball for one employs the language of randomness: "Understand that God was not randomly ordering battles and encouraging violence" (*How [Not] to Read the Bible*, 276).

38 Jones, "We Don't Hate Sin," 53–72.

39 Norman L. Geisler and Thomas Howe, *The Big Book of Bible Difficulties: Clear and Concise Answers from Genesis to Revelation* (Grand Rapids, MI: Baker Books, 1992), 137. They cite Leviticus 18 as evidence and conclude that "sometimes radical surgery is required to completely eliminate a deadly cancer from the body" (138).

40 Bible-redeemers mobilize Genesis 15:16 to make the claim that the Canaanites had a chance to repent but did not take it.

41 Andy Patton, "Why Did God Command the Invasion of Canaan in the Book of Joshua?" *The Bible Project* (blog), https://bibleproject.com/blog/why-did-god-command-the-invasion-of-canaan-in-the-book-of-joshua/.

42 Patton, "Why Did God Command."

43 Copan, *Is God a Moral Monster?*, 167.

44 For a critique of the biblical text that does empathize with the Canaanites, see Warrior, "A Native American Perspective: Canaanites, Cowboys, and Indians." White evangelical Christians likely avoid empathizing

with the Canaanites because they do not have to, given that in the power differential they are more analogous to Israel and the conquering deity than to victims of annihilation. Because of their hegemonic positionality, white evangelical Christians in the US can see violence against the Canaanites as principally an intellectual problem rather than as a terrifying proposition.

45 Copan, *Is God a Moral Monster?*, 170–71; Patton, "Why Did God Command"; Kimball, *How (Not) to Read the Bible*, 283.

46 Kimball, *How (Not) to Read the Bible*, 283.

47 Kimball, *How (Not) to Read the Bible*, 283.

48 They all give a sports analogy.

49 Bible benevolence projects make a similar move when it comes to enslavement (even in the face of the deity's portrayal throughout the Bible as a slaver god). Sarah Bessey, for example, acknowledges that "there is actually *no specific verse in Scripture that prohibits the buying and selling of human beings*" and that "some verses even affirm proper treatment and behaviors of slaves," and then asserts, as though it were axiomatic: "And yet we accept and understand that slavery is evil precisely *because* of the Bible and because we understand God's created purpose for humanity" (*Jesus Feminist: An Invitation to Revisit the Bible's View of Women* [New York: Howard Books, 2013], 29). Bessey is a Canadian who attended the conversative Christian Oral Roberts University in Tulsa, Oklahoma. Her writing has intervened in debates around gender that have been important to American evangelicals in recent decades.

50 Kimball, *How (Not) to Read the Bible*, 256.

51 Kimball, *How (Not) to Read the Bible*, 262.

52 Copan, *Is God a Moral Monster?*, 177.

53 Joshua Ryan Butler, *The Skeletons in God's Closet: The Mercy of Hell, the Surprise of Judgment, the Hope of Holy War* (Nashville: Thomas Nelson, 2014), 227.

54 Butler, *The Skeletons in God's Closet*, 227.

55 The same author spends fewer pages on the deaths of innocent Canaanite infants than on the question of whether the Israelite men who killed them would have suffered harmful psychological effects by executing God's command. Copan, *Is God a Moral Monster?*, starting on page 189.

56 Copan, *Is God a Moral Monster?*, 189.

57 Copan, *Is God a Moral Monster?*, 189.

58 Conservative evangelical Protestant Christians are essentialist in defining "woman" as a person who was designated a girl at birth based on

observation of external genitalia. Consistent with the history of First Wave Feminism's defense of white women's rights (see esp. Louise Michele Newman, *White Women's Rights: The Racial Origins of Feminism in the United States* [New York: Oxford University Press, 1999]), these contemporary Bible benevolence projects are poised principally to make the Bible good for white women. This phenomenon can be illustrated succinctly with white evangelical Wendy Alsup's quick dismissal of Hagar's oppression in Genesis, which she does not count as oppression worth investigating or explaining because it occurred at the hands of another woman rather than a man's: "Genesis has several hard stories about women. Hagar's abuse in Abraham's household in Genesis 16 and 21 gives me pause. But her persecution came primarily through another woman, Sarah" (Alsup, *Is the Bible Good for Women? Seeking Clarity and Confidence through a Jesus-Centered Understanding of Scripture* [New York: Multnomah, 2017], 96). Alsup does not acknowledge the power differential between Sarah and Hagar, who was enslaved to Sarah, nor appreciate that the relationship of Sarah and Hagar maps onto to the history of enslavement and subsequent oppression of Black women by white men and white women. See Renita J. Weems, *Just a Sister Away: A Womanist Vision of Women's Relationships in the Bible* (1988), 1–19; and Wil Gafney, "Hagar," *Bible Odyssey*, https://www.bibleodyssey.org/people/main-articles/hagar/.

59   This is not original to white evangelicals. It was an argument promoted by the earliest white women's rights advocates in the US, like Sarah Grimké and others. The argument is so common that they typically do not cite preexisting sources.

60   Alsup, *Is the Bible Good for Women?*, 97. Dinah was not always the "victim" of this story. On this, see particularly this accessible piece: Alison L. Joseph, "Who Is the Victim in the Dinah Story?" *TheTorah.com* https://www.thetorah.com/article/who-is-the-victim-in-the-dinah-story, and the literature cited therein. For a history of Christian interpretation, from early Christianity through the Reformation, of Dinah's story and other biblical stories of sexual violence, see Joy A. Schroeder, *Dinah's Lament: The Biblical Legacy of Sexual Violence in Christian Interpretation* (Minneapolis: Fortress, 2007).

61   Kimball, *How (Not) to Read the Bible*, 115.

62   Alsup, *Is the Bible Good for Women?*, 29. Italics original.

63   Kimball, *How (Not) to Read the Bible*, 132. Italics original.

64   Kimball, *How (Not) to Read the Bible*, 133.

Chapter 2

1   Beth Moore (@BethMooreLPM), "Above all else, we must search the attitudes & practices of Christ Jesus himself toward women," Twitter, May 11, 2019, https://twitter.com/bethmoorelpm/status/1127211070811197440.

2   Therese Huston, "'He's Like Tony Stark and She's Like My Mom': How Workplace Praise Diverges between Men and Women," *Fast Company,* January 21, 2021, https://www.fastcompany.com/90594770/hes-like-tony-stark-and-shes-like-my-mom-how-workplace-praise-is-diverges-between-men-and-women. Excerpted from Therese Huston, *Let's Talk: Make Effective Feedback Your Superpower* (Portfolio, 2021).

3   See my review essay, in which I also discuss the film and racism: Jill Hicks-Keeton, "The Christian Nationalism behind the New 'God's Not Dead' Film," *Religion & Politics,* October 26, 2021, https://religionandpolitics.org/2021/10/26/the-christian-nationalism-behind-the-new-gods-not-dead-film/. Some material is adopted or adapted from that article.

4   On sex and evangelicals, see especially Amy DeRogatis, *Saving Sex: Sexuality and Salvation in American Evangelicalism* (New York: Oxford University Press, 2014) and Sara Moslener, *Virgin Nation: Sexual Purity and American Adolescence* (New York: Oxford University Press, 2015). On sex scandals, see Leslie Dorrough Smith, *Compromising Positions: Sex Scandals, Politics, and American Christianity* (New York: Oxford University Press, 2020). For more on #ChurchToo, see Emily Joy Allison, *#ChurchToo: How Purity Culture Upholds Abuse and How to Find Healing* (Minneapolis: Broadleaf Books, 2021); Eliza Griswold, "Silence is Not Spiritual: The Evangelical #MeToo Movement," *The New Yorker,* June 15, 2018, https://www.newyorker.com/news/on-religion/silence-is-not-spiritual-the-evangelical-metoo-movement; Peter Smith and Holly Meyer, "#ChurchToo Revelations Growing, Years after Movement Began," *Religion News Service,* June 13, 2022, https://religionnews.com/2022/06/13/churchtoo-revelations-growing-years-after-movement-began/. For an explainer on the SBC sexual abuse scandals, see Emily St. James, "The Sexual Abuse Scandal Rocking the Southern Baptist Convention, Explained," *Vox.com,* June 7, 2022, https://www.vox.com/culture/23131530/southern-baptist-convention-sexual-abuse-scandal-guidepost. Enlightening ethnographic studies of evangelical women include R. Marie Griffith, *God's Daughters: Evangelical Women and the Power of Submission* (Berkeley: University of California Press, 2000) and Julie Ingersoll, *Evangelical Christian Women: War Stories in the Gender Battles* (New York: New York University Press, 2003).

5 The reactions of dominant white evangelical men to the critique they face in the wake of the widespread popularity of Kristin Kobes Du Mez's *Jesus and John Wayne* illustrates the point well. See Sarah Pulliam Bailey, "How a Book about Evangelicals, Trump, and Militant Masculinity Became a Surprise Bestseller," *Washington Post*, July 16, 2021, https://www.washingtonpost.com/religion/2021/07/16/jesus-and-john-wayne-evangelicals-surprise-bestseller/.

6 I offer evidence in this book that evangelical "egalitarianism" does not empower women to be released from the demands and expectations of patriarchal social order. Patriarchal normativity suffuses white evangelicalism. These arguments are consistent with the findings of Lisa Weaver Swartz, whose recent sociological study of two evangelical seminaries suggests that women in self-proclaimed egalitarian communities "celebrate freedom from policies and theologies based on male headship" but "find themselves constrained culturally and structurally by the same genderblind egalitarian framework that opens the institutional authority to them" (*Stained Glass Ceilings: How Evangelicals Do Gender and Practice Power* [New Brunswick, NJ: Rutgers University Press, 2022], 15). She goes on: "While women in both [complementarian and egalitarian] communities find creative ways to thrive, they often find it necessary to participate in their communities' male centering if they wish to succeed in churchly spaces" (15).

7 Kevin DeYoung, "Our Pro-Woman, Complementarian Jesus," *The Gospel Coalition,* February 15, 2006, https://www.thegospelcoalition.org/article/our-pro-woman-complementarian-jesus/.

8 Beth Allison Barr, *The Making of Biblical Womanhood: How the Subjugation of Women Became Gospel Truth* (Grand Rapids, MI: Brazos Press, 2021).

9 Barr, *The Making of Biblical Womanhood*, 28.

10 Barr, *The Making of Biblical Womanhood*, 31. Cf. the similar remarks in Philip B. Payne, *The Bible vs. Biblical Womanhood: How God's Word Consistently Affirms Gender Equality* (Grand Rapids, MI: Zondervan, 2023), esp. 27.

11 Barr, *The Making of Biblical Womanhood*, 76–77.

12 Barr, *The Making of Biblical Womanhood*, 85.

13 Kimball, *How (Not) to Read the Bible*, 120.

14 Kimball, *How (Not) to Read the Bible*, 121.

15 Bessey, *Jesus Feminist,* 16–17.

16 Kate Manne, *Down Girl: The Logic of Misogyny* (New York: Oxford University Press, 2017). See further Kate Manne, *Entitled: How Male*

Privilege Hurts Women (New York: Crown, 2020), which has also influenced my analysis.

17 Manne, *Down Girl*, 79.

18 Manne, *Down Girl*, 59.

19 Manne calls this the "naïve conception" of misogyny (*Down Girl*, 18–19, 27–28).

20 Not all women and girls are subject to the same experience of misogyny. Oppression is compounded by other social factors. Trans women, women of color, and trans women of color in particular are usually subject to different and more hostility and discrimination than are white cisgendered women. In Manne's words, her accounting of misogyny "leaves room for the diverse ways misogyny works on girls and women given their intersectional identities, in terms of the quality, quantity, intensity, experience, and impact of the hostility, as well as the agents and social mechanisms by means of which it is delivered" (*Down Girl*, 21). She goes on: "Misogyny may also involve *multiple* compounding forms of misogyny if she is (say) subject to different parallel systems of male dominance (depending, again, on other intersecting factors), or required to play incompatible roles in virtue of multiple social positions which she occupies simultaneously." Such an intersectional approach was pioneered by Kimberlé W. Crenshaw (see esp. "Demarginalizing the Intersection of Race and Sex: A Black Feminist Critique of Antidiscrimination Doctrine, Feminist Theory and Antiracist Politics," *University of Chicago Legal Forum* 1, no. 8 [1989], 139–67). The distinctive intersection of misogyny and anti-Black racism in the US led Moya Bailey to coin, in 2008, the term *misogynoir* to refer to hostilities faced in particular by Black women, especially through popular culture depictions (*Misogynoir Transformed: Black Women's Digital Resistance* [New York: New York University Press, 2021]).

21 Manne, *Down Girl*, 63–64, 78.

22 Manne, *Down Girl*, 83–84.

23 Manne, *Entitled*, 7.

24 Manne, *Down Girl*, 84.

25 Manne, *Down Girl*, xiv, 113–14.

26 See the example of Rush Limbaugh's treatment of Sandra Fluke in Manne, *Down Girl*, 55–62.

27 Manne, *Down Girl*, 110–13. See also the various chapters on what men within a patriarchal order are "entitled to" in Manne's *Entitled*.

28 Manne, *Down Girl*, 234–35.

29 See also Rhiannon Graybill's use of "peremption" as a way to understand harm in biblical texts, developed particularly in conversation with the

NOTES

story of David and Bathsheba in 2 Samuel 11 (*Texts after Terror,* 58–84). Graybill usefully applies this model from the work of Joseph J. Fischel, (*Sex and Harm in the Age of Consent* [Minneapolis: University of Minnesota Press, 2016]). Like Manne's model does, "peremption" centers the person harmed rather than the predator/perpetrator.

30   Manne, *Down Girl,* 73–75.

31   Manne, *Down Girl,* 44.

32   In the reading of gospel stories I offer in this chapter, I am not interested in articulating what an author, "Mark," thought about women, or what the narrator thinks about women, or whether the gospel of Mark gives evidence as to what the (elusive) "historical Jesus" thought about women. I am interested in how later readers use the gospel of Mark as an access point to a particular Jesus that is productive for their own arguments about women. I am interested in what kinds of creative negotiations they engage in and value judgments they must make in order to fashion such a Jesus on the basis of the available data in the gospels. While I will argue that such Bible-rehabilitation projects often reproduce misogyny even as they seek to exculpate the Bible from it, my point is not to present these white evangelical apologists' interpretations as "incorrect" but rather to show that they are not natural, comprehensive, or obvious based on the text itself. Work is required.

33   This power dynamic is common today as well. Dominant men empower others as long as those others are subordinates, people whose empowerment will not imperil the hierarchy (Manne, *Entitled,* 8).

34   Unless otherwise noted, translations are quoted from the NRSVUE.

35   "From a distance," biblical scholar Tat-siong Benny Liew observes, "may well be an apt description of the way these women have always followed and served Jesus" in Mark (*Politics of Parousia: Reading Mark Inter(con)textually,* Biblical Interpretation Series (Leiden: Brill, 1999), (142). And further: "When Jesus and his male disciples are in Galilee and then on the way to Jerusalem, these women are kept invisible, out of the way, until the male disciples have fallen away" (142).

36   Likely this is the result of a literary seam leftover from the gospel writer's use of a preexisting passion narrative, but composition history is not our task here. The gospel of Luke fixes this apparent problem by moving the women earlier in narrative time (8:1–3).

37   This is sometimes leveraged in support of the idea that Jesus was especially good to women. Philip Payne writes, for example, "Jesus demonstrated his respect for [women's] testimony by appearing first to Mary Magdalene after his resurrection (John 20:14–18) and instructing her to tell the others." (Philip B. Payne, *Man and Woman, One in Christ:*

An Exegetical and Theological Study of Paul's Letters [Grand Rapids, MI: Zondervan, 2009], 57). The exclusion of women from the highest levels of power is something many white evangelicals in the US are comfortable with, of course. Complementarian social order depends on it.

38   Susan Miller, *Women in Mark's Gospel* (London: T&T Clark International, 2004), 22.

39   See Tressie McMillan Cottom, *Thick: And Other Essays* (New York: The New Press, 2019), 77–97; Manne, *Entitled,* 75–96, and the literature cited therein; Anushay Hossain, *The Pain Gap: How Sexism and Racism in Healthcare Kill Women* (New York: Simon and Schuster, 2021).

40   Liew, *Politics of Parousia,* 144–45.

41   Some observe further that the labor Simon's mother-in-law performs is the same as that of the angels who ministered to Jesus in the wilderness, recounted just above in Mark's story (1:13). The translation of Simon's mother-in-law's verb is a site of contestation in which battles over women's ordination can be, and have been, fought. The ESV translation, for example, uses "ministering" to describe the angels' behavior but "serve" to describe Simon's mother-in-law's behavior, presumably in a bid to neutralize any claims that could be made on the basis of Mark 1 that women are allowed to be ministers. Yet, no matter which English word is used, it remains that both the angels and Simon's mother-in-law are performing labor for the benefit of someone else in a hierarchical regime in which that someone else is higher than they are. Moreover, while the angels serve Jesus alone, Simon's mother-in-law serves a plural *them.* This most naturally refers to Jesus and the other men who have been named as present, at the very least James and John. Probably also Simon and Andrew, whose home they are in.

42   See the survey of readings by feminist biblical scholars, for example, offered by Deborah Krause, "Simon Peter's Mother-in-Law—Disciple or Domestic Servant? Feminist Biblical Hermeneutics and the Interpretation of Mark 1.29–31," in *A Feminist Companion to Mark,* ed. Amy Jill-Levine and Marianne Blickenstaff (Sheffield, UK: Sheffield Academic Press, 2001), 37–53.

43   Krause, "Simon Peter's Mother-in-Law," 46.

44   On the leakiness of Jesus's body and its resulting parallel to the woman's, see Candida R. Moss, "The Man with the Flow of Power: Porous Bodies in Mark 5:25–34," *Journal of Biblical Literature* 129 no. 3 (2010): 507–19.

45   Bessey, *Jesus Feminist,* 19.

46   So also Liew, *Politics of Parousia*, 139.

47   According to online profiles, McLelland trained for a master's degree in Christian Education at Dallas Theological Seminary. She teaches at Williamson College in Franklin, TN, whose website lists her title as "Professor of Goals, Priorities, and Attitudes, The Life of Christ, Israel Biblical Study Program, and Living Free in Christ" (https://williamsoncc.edu/kristi-mclelland/). Part of her tagline reads, "There is more to scripture than what you're reading!" (https://www.newlensbiblicalstudies.com).

48   Kristi McLelland, *Jesus & Women: In the First Century and Now* (Nashville: Lifeway Press, 2019), 21.

49   Elaine Storkey, *Women in a Patriarchal World: Twenty-Five Empowering Stories from the Bible* (Great Britain: Society for Promoting Christian Knowledge, 2020), 114. Storkey is a British theologian whose work has become significant in white evangelicalism in the US. After her book *Scars across Humanity: Understanding and Overcoming Violence against Women* (originally published by the UK organization The Society for Promoting Christian Knowledge in 2015) was republished by InterVarsity Press in the US in 2018, it won the 2019 Book of the Year Award in Politics and Public Life given by *Christianity Today,* the publication founded by famed white evangelist Billy Graham (https://www.christianitytoday.com/ct/2019/january-february/christianity-today-2019-book-awards.html). Her book *Women in a Patriarchal World* was reviewed in *Eikon: A Journal for Biblical Anthropology,* a publication of the Council on Biblical Manhood and Womanhood (https://cbmw.org/2020/11/20/women-in-a-patriarchal-world-twenty-five-empowering-stories-from-the-bible-book-review/).

50   Storkey, *Women in a Patriarchal World*, 112.

51   For an intersectional analysis of this scene, taking into account both race and gender, see Liew, *Politics of Parousia,* 134–37. See also the work of Musa W. Dube, who has argued that white Western interpretations of the Matthean version of this story tend to ignore the imperialist logics of "mission" and/or do not treat gender as a factor in the power dynamics at play (*Postcolonial Feminist Interpretation of the Bible* [St. Louis: Chalice, 2000], 157–96). Dube insists that only a decolonized text can be a potentially liberative one.

52   The Rev. Wil Gafney, PhD, "Drag Queens and Did Jesus Just Call that Woman a B—," September 12, 2012, https://www.wilgafney.com/2012/09/12/drag-queens-and-did-jesus-just-call-that-woman-a-b/.

53 This phenomenon is common in translations and printed Bibles, when Mark 7:24–30 is presented under an editorial heading such as "The Syrophoenician Woman's Faith." Examples include the RSV, the ESV, the NIV, and the NRSVUE.

54 Kyle Butt, "Jesus, the Syrophoenician Woman, and Little Dogs," *Apologetics Press*, September 24, 2006, https://apologeticspress.org/jesus-the-syrophoenician-woman-and-little-dogs-317/.

55 I here play with Manne's title *Down Girl*. For a highly publicized example of misogynistic (and racist) use of "dog" language in recent history, see Christina Cauterucci, "Donald Trump Called Omarosa a Dog. Is That Racist, Sexist, or Both?" *Slate*, August 14, 2018, https://slate.com/news-and-politics/2018/08/donald-trump-called-omarosa-a-dog-is-that-racist-sexist-or-both.html.

56 T. A. Burkill, "The Historical Development of the Story of the Syrophoenician Woman (Mark VII:24–31)," *Novum Testamentum* 9, no. 3 (1967): 161–77 (quotation from 170). Sharon H. Ringe quotes this line from Burkill and herself adds: "even if the saying . . . is a proverb, and even if it was a metaphorical way of referring to the fact that the petitioner in this case is a Gentile, that saying addressed to the woman is offensive in the extreme. Metaphor or not, Jesus is depicted as comparing the woman and her daughter to dogs!" ("A Gentile Woman's Story," in *Feminist Interpretation of the Bible*, ed. Letty M. Russell [Louisville, KY: Westminster John Knox Press, 1985], 69). See also Sharon H. Ringe, "A Gentile Woman's Story Revisited: Rereading Mark 7.24–31," in *A Feminist Companion to Mark*, ed. Amy-Jill Levine (Sheffield, UK: Sheffield Academic Press, 2001), 79–100.

57 Barr, *The Making of Biblical Womanhood,* 120.

58 Examples are plentiful in treatments of both Mark's and Matthew's versions. The following are illustrative of the trend: James F. McGrath, *What Jesus Learned from Women* (Eugene, OR: Cascade Books, 2021), 87; Frances Taylor Gench, *Back to the Well: Women's Encounters with Jesus in the Gospels* (Louisville, KY: Westminster John Knox Press, 2004), 18; Holly Carey, "Women in Action: Models for Discipleship in Mark's Gospel," *Catholic Biblical Quarterly* 81 (2019): 438.

59 Bessey, *Jesus Feminist,* 22.

60 Bessey, *Jesus Feminist*, 11.

61 Bessey, *Jesus Feminist,* 21–22. She also writes this of Paul: "Paul believed women were people, too. As a follower of Jesus, of course he did. Of course he did" (69).

62 A reprint of the article is available online here: "Women Are People, Too!": The Groundbreaking Article by Betty Friedan," August 9, 2010,

https://www.goodhousekeeping.com/life/career/advice/a18890/1960-betty-friedan-article/. For more on this article, its reception, and its relation to *The Feminist Mystique*, see Stephanie Coontz, *A Strange Stirring: The Feminine Mystique and American Women at the Dawn of the 1960s* (New York: Basic Books, 2011). If Bessey is aware of this history, it is not apparent from her writing in *Jesus Feminist*. It is unclear whether Bessey's appropriation of Friedan's phrase is deliberate or accidental.

63   Friedan, "Women are People, Too!"

64   Bessey, *Jesus Feminist*, 34.

65   Kimball, *How (Not) to Read the Bible*, 122.

66   One example is Philip Payne, who puts it this way: Jesus "respected [women's] intelligence and spiritual capacity as is evident in the great spiritual truths he originally taught to women," especially the Samaritan woman in John 4 (*Man and Woman*, 57).

67   Meredith J. C. Warren, "Five Husbands: Slut-Shaming the Samaritan Woman," *The Bible & Critical Theory* 17, no. 2 (2021), 51–69. "This is not an inclusive Jesus," Warren writes, "when it comes to sexuality."

68   Warren ("Five Husbands") points out that professional biblical scholars do this as well.

69   Bessey, *Jesus Feminist*, 64.

70   See the research of Joanna Wolfe of Carnegie Mellon University, as discussed in Jason Maderer, "Women Interrupted: A New Strategy for Male-Dominated Discussions," *CMU News*, October 21, 2020. Wolfe summarizes the consensus this way: "The research is pretty clear: While both sexes interrupt, men talk and interrupt more often than women. Some of that is because society has accepted that it's normal and natural that men tend to talk more." This issue received widespread attention when during a vice presidential debate in 2020, Kamala Harris, who would go on to be elected, responded to then–vice president Mike Pence's interruption of her with "Mr. Vice President, I'm speaking." On gender and Donald Trump's repeated interruption of 2016 opponent Hillary Clinton (as one of other misogynistic regulatory behaviors), see Minita Sanghvi, *Gender and Political Marketing in the United States and the 2016 Election: An Analysis of Why She Lost* (Cham, Switzerland: Palgrave Macmillan, 2018), especially 133–45.

71   Warren, "Five Husbands," 63.

72   Warren observes that Jesus's "behaviour is comparably much less radical and less kind than that of the Samaritan community in which the woman lives" ("Five Husbands," 63).

73 Judith Plaskow showed decades ago the ease with which Christian feminists have problematically caricatured ancient Judaism as backward and oppressive to women in order to make the gospels evidence for Christian inclusion of women ("Blaming Jews for Inventing Patriarchy," *Lilith,* June 5, 1980, https://lilith.org/articles/debut-2/).

74 Plaskow, "Blaming Jews for Inventing Patriarchy."

75 See especially, Plaskow, "Blaming Jews for Inventing Patriarchy"; and Katharina von Kellenbach, *Anti-Judaism in Feminist Religious Writings* (New York: Oxford University Press, 1994). Von Kellenbach summarizes: "By equating the (Jewish) foes of Jesus with the (patriarchal) enemies of feminism, some scholars arrive at the conclusion that Christianity and feminism are fighting the same battle" (74).

76 See Rebecca Solnit, "Men Who Explain Things," *Los Angeles Times*, April 13, 2008; republished as *Men Explain Things to Me* (Chicago: Haymarket Books, 2014), 6–17.

77 See Jennifer Knust and Tommy Wasserman, *To Cast the First Stone: The Transmission of a Gospel Story* (Princeton: Princeton University Press, 2020).

78 Scot McKnight, *A New Vision for Israel: The Teachings of Jesus in National Context* (Grand Rapids, MI: Eerdmans, 1999), 222.

79 Scot McKnight, *A New Vision for Israel*, 222.

80 These monikers appear in editors' headings: "A [or The] Woman Caught in Adultery" appears in the ESV, Good News Translation, International Children's Bible, New Century Version, RSV, NRSV, the Voice, New English Translation, New Living Translation, and New Catholic Bible; "Mercy for a Sinful Woman" in the Tree of Life Version; "An Adulteress Faces the Light of the World" in the New King James Version; "The Adulteress" in the Evangelical Heritage Version; and "The Adulterous Woman" in the Amplified Bible and NASB.

81 As biblical scholar Jennifer Knust puts it, "The real question is not 'will the woman be saved?' so much as 'which man will win?'" (Jennifer Knust, "Can an Adulteress Save Jesus? The *Pericope Adulterae*, Feminist Interpretation, and the Limits of Narrative Agency," in *The Bible and Feminism: Remapping the Field*, ed. Yvonne Sherwood [New York: Oxford University Press, 2017], 410). "The text and its god," she observes, "are both quite willing to forge male homosocial bonds at a woman's expense" (402).

82 Holly J. Toensing, "Divine Intervention or Divine Intrusion? Jesus and the Adulteress in John's Gospel," in *A Feminist Companion to John, Vol 1.,*

ed. by Amy-Jill Levine with Marianne Blickenstaff (Sheffield, UK: Sheffield Academic Press, 2003), 159–72.

83 Bessey, *Jesus Feminist*, 19.

84 Toensing, "Divine Intervention or Divine Intrusion?," 167.

85 See Kate Manne on men's entitlement to admiration and its effects on women (*Entitled,* 14–32).

86 Bessey, *Jesus Feminist*, 18.

87 On the unequal treatment of men and women here, see Toensing, "Divine Intervention or Divine Intrusion?," 170–72).

88 As Toensing puts it: "The scribes and Pharisees maintain the power to define, assess and guide for themselves. The woman is told what to do, what not to do, and how to interpret what she does! She is firmly reminded that she continues to be held accountable to prevailing definitions of sin, governed by men" ("Divine Intervention or Divine Intrusion?," 170).

89 As Toensing comments, Jesus "risked the adulterous woman's life by agreeing that she deserved death" ("Divine Intervention or Divine Intrusion?," 168).

90 Alsup, *Is the Bible Good for Women?*, 113.

91 Bessey, *Jesus Feminist*, 18–19.

92 This is to say nothing of the gospel writers' own presentation of women or perpetuation of misogyny, which could also be critiqued. Many readers are so trained to read with trust, for example, that they might miss just how easy it is to raise legitimate questions about misogyny and patriarchy in the birth narratives. Reasonable cases have been made that Mary is instrumentalized, impregnated without her consent. See, for example, Michael Pope, "Gabriel's Entrance and Biblical Violence in Luke's Annunciation Narrative," *Journal of Biblical Literature* 137, no. 3 (2018): 701–10. The gospel of Luke enjoys a popular reputation as the gospel most friendly to women, but the portrayal is at best ambivalent. See Turid Karlsen Seim, *Patterns of Gender in Luke-Acts* (London: T&T Clark International, 1990). Scholars have noted that women following Jesus are "diminished" in the text. See Sara Parks, Shayna Sheinfeld, and Meredith J. C. Warren, *Jewish and Christian Women in the Ancient Mediterranean* (New York: Routledge, 2021), 166–69, and the literature cited therein.

93 See, for example, Sara Parks, *Gender in the Rhetoric of Jesus: Women in Q* (Lanham, MD: Lexington Books/Fortress Academic, 2019).

94 Parks, *Gender in the Rhetoric of Jesus*, esp. 3–5.

95 Susan Durber, "The Female Reader of the Parables of the Lost," *Journal for the Study of the New Testament* 45 (1992): 59–78.

96 Philip Payne uses this scene as evidence for the claim that Jesus "seems to be unconcerned with gender differences in the kingdom of God," which he sees as good for women (*Man and Woman*, 57).

Chapter 3

1 Biblical scholars question whether Paul is concerned in 1 Corinthians 11 with veiling or with how women wear their hair. See, for example, Elisabeth Schüssler Fiorenza, *In Memory of Her: A Feminist Theological Reconstruction of Christian Origins* (New York: Crossroad, 1983), 227–28; Troy W. Martin, "Paul's Argument from Nature for the Veil in 1 Corinthians 11:13–15: A Testicle Instead of a Head Covering," *Journal of Biblical Literature* 123, no. 1 (2004): 75–84; Carly Daniel-Hughes, "'Wear the Armor of Your Shame!': Debating Veiling and the Salvation of the Flesh in Tertullian of Carthage," *Studies in Religion* 39, no. 2 (2010): 179–201.

2 While historical critical scholars can dispense with criticism of Paul by deeming some of the marred writings to be post-Pauline, evangelicals are often reluctant to concede Pauline authorship because of the risk doing so might pose to biblical authority. To apprehend fully how white evangelicals make the Bible good, we must engage in the fiction that Paul wrote the letters in the Bible that claim to be written by Paul. Doing so in fact makes the task that much more interesting, since making Paul good is trickier when "Paul" is more voluminous. More potential for contradictions and for change over time exists than otherwise would if we limited our analysis only to the seven undisputed epistles of Paul. More contradictions and more change over time cannot help but give rise to more creative reconciliation projects, as difficult interpretive problems demand ingenious solutions. An expanded Paul is a Paul harder to explain—which makes attempts at explanation all the more intriguing. Yet for an interesting argument for how evangelicals can affirm both that some Pauline letters were forged in antiquity and that they should remain canonical, see Armin Baum, "A Theological Justification for the Canonical Status of Literary Forgeries: Jacob's Deceit (Genesis 27) and Petr Pokorny's *sola gratia* Argument," *Journal of the Evangelical Theological Society* 55, no. 2 (2012): 273–90.

3 See, for example, Philip B. Payne, "Vaticanus Distigme-Obelos Symbols Marking Added Text, Including 1 Corinthians 14.34–5," *New Testament Studies* 63 no. 4 (2017): 604–25.

4   Dan Kimball, *How (Not) to Read the Bible.* "Crazy" is a term often used to demean and/or regulate women. On this, see in particular Mary Pols, "Crazy," in *Pretty Bitches: On Being Called Crazy, Angry, Bossy, Frumpy, Feisty, and All the Other Words That Are Used to Undermine Women*, ed. Lizzie Skurnick (New York: Seal Press, 2020), 127–39.

5   Kimball, *How (Not) to Read the Bible*, 141.

6   Margaret M. Mitchell has shown how ancient arguments that, like Paul's, assert the importance of unity and cast disagreement as strife or disorder rely on hierarchical assumptions about patriarchy and social order (*Paul and the Rhetoric of Reconciliation: An Exegetical Investigation of the Language and Composition of 1 Corinthians* [Louisville, KY: Westminster/John Knox, 1991]).

7   Kimball's justification further assumes that there exists some behaviors so deplorable that they require drastic measures whose potential moral problems do not merit interrogating. The end justifies the means.

8   The film *God's Not Dead: We the People*, for example, relies on its (white, Christian, Western) viewers, "knowing" that making the congresswoman veil is a ridiculous proposition. The film likely relies on assumptions of many white evangelical Christians in the post-9/11 US that view veiling of women as fundamentally *other* and oppressive because of a (tired and inaccurate) dichotomy that associates the Middle East and Islam with oppressive patriarchy and sees the (Christian) West as, by contrast, liberating and progressive. Payne's assumption may be shared by many evangelical Christian readers in the post-9/11 US who associate veiling of women with Islam as "other," while ignoring or failing to apprehend the ways in which women's dress is regulated by men, or by women for the benefit of men, in their own communities. See Leila Ahmed, *A Quiet Revolution: The Veil's Resurgence, from the Middle East to America* (Cambridge: Harvard University Press, 2012). Muslim women at various times and places, according to Ahmed, have had interpretations of veiling that do not cohere with the patriarchal and traditionalist arguments of male religious leaders. Paul's argument, though, lacks any voices of women who might or might not choose to veil, or any of the reasons that they might offer for doing so.

9   The Bible itself preserves evidence that gentile Christianity's eschewing of biblical food laws was not inevitable—early Jesus followers debated over to what extent gentiles were to observe Jewish law, including food laws (see Gal 1–2 and Acts 15). But this is not a live debate today, even though evangelicals have become comfortable appropriating other aspects of

Jewish religious practice into their own (see John Dulin, "Reversing Rupture: Evangelicals' Practice of Jewish Rituals and Processes of Protestant Inclusion," *Anthropological Quarterly* 88, no. 3 [2015]: 601–34). For most Christians, it is not a moral issue either. Tying slavery to shrimp is rhetorically useful for Kimball, then, because Christians tend to think of the latter as a ritual issue rather than a moral one, and evangelical Protestants are disposed to regard any ritual as suspect.

10   Kimball, *How (Not) to Read the Bible*, 3. The "magical underwear" objection could be easily dispatched. The biblical verse itself, for example, is clear that the command was limited to one specific person and his descendants. Unless someone today could trace their lineage back to Aaron, they are not accountable for priestly vestments. One could also make the argument that a "tent of meeting" is antiquated and has no modern equivalent, or that the command has been superseded because when the ancient Israelite (and later Jewish) priesthood went under due to historical events—including the Jerusalem Temple's eventual destruction—their underwear was buried with them. But Kimball offers no explanation.

11   Kimball, *How (Not) to Read the Bible*, 4.

12   Kimball, *How (Not) to Read the Bible*, 7.

13   Kimball, *How (Not) to Read the Bible*, 9.

14   Kimball, *How (Not) to Read the Bible*, 10.

15   Kimball, *How (Not) to Read the Bible*, 21.

16   Kimball, *How (Not) to Read the Bible*, 24.

17   Philip Payne and Vince Huffaker, *Why Can't Women Do That? Breaking Down the Reasons Churches Put Men in Charge* (Boulder, CO: Vinati Press, 2021), 144.

18   So also Philip Payne: "The exciting conclusion is that it brings together a picture of Paul which makes sense as a coherent whole. You don't have this conflicted Paul who's torn between two issues but rather a Paul who speaks with a unified message concerning the standing of man and woman in Christ. It takes Paul and lets us see him for who he really was, Paul the apostle of liberty." This quotation is transcribed from a YouTube video promoting the book *Man and Woman, One in Christ*. The video was posted on March 7, 2012 (https://www.youtube.com/watch?v=yK2UBRoy1mY).

19   See Antoinette Clark Wire, *The Corinthian Woman Prophets: A Reconstruction through Paul's Rhetoric* (Minneapolis: Fortress Press, 1990).

20   Many academic biblical scholars have looked for ways to center the voices of those other than Paul in their readings of Paul's letters. See, for

example, Fiorenza, *In Memory of Her*; and Elisabeth Schüssler Fiorenza, *Rhetoric and Ethic: The Politics of Biblical Studies* (Minneapolis: Fortress Press, 1999); Elizabeth Castelli, "Interpretations of Power in 1 Corinthians," *Semeia* 54 (2006): 197–222; Joseph A. Marchal, *The Politics of Heaven: Women, Gender, and Empire in the Study of Paul* (Minneapolis: Fortress Press, 2008); Joseph A. Marchal, ed., *The People beside Paul: The Philippian Assembly and History from Below* (Atlanta: Society of Biblical Literature Press, 2015); Melanie Johnson-DeBaufre and Laura S. Nasrallah, "Beyond the Heroic Paul: Toward a Feminist and Decolonizing Approach to the Letters of Paul," in *The Colonized Apostle: Paul through Postcolonial Eyes*, ed. Christopher D. Stanley (Minneapolis: Fortress Press, 2011), 161–74; and Cavan W. Concannon, *"When you were Gentiles": Specters of Ethnicity in Roman Corinth and Paul's Corinthian Correspondence* (New Haven, CT: Yale University Press, 2014).

21 The men's ministry exists "for men to connect and come together on a unified mission to know God, to fellowship with each other, to serve their families and community, and to grow God's Kingdom," while the women's ministry exists "to create opportunities for women to know and love God more," and "to know, love and invest in each other and to study and dialogue about issues of life and faith." While the men's ministry holds its meeting exclusively outside of traditional working hours, either before the workday begins or after it ends, the women's ministry does not. A "Moms' MeetUp" is offered twice a month on Fridays during the day. No analogous meetup for dads is advertised. These quotations are taken from the church's website (https://www.vintagechurch.org) and are current as of December 2022.

22 On this point he invokes Scot McKnight, whom he calls a "Bible scholar guru and personal friend" (144). I analyze McKnight's book on the subject below.

23 With Christian anti-Jewish polemic, he suggests that Jewish worship practices in antiquity—which were "just a custom, not directed in the Bible"—led to the church having separate seating for men and women. Women in such an arrangement might have been "shouting across the room" to their husbands with questions.

24 Kimball, *How (Not) to Read the Bible*, 145.

25 Kimball, *How (Not) to Read the Bible*, 141.

26 Kimball's confusion of terms suggests unfamiliarity with how ancient Greco-Roman religions worked. He equates "Temple of Artemis" with "religion," despite the fact that the temple was a place, the setting for religious practice and not a religion itself. Kimball also equates "Artemis"

with "cult," though these are not interchangeable given that Artemis, as a goddess, was the object of veneration of the cult made of people doing the venerating.

27 Payne and Huffaker similarly sexualize women's reproductive capacity, even as they claim that the leaders were not men but women: "Remember from Acts 19 that Ephesus was the center for worship of the Greek goddess Artemis, the goddess of fertility. The people were lured by promises of fertility, sexuality, and protection during pregnancy and childbirth. The leaders of this cult were predominantly women" (*Why Can't Women Do That?*, 141).

28 Kimball, *How (Not) to Read the Bible*, 142.

29 S. M. Baugh notes that "neither Strabo, Pliny the Elder, Dio Chrysostom, Pausanias, Xenophon of Ephesus, Achilles Tatius, nor any other ancient author speaks explicitly or even hints at cult prostitution in either the narrow or broad sense in Ephesus of any period. Nor is it evidenced in the nearly 4,000 extant Greek and Latin inscriptions from Ephesus. This is an opinion found only in modern writers" ("Cult Prostitution in New Testament Ephesus: A Reappraisal." *Journal of the Evangelical Theological Society* 42, no. 3 [1999]: 449). Baugh, devastatingly, traces the idea of cult prostitution in Ephesus to a 1917 comment by a writer named Camdem Cobern, who cites no ancient evidence to support the claim (Camden M. Cobern, *New Archaeological Discoveries* [2nd edition; New York: Funk & Wagnalls, 1917], 465). Later writers then cite Cobern as evidence for the claim without, apparently, checking to see what evidence he was basing his claim on—which was none.

30 The interpreters I discuss in this chapter are not the originators or sole practitioners of what I call *pornodoxy*. My treatment of their work here is meant to be illustrative rather than genealogical. The phenomenon is widespread, both within and outside of evangelical Christianity—to include in many cases professional biblical scholarship that is ostensibly nonreligious.

31 McKnight previously taught at two other evangelical institutions, North Park University and Trinity Evangelical Divinity School, the latter of which he also counts as alma mater. His faculty webpage describes him as "a world-renowned speaker, writer, professor and equipper of the Church" and "a recognized authority on the historical Jesus, early Christianity, and the New Testament" ("Scot McKnight," *Northern Seminary*, https://www.seminary.edu/faculty/scot-mcknight/).

32 Scot McKnight, *The Blue Parakeet: Rethinking How You Read the Bible*, 2nd ed. (Grand Rapids, MI: Zondervan, 2018), 201–2.

33   So also Philip Payne, in a tweet on July 8, 2022: "I used to believe in male authority in the home and church. It was the Bible itself that convinced me otherwise." (https://twitter.com/PhilipBPayne/status/15454413286 70154755).

34   McKnight, *The Blue Parakeet*, 200.

35   McKnight, *The Blue Parakeet*, 250. He draws on New Testament scholar Bruce Winter's book *Roman Wives, Roman Widows: The Appearance of New Women and the Pauline Communities* (Grand Rapids, MI: Eerdmans, 2003). Winter's book, while positively reviewed by *The Gospel Coalition* (https://www.thegospelcoalition.org/themelios/review/roman-wives-roman-widows-the-appearance-of-new-women-and-the-pauline-communities/), received tentative or even harsh reviews from historians and feminist scholars when it came out in 2003. Shelly Matthews wrote, for example, a pointed critique in one of the leading journals in the field of biblical studies:

> Where would the field of women, gender, and Pauline studies be without Elisabeth Schüssler Fiorenza, Antionette Wire, Bernadette Brooten, Elizabeth Castelli, Luise Schottroff, Mary Rose D'Angelo, Dennis Ronald MacDonald . . . and Jouette Bassler, to name a sampling of the major contributors to this field in the last quarter century? Bruce Winter answers this question by writing a book on women and Pauline communities that makes no reference [to] any of these scholars (*Catholic Biblical Quarterly* 67 [2005]: 162).

And further: "The major problem with W.'s argument comes into focus in his suggestion that the New Woman lurks behind all the biblical passages he exegetes in part 2. To explain and defend these restrictions on women, W. repeatedly resorts to the specter of this sexually aggressive, inappropriately dominant, and otherwise immoral figure." Matthews goes on to observe that:

> W. never seriously entertains the notion that Scripture contains draconian, unjust, patriarchal restrictions against early Christian women, or that the passages he exegetes might stand in troubling conflict with other scriptural passages that contain more positive and/or fair assessments of women's place in early Christianity. The fault lies squarely with the Woman herself, who either always is, or has threatened to one day become, sexually promiscuous (162–63).

Mary R. D'Angelo's review of Winter's book points out that his use of secondary sources on the Roman material is "strangely selective" and that "larger arguments of the studies he uses often seem to differ from, even contradict, the conclusions he draws from them." ("Roman

Women, Roman Wives: The Appearance of New Women and the Pauline Communities by Winter, Bruce W.," *Journal of Religion* 85, no. 3 [2005]: 481). D'Angelo writes further that:

> Winter has also chosen to ignore the vast array of studies on this material by New Testament scholars, especially, though not exclusively, feminist scholars of the New Testament. Closer attention to this work might have reminded him that ancient Roman and Christian women virtually never speak for themselves: "values" attributed to them are deduced from literary, legal, and epigraphic representations. As it stands, Winter leaves ancient women as heavily veiled as ever (481).

36 McKnight, *The Blue Parakeet*, 251.

37 McKnight, *The Blue Parakeet*, 251.

38 McKnight, *The Blue Parakeet*, 251. The translation is by Graham Anderson (in *Collected Ancient Greek Novels*, 2nd ed., ed. B. P. Reardon [Berkeley: University of California Press, 2008], 125–69). All quotations below are from this translation.

39 McKnight, *The Blue Parakeet*, 251.

40 McKnight, *The Blue Parakeet*, 251.

41 Puzzlingly, McKnight describes their relationship as a "love affair" again when describing scenes in which they are faithfully married to one another (*The Blue Parakeet,* 251). This word choice conceals from the reader the actual nature of the relationship between Anthia and Habrocomes.

42 Christine M. Thomas points out that Xenophon's story portrays Artemis only as virginal huntress, representing her as the Greek goddess who was the sister of Apollo, without appeal to the fertility connotations associated with cult statues of Artemis Ephasia, whose numerous protuberances are sometimes interpreted as breasts ("At Home in the City of Artemis: Religion in Ephesos in the Literary Imagination of the Roman Period," in *Ephesos, Metropolis of Asia: An Interdisciplinary Approach to its Archaeology, Religion, and Culture,* ed. Helmut Koester [Cambridge: Harvard University Press, 2004], 87–88).

43 Thomas observes this well: "Since the pleasure of reading ancient novels was what made them marketable, one can safely assume that the attitudes depicted in them are widespread and generic, meant to attract and entrance, rather than to provoke, and to create a common ground against which to present the events of the story. In this sense, the novels are a reliable index of 'popular' religious attitudes" ("At Home in the City of Artemis," 82).

44 McKnight, *The Blue Parakeet*, 252.

45   The translation McKnight cites is that of G. G. Ramsay in *Juvenal and Perseus*, Loeb Classical Library 91 (Cambridge: Harvard University Press, 1961 reprint [orig. 1918]), 6.434–44. This translation may also be found online, here: "Juvenal and Persius/The Satires of Juvenal/Satire 6," *Wikisource*, https://en.wikisource.org/wiki/Juvenal_and_Persius/The_Satires_of_Juvenal/Satire_6. Because I am analyzing McKnight's source text, I quote Ramsay's translation in subsequent citations. A more recent translation, which I have also consulted, is now available in Susanna Morton Braund, ed. and trans., *Juvenal and Persius*, Loeb Classical Library, (Cambridge: Harvard University Press, 2004).

46   Braund, "Note on Satire 6," in *Juvenal and Perseus*, 230.

47   Susanna H. Braund, "Juvenal—Misogynist or Misogamist?" *The Journal of Roman Studies* 82 (1992): 83–84. Braund comments that the speaker's "hyperbole is not reliable *reportage* but one of his strategies of persuasion."

48   Braund, "Juvenal—Misogynist or Misogamist?," 84.

49   Braund, "Juvenal—Misogynist or Misogamist?," 84.

50   McKnight, *The Blue Parakeet*, 252.

51   He cites Bruce Winter (*Roman Wives, Roman Widows*) and Philip H. Towner, *Letters to Timothy and Titus*, The New International Commentary on the New Testament (Grand Rapids, MI: Eerdmans, 2006).

52   Suzanne Dixon, *Reading Roman Women* (London: Bristol Classical Press, 2001), 55–56.

53   Dixon, *Reading Roman Women*, 56.

54   Dixon, *Reading Roman Women*, 56.

55   Dixon writes: "This is the classic mark of a stereotype: counter-examples are treated as exceptions, while transgressive women are cited with some relish as confirmation. The secrecy of abortion, its disreputability and its strong association with adultery make it highly improbable that any of Seneca's women friends actually told him (or anyone else) that she had had an abortion to preserve her looks" (*Reading Roman Women*, 57).

56   Dixon, *Reading Roman Women*, 61. Dixon also points out: "Men's ideas on how abortions might have been induced were vague, but their views on women's motives for procuring them were definite. That alone should give us pause about treating the literary commonplaces as evidence" (63).

57   McKnight, *The Blue Parakeet*, 254.

58   It may be that McKnight is eliding 1 Timothy 5 and 2 Timothy 3:6–7, but even that passage notes that women are spurred by desire to be taught theology by disciples that Paul does not approve of.

59   McKnight, *The Blue Parakeet*, 255.

60   McKnight, *The Blue Parakeet*, 255.

61 Philip B. Payne, *Man and Woman: One in Christ: An Exegetical and Theological Study of Paul's Letters* (Grand Rapids, MI: Zondervan, 2009). See also his 2023 book *The Bible vs. Biblical Womanhood*. Payne states in the introduction to the latter: "This book simplifies my 511-page book on this topic, *Man and Woman: One in Christ*. It puts cookies on the lower shelf for everyone to enjoy" (xiv). In my analysis of Payne's arguments, I have started on the top shelf and moved down.

62 Payne, *Man and Woman*, 112–268. A digest of the argument appears in Philip B. Payne, "Wild Hair and Gender Equality in 1 Corinthians 11:2–16," *Priscilla Papers* 20, no. 3 (2006): 9–18. The argument also appears in *The Bible vs. Biblical Womanhood*, 61–64.

63 For discussion of the complicated argument of 1 Corinthians 11, see Jill E. Marshall, "Uncovering Traditions in 1 Corinthians 11:2–16," *Novum Testamentum* 2019, no. 1 (2018): 70–87; Jason David BeDuhn, "Because of the Angels: Unveiling Paul's Anthropology in 1 Corinthians 11," *Journal of Biblical Literature* 118, no. 2 (1999): 295–320.

64 See, for example, the treatment in Thomas R. Schreiner, "Head Coverings," in *Recovering Biblical Manhood and Womanhood: A Response to Evangelical Feminism*, ed. John Piper and Wayne Grudem (Wheaton, IL: Crossway, 1991), 124–39.

65 Payne, *Man and Woman*, 160.

66 Elsewhere he uses "well-bred women," which he adopts from BDAG (*Man and Woman*, 204).

67 Payne, *Man and Woman*, 164.

68 Payne, *Man and Woman*, 164.

69 Payne, *Man and Woman*, 164.

70 Numbers 5:11–31 prescribes a ritual through which a man, with a priest's help, can "test" the veracity of his suspicions around his wife's sexual infidelity (and thereby determine whether or not she is an acceptable repository for his seed that will become heirs). Regardless of whether the accused woman has been compliant with the patriarchal expectation of her body—that is, regardless of her "guilt" or "innocence" with respect to the charge of adultery—she is humiliated and tortured in the ritual, which includes disheveling her hair and compelling her to drink dirty water.

71 Payne, *Man and Woman*, 187.

72 Payne, *Man and Woman*, 164.

73 Payne, *Man and Woman*, 169.

74 Perhaps not incidentally, Payne explains that Paul forbids men from having long hair (1 Cor 11:14) because it marks men as outside his bounds

of proper gender presentation and sexual behavior. In the 2023 rendition of his argument, Payne puts it this way: "In many cases, effeminate hairstyles solicited illicit sexual hook-ups" (*The Bible vs. Biblical Womanhood*, 60). "Effeminate hair" for men, Payne writes in the earlier work on which his 2023 book is based, "symbolizes rejection of God's moral standards" ("Wild Hair and Gender Equality," 12). In a particularly cringe-inducing sentence, he goes on to say that long hair on men "undermines procreation by blurring the distinction between the sexes and by symbolizing homosexual relations" ("Wild Hair and Gender Equality," 12). This, too, has consequences for women, who are defined by their reproductive capacity and by implication framed as givers of reproductive labor to men. Payne reads Paul's statement in 1 Corinthians 11:7 that "woman is the glory of man" as Paul's way of enforcing heterosexuality. "Woman is depicted," Payne summarizes, "as the crowning glory of creation made specifically to be man's partner" ("Wild Hair and Gender Equality," 13). He does something similar when he writes in relation to "saved by childbearing" in the pastorals: "By affirming that God became incarnate through a woman, this passage ennobles all women and their role in childbirth" (Payne, *Men and Women*, 440).

75   See Mitzi J. Smith, "Paul, Timothy, and the Respectability Politics of Race: A Womanist Inter(con)textual Reading of Acts 16:1–5" *Religions* 10, no. 3 (2019):

> The contextually superior and dominant group is the privileged race and the other subordinated race is compelled to submit to the will and rules of the dominant group, especially if they expect to experience any degree of inclusion or access to resources and privileges . . . Respectability politics has driven black women (men and children) to seek to be pure and acceptable by other people's standards, particularly the dominant white culture and to be blemish free, even as the dominant white culture nudges the yardstick forward to ensure that black people never measure up or the goal is placed out of reach for the masses of non-white people—only the exceptional black people achieve.

See also the work of Evelyn Brooks Higginbotham, who coined the phrase "politics of respectability" (*Righteous Discontent: The Women's Movement in the Black Baptist Church, 1880–1920* [Cambridge: Harvard University Press, 1994]).

76   Though Payne tries at one point, when he writes about the pastorals. The result is an uncomfortable mess. Paul "writes against behaviors that would bring discredit to Christ and the gospel and advocates behavior that will

advance the testimony and freedom of believers living within these social structures. One of the motivations for encouraging slaves to respect their masters is 'so that God's name and our teaching may not be slandered' (1 Tim 6:1) and to make the gospel 'attractive' (Titus 2:9–10)" (*Man and Woman*, 271). In more recent presentations of this argument, Payne has dropped "slaves" from this list and added the category of disabled persons. See, for example, this post penned by Payne in response to Kevin DeYoung, published on the blog of Scot McKnight: Scot McKnight, "Phil Payne vs. Kevin DeYoung," *Patheos* (blog), March 7, 2016, https://www.patheos.com/blogs/jesuscreed/2016/03/07/phil-payne-vs-kevin-deyoung/ (which Payne ends with the magnificent non sequitur: "One wonders how the photo of a woman with no head perched on a stump in DeYoung's article relates to his thesis." Photo here: Kevin DeYoung, "Our pro-Woman, Complementarian Jesus," February 15, 2016, https://www.thegospelcoalition.org/article/our-pro-woman-complementarian-jesus/).

77   In another passage, Payne adds white supremacist aesthetics to the leering: "The history of art typically exalts woman as the fairest of God's creation" (*Man and Woman*, 179). For a critical interrogation of white supremacy in biblical studies, see Wil Gafney's short video at https://www.wilgafney.com/2020/09/08/white-supremacy-in-biblical-interpretation/.

78   Payne, *Men and Women*, 34.

79   Payne, *Men and Women*, 34–35.

80   Payne, *Man and Woman*, 35.

81   Payne, *Man and Woman*, 35.

82   It is not difficult to find critiques of the Billy Graham Rule as sexist. Many were published in 2019 in the wake of a *Mississippi Today* journalist reporting that a gubernatorial candidate had refused to allow her to shadow him because he feared it would lead to accusations of sexual impropriety. See, for example, this opinion piece from the *Los Angeles Times* editorial board: "Following the Billy Graham Rule Doesn't Make You Noble. It Makes You a Sexist Dinosaur," *Los Angeles Times*, July 16, 2019, https://www.latimes.com/opinion/editorials/la-ed-billy-graham-rule-sexist-20190716-story.html. Mike Pence set off a similar series of critiques in 2017. See Emma Green, "How Mike Pence's Marriage Became Fodder for the Culture Wars," *The Atlantic*, March 20, 2017, https://www.theatlantic.com/politics/archive/2017/03/pence-wife-billy-graham-rule/521298/. See also Sara J. Moslener, "#MeToo and the Problem with the 'The Billy Graham Rule,'" *Religion Dispatches*, February 27, 2018, https://religiondispatches.org/metoo-and-the-problem-with-the-the-billy-graham-rule/.

83 Payne, *Man and Woman,* 59. See the similar statement his *The Bible vs. Biblical Womanhood,* 30.

84 Payne, *Man and Woman,* 59. See the similar statement his *The Bible vs. Biblical Womanhood,* 29–30.

85 Payne, *Man and Woman,* 92.

86 Both Payne and McKnight, for example, suggest in their writings that Christian practices that oppress women are dangerous because they could damage the appeal of Christianity. As a way of explaining why his book is needed, Payne writes: "Prohibiting women from exercising their leadership and teaching gifts limits the proclamation of the gospel and the advancement of God's kingdom. It is not just a waste of resources. Many people hate the gospel because they associate it with the subjugation of women (*The Bible vs. Biblical Womanhood,* xviii). See also McKnight, *The Blue Parakeet,* 250.

87 In another book, Kimball reflects on his rise to ministry within the church, which he frames as a result of homosocial friendship rather than traditional forms of merit like "calling" from God or any kind of training:

> I developed a good friendship with one of the pastors who led the worship ministry. I got involved in a Bible study group with some other people my age, and this pastor and I used to meet to go over the study together. After a while, he asked me if I would be willing to help out with the youth group. At first, I was overwhelmed and humbled that anyone would even think of asking me to help. After all, I had never set foot in a church youth meeting before (*Adventures in Churchland: Finding Jesus in the Mess of Organized Religion* [Grand Rapids, MI: Zondervan, 2012], 75).

88 In an interview given to Kirk Cameron aired on Trinity Broadcasting Network (May 23, 2022, https://www.youtube.com/watch?v=zkBi-U1q-7As), Kimball diminished the real-world impact that the silencing passages have had and stand to have on women in Christianity when he complained that Bible-detractors "are taking *little verses* and then trying to make a case against the scriptures [as misogynistic] from isolated verses like that" [emphasis mine]. Cameron responds confidently to Kimball with brash affirmation invoking a feminist-by-contrast argument dependent on biblical exceptionalism:

> Context is always the king when it comes to understanding what Bible verses mean. And we're talking about the ancient culture where women and children were degraded, and they were marginalized. There is nothing in all of ancient history that elevated the dignity and

value of women than the Bible itself [sic]. And I'm so glad that you've got a book that is *explaining* this to people.

In an interview given to the *Christian Post* in 2016, Kirk Cameron stated, "A lot of people don't know that marriage comes with instructions . . . And, we find them right there in God's word." He went on: "Wives are to honor and respect and follow their husband's lead, not to tell their husband how he ought to be a better husband . . . When each person gets their part right, regardless of how their spouse is treating them, there is hope for real change in their marriage" (Samuel Smith, "Kirk Cameron on Marriage: Worry More about Your Own Responsibilities than Your Spouse's," April 9, 2016).

89 Kimball, *Adventures in Churchland,* 77.

Chapter 4

1 Kate Bowler, *The Preacher's Wife: The Precarious Power of Evangelical Women Celebrities* (Princeton: Princeton University Press, 2019).

2 On the podcast's refusal to entertain that Driscoll's bad behavior could be consistent with the Bible, see Cavan Concannon, "Who Killed Mars Hill Church? There's One Suspect Evangelicals Simply Aren't Prepared to Interrogate," *Religion Dispatches,* October 4, 2021, https://religiondispatches.org/who-killed-mars-hill-church-theres-one-suspect-evangelicals-simply-arent-prepared-to-interrogate/. See also Jessica Johnson, "Sharing Many of the Same Flaws as Its Subject 'The Rise and Fall of Mars Hill' Podcast Puts Blame Anywhere but Where it Belongs," *Religion Dispatches,* October 1, 2021, https://religiondispatches.org/sharing-many-of-the-same-flaws-as-its-subject-the-rise-and-fall-of-mars-hill-podcast-puts-blame-anywhere-but-where-it-belongs/.

3 See the indispensable work of Jessica Johnson, *Biblical Porn: Affect, Labor, and Pastor Mark Driscoll's Evangelical Empire* (Durham, NC: Duke University Press, 2018).

4 A recording of this sermon, delivered in 2007 in Edinburgh, Scotland, is available here: "Mark Driscoll | Sex: A Study of the Good Bits of Song of Solomon," published March 13, 2014, YouTube video, https://www.youtube.com/watch?v=J8sNVDyW-ws.

5 Wendy Alsup, "Blessings and Cursing: Reflections on Mark Driscoll Stepping Down," *Practical Theology for Women,* August 26, 2014, https://theologyforwomen.org/2014/08/blessings-and-cursing-reflections-on-mark-driscoll-stepping-down.html.

6 Alsup, "Blessings and Cursing."

7 Alsup, "Blessings and Cursing."

8 Wendy Alsup, "The Roots of Bitterness at Mars Hill Church," *Practical Theology for Women,* June 4, 2014, https://theologyforwomen.org/2014/06/the-root-of-bitterness-at-mars-hill-church.html; Alsup made similar comments in this article: Stacy Solie, "Inside Mars Hill's Massive Meltdown," *Crosscut,* July 15, 2014, https://crosscut.com/2014/07/inside-mars-hills-big-meltdown.

9 I have benefited from this blog post: "Wendy Alsup in 2019 Shared That Mark Driscoll Has Considered Her a Contentious Women, So We Revisit Driscoll's February 2008 Declaration That She Was Fantastic and Not Like Demonic Busybody Gossips in His Spiritual Warfare Session. So, What Happened?" *WenatcheeTheHatchet,* November 16, 2019, https://wenatcheethehatchet.blogspot.com/2019/11/wendy-alsup-in-2019-shared-that-mark.html.

10 Mark Driscoll, "Spiritual Warfare pt 2 The Devil 2/5/2008" https://www.youtube.com/watch?v=JH65XFaW6ao.

11 Alsup, "Blessings and Cursing."

12 Elizabeth Dias and Sam Roberts, "Rachel Held Evans, Voice of the Wandering Evangelical, Dies at 37," *New York Times,* May 4, 2019, https://www.nytimes.com/2019/05/04/us/rachel-held-evans.html.

13 Aimee Byrd was similarly a target of conservative Christian men who felt threatened by her challenge to the construction and enforcement of traditional gender norms in evangelicalism. See *Recovering from Biblical Manhood and Womanhood* (Grand Rapids, MI: Zondervan, 2020) and her blog post "Leaving the OPC," October 22, 2021, https://aimeebyrd.com/2021/10/22/leaving-the-opc/.

14 Alsup, "RHE and Women Who Question," *Practical Theology for Women,* May 24, 2019, https://theologyforwomen.org/2019/05/rhe-and-women-who-question.html.

15 Alsup, *Is the Bible Good for Women?*, 7–8.

16 Alsup here repeats a common apologetic to establish the Bible as a reliable revelation. This is a rhetorical tactic that likely stands to be successful only with readers already sympathetic to these truth-claims.

17 Alsup, *Is the Bible Good for Women?*, 9.

18 Alsup, *Is the Bible Good for Women?*, 85.

19 Alsup, *Is the Bible Good for Women?*, 85.

20 Alsup, *Is the Bible Good for Women?*, 141.

21 Alsup considers these alongside comparable Petrine passages.

22 Alsup, *Is the Bible Good for Women?*, 139–40.

23 Alsup, *Is the Bible Good for Women?*, 85–86.

24 Alsup, *Is the Bible Good for Women?*, 146.

25 Alsup, *Is the Bible Good for Women?*, 146–47.

26 Alsup, *Is the Bible Good for Women?*, 154.

27 Alsup, *Is the Bible Good for Women?*, 150.

28 Alsup, *Is the Bible Good for Women?*, 165.

29 Wendy Alsup, *Companions in Suffering: Comfort for Times of Loss and Loneliness* (Downers Grove, IL: InterVarsity Press, 2020).

30 Wendy Alsup, "Why I'm Going Back to Church after My Divorce," *The Gospel Coalition,* September 5, 2021, https://www.thegospelcoalition.org/article/church-after-divorce/. She wrote of the pain of her divorce also for *Christianity Today:* "My Coparent in Heaven," August 23, 2021, https://www.christianitytoday.com/ct/2021/teach-us-to-pray/single-parent-prayer-reminds-me-im-not-alone-wendy-alsup.html. In her 2020 book, Alsup wrote that despite the fact that "widowhood and even unwanted divorce are not communicable diseases," "the alienation felt by those who have gone through either is real" (*Companions in Suffering,* 1).

31 Wendy Alsup, "Review: *The Making of Biblical Womanhood,*" *Practical Theology for Women,* May 22, 2021, https://theologyforwomen.org/2021/05/review-the-making-of-biblical-womanhood.html.

32 Alsup, *Is the Bible Good for Women?*, 196.

33 Alsup, "Review: *The Making of Biblical Womanhood.*"

34 Though traces remain of a social media disagreement between the two authors about whether Barr's book dismisses inerrancy (Wendy Alsup [@WendyAlsup], "Woah! I never said you were undermining Scriptural authority in my review, Beth," Twitter, May 24, 2021, https://twitter.com/WendyAlsup/status/1396970498953785353). On the entanglement of inerrancy discourses with white patriarchy, see Stephen Young, "Biblical Inerrancy's Long History as an Evangelical Activist for White Patriarchy," *Religion Dispatches,* February 8, 2022, https://religiondispatches.org/biblical-inerrancys-long-history-as-an-evangelical-activist-for-white-patriarchy/. See also Young's work on inerrancy and evangelical protectionist strategies (Stephen L. Young, "Protective Strategies and the Prestige of the 'Academic': A Religious Studies and Practice Theory Redescription of Evangelical Inerrantist Scholarship," *Biblical Interpretation* 23, no. 1 [2015]: 1–35).

35 Eliza Griswold, "The Unmaking of Biblical Womanhood," *New Yorker,* July 25, 2021, https://www.newyorker.com/news/on-religion/the-unmaking-of-biblical-womanhood. Barr was featured alongside Calvin University professor Kristin Kobes Du Mez, author of *Jesus and John Wayne,* which was published one year before.

36 Rachel Martin, "'The Making of Biblical Womanhood' Tackles Contradictions in Religious Practice," *Morning Edition*, April 15, 2021, https://www.npr.org/2021/04/15/987552105/the-making-of-biblical-womanhood-tackles-contradictions-in-religious-practice. I wrote a review of Barr's book for *Religion Dispatches* ("The Breaking of Biblical Womanhood: The Problem with the Hot New Book Taking Aim at the Subjugation of Women in Evangelicalism," *Religion Dispatches*, April 29, 2021, https://religiondispatches.org/the-breaking-of-biblical-womanhood-the-problem-with-the-hot-new-book-taking-aim-at-the-subjugation-of-women-in-evangelicalism/). Some material here is adapted from that review.

37 "Pastor's wife" is Barr's frequent designation for herself.

38 Barr, *The Making of Biblical Womanhood*, 59.

39 Barr, *The Making of Biblical Womanhood*, 66.

40 Barr, *The Making of Biblical Womanhood,* 70.

41 Barr, *The Making of Biblical Womanhood*, 66.

42 Barr, *The Making of Biblical Womanhood,* 93–94.

43 Cato's speech, and the other to which I refer below, can be found in Livy, *History of Rome, Volume IX: Books 31–34,* ed. and trans. J. C. Yardley. Loeb Classical Library 295 (Cambridge, MA: Harvard University Press, 2017).

44 Cato and 1 Corinthians 14:34–35 have different arenas in mind in which they seek to limit women's speech—the streets and the church—but they do offer the same solution to the perceived problem of women's speaking in places men do not think they belong. They are to ask their husbands at home.

45 Barr, *The Making of Biblical Womanhood,* 97. Following Charles Talbert, Barr also points to Juvenal's *Satires* 6 as an example of ancient Roman writers telling women to be quiet (Charles H. Talbert, "Biblical Criticism's Role: The Pauline View of Women as a Case in Point," in *The Unfettered Word: Southern Baptists Confront the Authority-Inerrancy Question*, ed. Robison B. James [Waco, TX: Word Books, 1987], 66). See my discussion of the problems associated with using Juvenal's *Satire* this way in the previous chapter.

46 Identifying the slogans is important for conservative biblicists since only by doing so can they be assured they know what Paul (as an authority figure) was supporting and what Paul was arguing against. See, as an example, Edward W. Watson and Martin M. Culy, *Quoting Corinthians: Identifying Slogans and Quotations in 1 Corinthians* (Eugene, OR: Pickwick Press, 2018).

47 Barr, *The Making of Biblical Womanhood*, 92–93.

48 Barr, *The Making of Biblical Womanhood*, 92.

49 In this case, blame falls to the Romans and ancient Jews ("Pharisees"). These others are the ones who constructed societies around evolving patriarchal values, while Christianity, when done rightly, has fought against them. In specific examples, Barr focuses on the Romans when it comes to positively contrasting Christianity. She does not elaborate on how Jews in antiquity were patriarchal. But their inclusion in the introduction contributes to the history of anti-Jewish Christian feminism (see the previous chapter).

50 In the end she undoes all this work by saying that she might be wrong, which suggests that she knows it's vulnerable. If she is wrong, she has another trick up her sleeve to get her still to where she wants to go: "As a historian, I find it hard to ignore how similar Paul's words are to the Greco-Roman world in which he lives. Yet, even if I am wrong and Paul is only drawing on Roman sources instead of intentionally quoting them for the purpose of refutation, I would still argue that the directives Paul gave to Corinthian women are limited to their historical context" (*The Making of Biblical Womanhood*, 101). This introduces a new apologetic strategy that does not fit easily with the others Barr has already deployed. Here, she considers the possibility that the problematic words actually *do* come from Paul. In that case, Paul, failing to live up to Barr's fourth heading ("Because Paul Didn't Tell Women to Be Silent"), is conceived to have only silenced some women at a particular place and time. Paul didn't tell (all) women to be silent (forever).

51 See the work of Jill E. Marshall in which she compares these men's regulation of women's speech (*Women Praying and Prophesying in Corinth: Gender and Inspired Speech in First Corinthians* [Tübingen: Mohr Siebeck, 2017], 76).

52 Livy 34.7.12; Marshall, 81. Marshall argues that ambivalence toward women's speech characterizes many ancient men's surviving literary corpuses, including that of Livy and Paul (*Women Praying and Prophesying in Corinth*, esp. 73–108.)

53 Scholars of early Christianity have shown that the earliest Christians accepted, endorsed, and practiced enslavement and, further, used enslavement language in their texts to advance the interests of elite slavers. See, for example, Jennifer Glancy, *Slavery in Early Christianity* (New York: Oxford University Press, 2002); Chris L. de Wet, *The Unbound God: Slavery and the Formation of Early Christian Thought* (New York:

Taylor & Francis, 2017); Katherine Shaner, *Enslaved Leadership in Early Christianity* (New York: Oxford University Press, 2018); Chance Everett Bonar, "Enslaved to God: Slavery and Divine Despotics in the *Shepherd of Hermas*," PhD diss., Harvard University (2023). Much of this work was influenced by a shift in how scholars understood the workings of the Roman slave system, spurred by the work of Keith Bradley, *Slavery and Society at Rome* (Cambridge: Cambridge University Press, 1994).

54 Barr, *The Making of Biblical Womanhood*, 72.

55 This includes Rachel Held Evans, "Aristotle vs. Jesus: What Makes the New Testament Household Codes Different," August 28, 2013, https://rachelheldevans.com/blog/aristotle-vs-jesus-what-makes-the-new-testament-household-codes-different; Carolyn Osiek and Margaret Y. MacDonald, *A Woman's Place: House Churches in Earliest Christianity* (Minneapolis: Fortress Press, 2006); Shi-Min Lu, "Women's Role in New Testament Household Codes: Transforming First-Century Roman Culture," *Priscilla Papers* 30, no. 1 (2016): 9–15; Lucy Peppiatt, *Rediscovering Scripture's Vision for Women: Fresh Perspectives on Disputed Texts* (Downer's Grove, IL: IVP Academic, 2019).

56 Barr, *The Making of Biblical Womanhood*, 81. So also Payne, *The Bible vs. Biblical Womanhood*, 113.

57 Barr, *The Making of Biblical Womanhood*, 81.

58 Barr, *The Making of Biblical Womanhood*, 77.

59 Barr gets "Jesus Remix" from Rachel Held Evans, who, like many interpreters discussed above, offers a rosy portrayal of Jesus as exemplar that holds out a rope to pull Paul toward progressivism; Evans, "Aristotle vs. Jesus."

60 On the trend of white feminists invoking racism as a way of amplifying their own oppression rather than interrogating the privileges accorded to them by whiteness, see in particular Rahki Ruparelia, "The Invisibility of Whiteness in the White Feminist Imagination," in *Shades of Whiteness*, ed. Ewan Kirkland (Oxfordshire, UK: Interdisciplinary Press, 2016), 77–89.

61 This is one reason why feminist biblical scholars, following in the lead of Elisabeth Schüssler Fiorenza, have moved away from a focus on patriarchy, preferring Fiorenza's neologism "kyriarchy," which refers to the multiple, overlapping hierarchies and inequalities that exist within a given social field (see the foundational work collected in Fiorenza, *Rhetoric and Ethic*. Kyriarchy refers to a social system that involves layers of mastery and submission: men over women, husbands over wives, free persons over

enslaved persons, elite women over lower-class men, and so on. As an analytical term, kyriarchy anticipated and folds well into more recent discussions of intersectionality, which similarly looks at issues of dominance and inequality by attending to the multiple intersections of class, gender, race, and status that shape particular experiences of oppression (on this see Fiorenza's "Exploring the Intersections of Race, Gender, Status, and Ethnicity in Early Christian Studies," in *Prejudice and Christian Origins*, ed. Laura Nasrallah and Elisabeth Schüssler Fiorenza [Minneapolis: Fortress Press, 2009], 1–25).

62   Scholars of sociology have shown that how these verses are printed correlates with whether readers see complementarian or egalitarian meanings in the text. See Samuel L. Perry and Elizabeth E. McElroy, "Does the Bible Tell Me So? Weighing the Influence of Content versus Bias on Bible Interpretation Using Survey Experiments," *Journal for the Scientific Study of Religion* 59, no. 3 (2020). When verse 21 is visibly separated from verse 22 and following, complementarian readings are more likely. If the printed Bible does not mark a separation, egalitarian readings are more likely. There is thus evidence that how one visibly presents the position of these two verses can change how readers interpret the Ephesian code as a whole. No such textual possibilities exist for the Colossian code.

63   Barr, *The Making of Biblical Womanhood*, 83.

64   Barr, *The Making of Biblical Womanhood*, 78.

65   Whereas no Roman god had total power, Paul presents his god as the ultimate slaver patriarch. The gods that populated the pagan world were capricious, in part because their power was not absolute. It was constrained or potentially constrained, whether by affection, competition, jealousy, pride, desire, or even nature and fate. There were other gods they had to contend with. Paul's god, by contrast, has little accountability.

66   The sexism inherent here comes out when self-described egalitarians attempt to explain why Paul would tell wives to *submit* and husbands to *love* if what Paul had in mind was *mutual submission*. Why not tell wives to submit and husbands to submit too? Philip Payne answers, "Paul highlights for women and men what each tends to need to hear most. Women tend to need a call to submit, men to love" (*Man and Woman, 277*).

67   The translation is taken from Philo, *Every Good Man is Free. On the Contemplative Life. On the Eternity of the World. Against Flaccus. Apology for the Jews. On Providence*, Loeb Classical Library 363, trans. F. H. Colson, (Cambridge, MA: Harvard University Press, 1941).

68   The translation is taken from Plutarch, *Moralia, Volume II,* Loeb Classical Library 222, trans. Frank Cole Babbitt, (Cambridge, MA: Harvard University Press, 1928).

69   Barr invokes Osiek and MacDonald on this point.

70   Barr, *The Making of Biblical Womanhood*, 88.

71   Barr, *The Making of Biblical Womanhood*, 83.

72   Manne, *Down Girl*, 209–14; *Entitled*, 37–38.

73   Kevin DeYoung, a staunch proponent of patriarchal hierarchy, suggests in a review of Barr's book published by *The Gospel Coalition* that she cannot be trusted to assess complementarianism because she was harmed by people who ascribe to it. Responding to Barr's experience of abuse (which she mentions in her book), DeYoung invokes the Bible to cast doubt on the truthfulness of her experience: "Others," he writes, "might be curious to know if there is another side to these stories (Prov 18:17) and, more importantly, might wonder whether the author's scars get in the way of giving complementarianism a fair hearing." Then this review goes on to make a legitimate critique of Barr's historical method. A legitimate critique of her historical method was apparently insufficient to accomplish DeYoung's aims. Kevin DeYoung, "*The Making of Biblical Womanhood*: A Review," *Themelios* 46, no. 2 (2022): https://www.thegospelcoalition.org/themelios/article/the-making-of-biblical-womanhood-a-review/.

74   May 22, 2021; https://twitter.com/bethallisonbarr/status/1396308647538565121.

75   Barr, *The Making of Biblical Womanhood*, 33.

76   Examples may be found here: https://twitter.com/bethallisonbarr/status/1395088800452317186; https://twitter.com/bethallisonbarr/status/1577487339873525761; https://twitter.com/bethallisonbarr/status/1487101075672997890; https://twitter.com/bethallisonbarr/status/1474422113712807936; https://twitter.com/bethallisonbarr/status/1275634761374072835

77   April 30, 2021; https://twitter.com/bethallisonbarr/status/1388228330944704517

78   For an analysis of how whiteness has historically shaped acceptable epistemologies in the field of biblical studies, see Angela N. Parker, *If God Still Breathes, Why Can't I? Black Lives Matter and Biblical Authority* (Grand Rapids, MI: Eerdmans, 2021).

79   See, for example, Athalya Brenner-Idan and Carole Fontaine, eds., *A Feminist Companion to Reading the Bible: Approaches, Methods and Strategies* (Sheffield, UK: Sheffield Academic Press, 1997); Fiorenza, *Rhetoric and Ethic*; Randall C. Bailey, Tat-Siong Benny Liew, and Fernando F. Segovia, eds., *They Were All Together in One Place? Toward Minority Biblical Criticism* (Atlanta: Society of Biblical Literature Press, 2009); Nyasha Junior, *An Introduction to Womanist Biblical Interpretation* (Louisville, KY: Westminster John Knox Press, 2015).

80 Beth Allison Barr, PhD (@bethallisonbarr), "It doesn't matter how good a scholar I am," Twitter, Feb 05, 2022, https://twitter.com/bethallisonbarr/status/1490117786051485696; Beth Allison Barr, PhD (@bethallisonbarr), "well, I am a feminist and a mother and a wife who loves her husband very much," Twitter, August 13, 2021, https://twitter.com/bethallisonbarr/status/1426209817153134596; Beth Allison Barr, PhD (@bethallisonbarr), "I have a lot of new folk! Welcome," Twitter, October 16, 2020, https://twitter.com/bethallisonbarr/status/1317099510691233792; Beth Allison Barr, PhD (@bethallisonbarr), "Welcome y'all! I appreciate the new follows and hope you like learning about history and fighting for women," Twitter, July 24, 2020, https://twitter.com/bethallisonbarr/status/1286660029786075136.

81 Beth Allison Barr, PhD (@bethallisonbarr), "And now I think it is time for me to take a page from @BethMooreLPM and step away tonight before I say anything I might regret," Twitter, December 22, 2021, https://twitter.com/bethallisonbarr/status/1473803776104583182; Beth Allison Barr, PhD (@bethallisonbarr), "I'd give you a cookie I'd just made, but since I can't I'll eat it for you," Twitter, May 23, 2021, https://twitter.com/bethallisonbarr/status/1396672132978036736.

82 Beth Allison Barr, PhD (@bethallisonbarr), "Mother son bonding," Twitter, July 19, 2021, https://twitter.com/bethallisonbarr/status/1417324287304863744.

83 Beth Allison Barr, PhD (@bethallisonbarr), "Found this in my office today," Twitter, August 28, 2020, https://twitter.com/bethallisonbarr/status/1299526909836001281.

Chapter 5

1 I here adopt Vincent Wimbush's term (*White Men's Magic*).

2 A number of recent studies have shown the ways in which Christian theology and biblical interpretation were shaped by the intertwined developments of racism and capitalism. See, for example, Vincent L. Wimbush, *White Men's Magic*; Willie James Jennings, *The Christian Imagination: Theology and the Origins of Race* (New Haven, CT: Yale University Press, 2010); J. Kameron Carter, *Race: A Theological Account* (New York: Oxford University Press, 2008). Both biblical studies and Bible publishing were influenced by the spread of European colonialism and the emergence of capitalist distribution networks within those colonial systems. See Mary W. Carpenter, *Imperial Bibles, Domestic Bodies: Women, Sexuality and Religion in the Victorian Market* (Athens, OH: Ohio University Press, 2003) and Gregory L. Cuéllar, *Empire, the British Museum, and the Making of*

the Biblical Scholar in the Nineteenth Century (Cham, Switzerland: Palgrave Macmillan, 2019).

3   Steve Green and Jackie Green, *This Dangerous Book: How the Bible Has Shaped Our World and Why It Still Matters Today* (Grand Rapids, MI: Zondervan, 2017), 10.

4   This Bible benevolence strategy is common. As one example, see Michael and Lauren Green McAfee, *Not What You Think: Why the Bible Might Be Nothing We Expected Yet Everything We Need* (Grand Rapids, MI: Zondervan, 2019), esp. 123.

5   On the Bible as cultural icon, see Timothy Beal, *The Rise and Fall of the Bible: The Unexpected History of an Accidental Book* (New York: HarperOne, 2012).

6   Michael McAfee and Lauren Green McAfee, *Not What You Think*, 111. Jerry Pattengale's Bible redemption project *Is the Bible at Fault?* uses the same formula. On the use of this strategy in the Museum of the Bible in Washington, DC, particularly when it comes to the history of slavery in the US, see Mitchell, "'It's Complicated.' 'No, It's Not,'" 3–36; and Hicks-Keeton and Concannon, *Does Scripture Speak for Itself?*, 47–75.

7   Kimball, *How (Not) to Read the Bible*, 147.

8   Jerry Pattengale, *Is the Bible at Fault? How the Bible Has Been Misused to Justify Evil, Suffering, and Bizarre Behavior* (Franklin, TN: Worthy, 2018).

9   Pattengale, *Is the Bible at Fault?*, 8.

10   The-Bible-as-ever-benevolent rhetoric among white evangelicals functions similarly to how "religious freedom" gets deployed to protect the interests of the hegemonic. See, for example, Tisa Wenger, *Religious Freedom: The Contested History of an American Ideal* (Chapel Hill: University of North Carolina Press, 2017).

Bibliography

Ahmed, Leila. *A Quiet Revolution: The Veil's Resurgence, from the Middle East to America*. Cambridge: Harvard University Press, 2012.

Allison, Emily Joy. *#ChurchToo: How Purity Culture Upholds Abuse and How to Find Healing*. Minneapolis: Broadleaf Books, 2021.

Alsup, Wendy. *Companions in Suffering: Comfort for Times of Loss and Loneliness*. Downers Grove, IL: InterVarsity Press, 2020.

———. *Is the Bible Good for Women? Seeking Clarity and Confidence through a Jesus-Centered Understanding of Scripture*. New York: Multnomah, 2017.

Bailey, Moya. *Misogynoir Transformed: Black Women's Digital Resistance*. New York: New York University Press, 2021.

Bailey, Randall C., Tat-Siong Benny Liew, and Fernando F. Segovia, eds. *They Were All Together in One Place? Toward Minority Biblical Criticism*. Atlanta: Society of Biblical Literature Press, 2009.

Bailey, Sarah Pulliam. "How a Book about Evangelicals, Trump, and Militant Masculinity Became a Surprise Bestseller." *Washington Post*, July 16, 2021. https://www.washingtonpost.com/religion/2021/07/16/jesus-and-john-wayne-evangelicals-surprise-bestseller/.

Barr, Beth Allison. *The Making of Biblical Womanhood: How the Subjugation of Women Became Gospel Truth*. Grand Rapids, MI: Brazos Press, 2021.

Baum, Armin. "A Theological Justification for the Canonical Status of Literary Forgeries: Jacob's Deceit (Genesis 27) and Petr Pokorny's *sola gratia* Argument." *Journal of the Evangelical Theological Society* 55, no. 2 (2012): 273–90.

Beal, Timothy. *The Rise and Fall of the Bible: The Unexpected History of an Accidental Book.* New York: Houghton Mifflin Harcourt, 2011.

———. "Reception History and Beyond: Toward the Cultural History of Scriptures." *Biblical Interpretation* 19 (2011): 357–72.

BeDuhn, Jason David. "Because of the Angels: Unveiling Paul's Anthropology in 1 Corinthians 11." *Journal of Biblical Literature* 118, no. 2 (1999): 295–320.

Bessey, Sarah. *Jesus Feminist: An Invitation to Revisit the Bible's View of Women.* New York: Howard Books, 2013.

Bonar, Chance Everett. "Enslaved to God: Slavery and Divine Despotics in the *Shepherd of Hermas*," PhD diss., Harvard University, 2023.

Bowler, Kate. *The Preacher's Wife: The Precarious Power of Evangelical Women Celebrities.* Princeton: Princeton University Press, 2019.

Bradley, Keith. *Slavery and Society at Rome.* Cambridge: Cambridge University Press, 1994.

Braund, Susanna H. "Juvenal—Misogynist or Misogamist?" *The Journal of Roman Studies* 82 (1992): 71–86.

Braund, Susanna Morton, ed. and trans. *Juvenal and Persius,* Loeb Classical Library, Cambridge: Harvard University Press, 2004.

Brenner-Idan, Athalya, and Carole Fontaine, eds. *A Feminist Companion to Reading the Bible: Approaches, Methods and Strategies.* Sheffield, UK: Sheffield Academic Press, 1997.

Butler, Anthea. *White Evangelical Racism: The Politics of Morality in America.* Chapel Hill: University of North Carolina Press, 2021.

Butler, Joshua Ryan. *The Skeletons in God's Closet: The Mercy of Hell, the Surprise of Judgment, the Hope of Holy War.* Nashville: Thomas Nelson, 2014.

Burkill, T. A. "The Historical Development of the Story of the Syrophoenician Woman (Mark VII:24–31)." *Novum Testamentum* 9, no. 3 (1967).

Butt, Kyle. "Jesus, the Syrophoenician Woman, and Little Dogs." *Apologetics Press.* September 24, 2006. https://apologeticspress.org/jesus-the-syrophoenician-woman-and-little-dogs-317/.

Byrd, Aimee. *Recovering from Biblical Manhood and Womanhood.* Grand Rapids, MI: Zondervan, 2020.

Callahan, Allen Dwight. *The Talking Book: African Americans and the Bible.* New Haven, CT: Yale University Press, 2006.

Carey, Holly. "Women in Action: Models for Discipleship in Mark's Gospel." *Catholic Biblical Quarterly* 81 (2019).

Carter, J. Kameron. *Race: A Theological Account.* New York: Oxford University Press, 2008.

Carpenter, Mary W. *Imperial Bibles, Domestic Bodies: Women, Sexuality and Religion in the Victorian Market.* Athens: Ohio University Press, 2003.

Castelli, Elizabeth. "Interpretations of Power in 1 Corinthians." *Semeia* 54 (2006): 197–222.

Cauterucci, Christina. "Donald Trump Called Omarosa a Dog. Is That Racist, Sexist, or Both?" *Slate.* August 14, 2018. https://slate.com/news-and-politics/2018/08/donald-trump-called-omarosa-a-dog-is-that-racist-sexist-or-both.html.

Concannon, Cavan. "Who Killed Mars Hill Church? There's One Suspect Evangelicals Simply Aren't Prepared to Interrogate." *Religion Dispatches.* October 4, 2021. https://religiondispatches.org/who-killed-mars-hill-church-theres-one-suspect-evangelicals-simply-arent-prepared-to-interrogate/.

Concannon, Cavan W. *Profaning Paul*. Chicago: University of Chicago Press, 2021.

———. *"When you were Gentiles": Specters of Ethnicity in Roman Corinth and Paul's Corinthian Correspondence*. New Haven, CT: Yale University Press, 2014.

Coontz, Stephanie. *A Strange Stirring: The Feminine Mystique and American Women at the Dawn of the 1960s*. New York: Basic Books, 2011.

Copan, Paul. *Is God a Moral Monster? Making Sense of the Old Testament God*. Grand Rapids, MI: Baker Books, 2011.

Cottom, Tressie McMillan. *Thick: And Other Essays*. New York: The New Press, 2019.

Crenshaw, Kimberlé W. "Demarginalizing the Intersection of Race and Sex: A Black Feminist Critique of Antidiscrimination Doctrine, Feminist Theory and Antiracist Politics." *University of Chicago Legal Forum* 1, no. 8 (1989): 139–67.

Cuéllar, Gregory L. *Empire, the British Museum, and the Making of the Biblical Scholar in the Nineteenth Century*. Cham, Switzerland: Palgrave Macmillan, 2019.

Curtis, Jesse. *The Myth of Colorblind Christians: Evangelicals and White Supremacy in the Civil Rights Era*. New York: New York University Press, 2021.

D'Angelo, Mary R. "Review of Bruce Winter, *Roman Widows: The Appearance of New Women and the Pauline Communities* (Grand Rapids, MI: Eerdmans, 2003)." *Journal of Religion* 85 (2005).

Daniel-Hughes, Carly "'Wear the Armor of Your Shame!': Debating Veiling and the Salvation of the Flesh in Tertullian of Carthage." *Studies in Religion* 39, no. 2 (2010): 179–201.

Dawkins, Richard. *The God Delusion*. London: Bantam Press, 2006.

DeRogatis, Amy. *Saving Sex: Sexuality and Salvation in American Evangelicalism*. New York: Oxford University Press, 2014.

De Wet, Chris L. *The Unbound God: Slavery and the Formation of Early Christian Thought.* New York: Taylor & Francis, 2017.

DeYoung, Kevin. "Our Pro-Woman, Complementarian Jesus." *The Gospel Coalition.* February 15, 2006. https://www.thegospelcoalition.org/article/our-pro-woman-complementarian-jesus/.

―――. "*The Making of Biblical Womanhood:* A Review," *Themelios* 46, no. 2 (2022).

Dias, Elizabeth, and Sam Roberts. "Rachel Held Evans, Voice of the Wandering Evangelical, Dies at 37." *New York Times,* May 4, 2019. https://www.nytimes.com/2019/05/04/us/rachel-held-evans.html.

Dixon, Suzanne. *Reading Roman Women.* London: Bristol Classical Press, 2001.

Dube, Musa W. *Postcolonial Feminist Interpretation of the Bible.* St. Louis: Chalice, 2000.

Dulin, John. "Reversing Rupture: Evangelicals' Practice of Jewish Rituals and Processes of Protestant Inclusion." *Anthropological Quarterly* 88, no. 3 (2015): 601–34.

Du Mez, Kristin Kobes. *Jesus and John Wayne: How White Evangelicals Corrupted a Faith and Fractured a Nation.* New York: Liveright, 2020.

Durber, Susan. "The Female Reader of the Parables of the Lost." *Journal for the Study of the New Testament* 45 (1992): 59–78.

Ehrman, Bart D. *God's Problem: How the Bible Fails to Answer Our Most Important Question—Why We Suffer.* New York: HarperOne, 2009.

Emanuel, Sarah. "When Women of the Bible Say #MeToo," *Feminist Studies in Religion* (blog), January 26, 2018. https://www.fsrinc.org/women-of-the-bible-say-metoo/.

Evans, Rachel Held. "Aristotle vs. Jesus: What Makes the New Testament Household Codes Different." August 28, 2013. https://rachelheldevans.com/blog/

aristotle-vs-jesus-what-makes-the-new-testament-house-hold-codes-different.

Fea, John. *Believe Me: The Evangelical Road to Trump.* Grand Rapids, MI: Eerdmans, 2018.

Fischel, Joseph J. *Sex and Harm in the Age of Consent.* Minneapolis: University of Minnesota Press, 2016.

Fitch, Suzanne P., and Roseann Mandziuk. *Sojourner Truth as Orator: Wit, Story, and Song.* Westport, CT: Greenwood Press, 1997.

Gafney, Wil. "Drag Queens and Did Jesus Just Call that Woman a B—." September 12, 2012. https://www.wilgafney.com/2012/09/12/drag-queens-and-did-jesus-just-call-that-woman-a-b/.

———. "Hagar." *Bible Odyssey.* https://www.bibleodyssey.org/people/main-articles/hagar/.

Geisler, Norman L., and Thomas Howe. *The Big Book of Bible Difficulties: Clear and Concise Answers from Genesis to Revelation.* Grand Rapids, MI: Baker Books, 1992.

Gench, Frances Taylor. *Back to the Well: Women's Encounters with Jesus in the Gospels.* Louisville, KY: Westminster John Knox Press, 2004.

Glancy, Jennifer. *Slavery in Early Christianity.* New York: Oxford University Press, 2002.

Graybill, Rhiannon. *Texts after Terror: Rape, Sexual Violence, and the Hebrew Bible.* New York: Oxford University Press, 2021.

Green, Emma. "How Mike Pence's Marriage Became Fodder for the Culture Wars." *The Atlantic,* March 20, 2017. https://www.theatlantic.com/politics/archive/2017/03/pence-wife-billy-graham-rule/521298/.

Green, Steve, and Jackie Green. *This Dangerous Book: How the Bible Has Shaped Our World and Why It Still Matters Today.* Grand Rapids, MI: Zondervan, 2017.

Griffith, R. Marie. *God's Daughters: Evangelical Women and the Power of Submission.* Berkeley: University of California Press, 2000.

Griswold, Eliza. "Silence is Not Spiritual: The Evangelical #MeToo Movement." *New Yorker,* June 15, 2018. https://www.newyorker.com/news/on-religion/silence-is-not-spiritual-the-evangelical-metoo-movement.

———. "The Unmaking of Biblical Womanhood." *New Yorker,* July 25, 2021. https://www.newyorker.com/news/on-religion/the-unmaking-of-biblical-womanhood.

Harrill, J. Albert. "The Use of the New Testament in the American Slave Controversy: A Case History in the Hermeneutical Tension between Biblical Criticism and Christian Moral Debate." *Religion and American Culture: A Journal of Interpretation* 10 no. 2 (2000): 149–86.

Hawkins, J. Russell. *The Bible Told Them So: How Southern Evangelicals Fought to Preserve White Supremacy.* New York: Oxford University Press, 2021.

Hicks-Keeton, Jill. "The Breaking of Biblical Womanhood: The Problem with the Hot New Book Taking at Aim at the Subjugation of Women in Evangelicalism." *Religion Dispatches,* April 29, 2021, https://religiondispatches.org/the-breaking-of-biblical-womanhood-the-problem-with-the-hot-new-book-taking-aim-at-the-subjugation-of-women-in-evangelicalism/.

———. "The Christian Nationalism behind the New 'God's Not Dead' Film." *Religion & Politics,* October 26, 2021. https://religionandpolitics.org/2021/10/26/the-christian-nationalism-behind-the-new-gods-not-dead-film/.

Hicks-Keeton, Jill, and Cavan Concannon. *Does Scripture Speak for Itself? The Museum of the Bible and the Politics of Interpretation.* Cambridge: Cambridge University Press, 2022.

Higginbotham, Evelyn Brooks. *Righteous Discontent: The Women's Movement in the Black Baptist Church,*

1880–1920. Cambridge: Harvard University Press, 1994.

Hitchens, Christopher. *God is Not Great: How Religion Poisons Everything.* Toronto: McClelland & Stewart, 2007.

Hossain, Anushay. *The Pain Gap: How Sexism and Racism in Healthcare Kill Women.* New York: Simon & Schuster, 2021.

Huston, Therese. "'He's Like Tony Stark and She's Like My Mom': How Workplace Praise Diverges between Men and Women." *Fast Company,* January 21, 2021. https://www. fastcompany.com/90594770/hes-like-tony-stark-and-shes-like-my-mom-how-workplace-praise-is-diverges-between-men-and-women.

———. *Let's Talk: Make Effective Feedback Your Superpower.* New York: Portfolio, 2021.

Ingersoll, Julie. *Evangelical Christian Women: War Stories in the Gender Battles.* New York: New York University Press, 2003.

Jennings, Willie James. *The Christian Imagination: Theology and the Origins of Race.* New Haven, CT: Yale University Press, 2010.

Johnson, Jessica. *Biblical Porn: Affect, Labor, and Pastor Mark Driscoll's Evangelical Empire.* Durham, NC: Duke University Press, 2018.

———. "Sharing Many of the Same Flaws as Its Subject 'The Rise and Fall of Mars Hill' Podcast Puts Blame Anywhere but Where it Belongs." *Religion Dispatches,* October 1, 2021. https://religiondispatches.org/sharing-many-of-the-same-flaws-as-its-subject-the-rise-and-fall-of-mars-hill-podcast-puts-blame-anywhere-but-where-it-belongs/.

Johnson-DeBaufre, Melanie, and Laura S. Nasrallah. "Beyond the Heroic Paul: Toward a Feminist and Decolonizing Approach to the Letters of Paul." In *The Colonized Apostle: Paul through Postcolonial Eyes,* edited by Christopher D. Stanley. Minneapolis: Fortress Press, 2011.

Jones, Clay. "We Don't Hate Sin So We Don't Understand What Happened to the Canaanites: An Addendum to 'Divine Genocide' Arguments." *Philosophia Christi* 11, no. 1 (2009): 53–72.

Jones, Robert P. *White Too Long: The Legacy of White Supremacy in American Christianity.* New York: Simon & Schuster, 2020.

Joseph, Alison L. "Who Is the Victim in the Dinah Story?" *TheTorah.com.* https://www.thetorah.com/article/who-is-the-victim-in-the-dinah-story.

Junior, Nyasha. *An Introduction to Womanist Biblical Interpretation.* Louisville, KY: Westminster John Knox Press, 2015.

Kimball, Dan. *Adventures in Churchland: Finding Jesus in the Mess of Organized Religion.* Grand Rapids, MI: Zondervan, 2012.

———. *How (Not) to Read the Bible: Making Sense of the Anti-Women, Anti-Science, Pro-Violence, Pro-Slavery and Other Crazy-Sounding Parts of Scripture.* Grand Rapids, MI: Zondervan, 2020.

Knust, Jennifer Wright. "Can an Adulteress Save Jesus? the *Pericope Adulterae*, Feminist Interpretation, and the Limits of Narrative Agency." In *The Bible and Feminism: Remapping the Field*, edited by Yvonne Sherwood. New York: Oxford University Press, 2017.

———. *Unprotected Texts: The Bible's Surprising Contradictions about Sex and Desire.* New York: HarperOne, 2012.

Knust, Jennifer, and Tommy Wasserman, *To Cast the First Stone: The Transmission of a Gospel Story.* Princeton: Princeton University Press, 2020.

Krause, Deborah. "Simon Peter's Mother-in-Law—Disciple or Domestic Servant? Feminist Biblical Hermeneutics and the Interpretation of Mark 1.29–31." In *A Feminist Companion to Mark*, edited by Amy Jill-Levine and Marianne Blickenstaff, 37–53. Sheffield, UK: Sheffield Academic Press, 2001.

Liew, Tat-siong Benny. *Politics of Parousia: Reading Mark Inter(con)textually.* Biblical Interpretation Series. Leiden: Brill, 1999.

Long, Michael G. *Billy Graham and the Beloved Community: America's Evangelist and the Dream of Martin Luther King, Jr.* Cham, Switzerland: Palgrave Macmillan, 2006.

Los Angeles Times Editorial Team. "Following the Billy Graham Rule Doesn't Make You Noble. It Makes You a Sexist Dinosaur." *Los Angeles Times,* July 16, 2019. https://www.latimes.com/opinion/editorials/la-ed-billy-graham-rule-sexist-20190716-story.html.

Lu, Shi-Min. "Women's Role in New Testament Household Codes: Transforming First-Century Roman Culture." *Priscilla Papers* 30, no. 1 (2016): 9–15.

Maderer, Jason. "Women Interrupted: A New Strategy for Male-Dominated Discussions." *CMU News*, October 21, 2020.

Manne, Kate. *Down Girl: The Logic of Misogyny.* New York: Oxford University Press, 2017.

———. *Entitled: How Male Privilege Hurts Women.* New York: Crown, 2020.

Marchal, Joseph A., ed. *The People beside Paul: The Philippian Assembly and History from Below.* Atlanta: Society of Biblical Literature Press, 2015.

———. *The Politics of Heaven: Women, Gender, and Empire in the Study of Paul.* Minneapolis: Fortress Press, 2008.

Marshall, Jill E. "Uncovering Traditions in 1 Corinthians 11:2–16." *Novum Testamentum* 2019, no. 1 (2018): 70–87.

———. *Women Praying and Prophesying in Corinth: Gender and Inspired Speech in First Corinthians*. Tübingen: Mohr Siebeck, 2017.

Martin, Rachel. "'The Making of Biblical Womanhood' Tackles Contradictions in Religious Practice," *Morning Edition*. National Public Radio. April 15, 2021. https://www.npr.org/2021/04/15/987552105/the-making-of-biblical-womanhood-tackles-contradictions-in-religious-practice.

Martin, Troy W. "Paul's Argument from Nature for the Veil in 1 Corinthians 11:13–15: A Testicle Instead of a Head Covering." *Journal of Biblical Literature* 123, no. 1 (2004): 75–84.

Matthews, Shelly. "Review of Bruce Winter, *Roman Widows: The Appearance of New Women and the Pauline Communities* (Grand Rapids, MI: Eerdmans, 2003)." *Catholic Biblical Quarterly* 67 (2005).

McAfee, Michael, and Lauren Green McAfee. *Not What You Think: Why the Bible Might Be Nothing We Expected Yet Everything We Need*. Grand Rapids, MI: Zondervan, 2019.

McGrath, James F. *What Jesus Learned from Women*. Eugene, OR: Cascade Books, 2021.

McKnight, Scot. *A New Vision for Israel: The Teachings of Jesus in National Context*. Grand Rapids, MI: Eerdmans, 1999.

———. *The Blue Parakeet: Rethinking How You Read the Bible*, 2nd ed. Grand Rapids, MI: Zondervan, 2018.

McLelland, Kristi. *Jesus & Women: In the First Century and Now*. Nashville: Lifeway Press, 2019.

Miller, Susan. *Women in Mark's Gospel*. London: T&T Clark International, 2004.

Mitchell, Margaret M. "'It's Complicated.' 'No, It's Not.': The Museum of the Bible, Problems and Solutions." In *The Museum of the Bible: A Critical Introduction*, edited by Jill Hicks-Keeton and Cavan Concannon, 3–36. Lanham, MD: Lexington/Fortress Academic.

———. *Paul and the Rhetoric of Reconciliation: An Exegetical Investigation of the Language and Composition of 1 Corinthians*. Louisville, KY: Westminster/John Knox, 1991.

Moslener, Sara. "#MeToo and the Problem with the 'The Billy Graham Rule.'" *Religion Dispatches*, February 27, 2018. https://religiondispatches.org/metoo-and-the-problem-with-the-the-billy-graham-rule/.

———. *Virgin Nation: Sexual Purity and American Adolescence*. New York: Oxford University Press, 2015.

Moss, Candida R. "The Man with the Flow of Power: Porous Bodies in Mark 5:25–34." *Journal of Biblical Literature* 129, no. 3 (2010): 507–19.

Moss, Candida R., and Joel S. Baden. *Bible Nation: The United States of Hobby Lobby*. Princeton: Princeton University Press, 2017.

Newman, Louise Michele. *White Women's Rights: The Racial Origins of Feminism in the United States*. New York: Oxford University Press, 1999.

Onishi, Bradley. *Preparing for War: The Extremist History of White Christian Nationalism—And What Comes Next*. Minneapolis: Broadleaf Books, 2023.

Osiek, Carolyn, and Margaret Y. MacDonald. *A Woman's Place: House Churches in Earliest Christianity*. Minneapolis: Fortress Press, 2006.

Parker, Angela N. *If God Still Breathes, Why Can't I? Black Lives Matter and Biblical Authority*. Grand Rapids, MI: Eerdmans, 2021.

Parks, Sara, Shayna Sheinfeld, and Meredith J. C. Warren. *Jewish and Christian Women in the Ancient Mediterranean.* New York: Routledge, 2021.

Parks, Sara. *Gender in the Rhetoric of Jesus: Women in Q.* Lanham, MD: Lexington Books/Fortress Academic, 2019.

Pattengale, Jerry. *Is the Bible at Fault? How the Bible Has Been Misused to Justify Evil, Suffering, and Bizarre Behavior.* Franklin, TN: Worthy, 2018.

Patton, Andy. "Why Did God Command the Invasion of Canaan in the Book of Joshua?" *The Bible Project* (blog). https://bibleproject.com/blog/why-did-god-command-the-invasion-of-canaan-in-the-book-of-joshua/.

Payne, Philip B. *Man and Woman, One in Christ: An Exegetical and Theological Study of Paul's Letters.* Grand Rapids, MI: Zondervan, 2009.

———. "Wild Hair and Gender Equality in 1 Corinthians 11:2–16." *Priscilla Papers* 20, no. 3 (2006): 9–18.

———. "Vaticanus Distigme-Obelos Symbols Marking Added Text, Including 1 Corinthians 14.34–5." *New Testament Studies* 63, no. 4 (2017): 604–25.

Payne, Philip, and Vince Huffaker. *Why Can't Women Do That? Breaking Down the Reasons Churches Put Men in Charge.* Boulder, CO: Vinati Press, 2021.

Peppiatt, Lucy. *Rediscovering Scripture's Vision for Women: Fresh Perspectives on Disputed Texts.* Downers Grove, IL: IVP Academic, 2019.

Perry, Samuel L., and Elizabeth E. McElroy. "Does the Bible Tell Me So? Weighing the Influence of Content versus Bias on Bible Interpretation Using Survey Experiments." *Journal for the Scientific Study of Religion* 59, no. 3 (2020).

Philo. *Every Good Man is Free. On the Contemplative Life. On the Eternity of the World. Against Flaccus. Apology for the Jews. On Providence.* Loeb Classical Library 363. Translated by F. H. Colson. Cambridge, MA: Harvard University Press, 1941.

Plaskow, Judith. "Blaming Jews for Inventing Patriarchy." *Lilith,* June 5, 1980.

Plotz, David. *Good Book: The Bizarre, Hilarious, Disturbing, Marvelous and Inspiring Things I Learned When I Read Every Single Word of the Bible.* New York: Harper, 2009.

Plutarch. *Moralia, Volume II.* Loeb Classical Library 222. Translated by Frank Cole Babbitt. Cambridge, MA: Harvard University Press, 1928.

Pols, Mary. "Crazy." In *Pretty Bitches: On Being Called Crazy, Angry, Bossy, Frumpy, Feisty, and All the Other Words That Are Used to Undermine Women,* edited by Lizzie Skurnick. New York: Seal Press, 2020.

Pope, Michael. "Gabriel's Entrance and Biblical Violence in Luke's Annunciation Narrative." *Journal of Biblical Literature* 137, no. 3 (2018): 701–10.

Posner, Sarah. *Unholy: Why White Evangelicals Worship at the Altar of Donald Trump.* New York: Random House, 2020.

Powery, Emerson B., and Rodney S. Sadler, Jr. *The Genesis of Liberation: Biblical Interpretation in the Antebellum Narratives of the Enslaved.* Louisville, KY: Westminster John Knox Press, 2016.

Ringe, Sharon H. "A Gentile Woman's Story." In *Feminist Interpretation of the Bible,* edited by Letty M. Russell. Louisville, KY: Westminster John Knox Press, 1985.

———. "A Gentile Woman's Story Revisited: Rereading Mark 7.24–31." In *A Feminist Companion to Mark,* edited by Amy-Jill Levine, 79–100. Sheffield, UK: Sheffield Academic Press, 2001.

Ruparelia, Rahki. "The Invisibility of Whiteness in the White Feminist Imagination." In *Shades of Whiteness,* edited by Ewan Kirkland, 77–89. Oxfordshire, UK: Interdisciplinary Press, 2016.

Sanghvi, Minita. *Gender and Political Marketing in the United States and the 2016 Election: An Analysis of Why She Lost.* Cham, Switzerland: Palgrave Macmillan, 2018.

Schreiner, Thomas R. "Head Coverings." In *Recovering Biblical Manhood and Womanhood: A Response to Evangelical Feminism,* edited by John Piper and Wayne Grudem, 124–39. Wheaton, IL: Crossway, 1991.

Schroeder, Joy A. *Dinah's Lament: The Biblical Legacy of Sexual Violence in Christian Interpretation.* Minneapolis: Fortress, 2007.

Schüssler Fiorenza, Elisabeth. "Exploring the Intersections of Race, Gender, Status, and Ethnicity in Early Christian Studies." In *Prejudice and Christian Origins,* edited by Laura Nasrallah and Elisabeth Schüssler Fiorenza. Minneapolis: Fortress Press, 2009.

———. *Rhetoric and Ethic: The Politics of Biblical Studies.* Minneapolis: Fortress Press, 1999.

———. *In Memory of Her: A Feminist Theological Reconstruction of Christian Origins.* New York: Crossroad, 1983.

Seim, Turid Karlsen. *Patterns of Gender in Luke-Acts.* London: T&T Clark International, 1990.

Setzer, Claudia. "The Bible and the Legacy of First Wave Feminism." In *The Bible in American Life,* edited by Philip Goff, Arthur E. Farnsley II, and Peter J. Thuesen, 183–91. New York: Oxford University Press, 2017.

———. "Slavery, Women's Rights, and the Beginnings of Feminist Biblical Interpretation in the Nineteenth Century." *Postscripts* 5, no. 2 (2009): 145–69.

Shaner, Katherine. *Enslaved Leadership in Early Christianity.* New York: Oxford University Press, 2018.

Smith, Leslie Dorrough. *Compromising Positions: Sex Scandals, Politics, and American Christianity.* New York: Oxford University Press, 2020.

Smith, Mitzi J. "Paul, Timothy, and the Respectability Politics of Race: A Womanist Inter(con)textual Reading of Acts 16:1–5." *Religions* 10, no. 3 (2019).

Smith, Peter, and Holly Meyer. "#ChurchToo Revelations Growing, Years after Movement Began." *Religion News Service,* June 13, 2022. https://religionnews. com/2022/06/13/churchtoo-revelations-growing-years-after-movement-began/.

Smith, Samuel. "Kirk Cameron on Marriage: Worry More about Your Own Responsibilities than Your Spouse's." *The Christian Post*, April 9, 2016.

Solnit, Rebecca. *Men Explain Things to Me.* Chicago: Haymarket Books, 2014.

———. "Men Who Explain Things." *Los Angeles Times,* April 13, 2008.

St. James, Emily. "The Sexual Abuse Scandal Rocking the Southern Baptist Convention, Explained." *Vox.com,* June 7, 2022. https://www.vox.com/culture/23131530/southern-baptist-convention-sexual-abuse-scandal-guidepost.

Stanton, Elizabeth Cady. *The Woman's Bible: A Classic Feminist Perspective.* Mineaola, New York: Dover Publications, 2002.

Storkey, Elaine. *Women in a Patriarchal World: Twenty-Five Empowering Stories from the Bible.* Great Britain: Society for Promoting Christian Knowledge, 2020.

Swartz, Lisa Weaver. *Stained Glass Ceilings: How Evangelicals Do Gender and Practice Power.* New Brunswick, NJ: Rutgers University Press, 2022.

Talbert, Charles H. "Biblical Criticism's Role: The Pauline View of Women as a Case in Point." In *The Unfettered Word: Southern Baptists Confront the Authority-Inerrancy Question*, edited by Robison B. James. Waco, TX: Word Books, 1987.

Thomas, Christine M. "At Home in the City of Artemis: Religion in Ephesos in the Literary Imagination of the Roman Period." In *Ephesos, Metropolis of Asia: An Interdisciplinary Approach to its Archaeology, Religion, and Culture*, edited by Helmut Koester. Cambridge: Harvard University Press, 2004.

Thomas, Rhondda Robinson. *Claiming Exodus: A Cultural History of Afro-Atlantic Identity, 1774-1903*. Waco, TX: Baylor University Press, 2013.

Thurman, Howard. *Jesus and the Disinherited*. Boston: Beacon Press, 1996.

Tisby, Jemar. *The Color of Compromise: The Truth about the American Church's Complicity in Racism*. Grand Rapids, MI: Zondervan, 2020.

Toensing, Holly J. "Divine Intervention or Divine Intrusion? Jesus and the Adulteress in John's Gospel." In *A Feminist Companion to John, Vol 1*, edited by Amy-Jill Levine and Marianne Blickenstaff, 159–72. Sheffield, UK: Sheffield Academic Press, 2003.

Trible, Phyllis. *Texts of Terror: Literary-Feminist Readings of Biblical Narratives*. Philadelphia: Fortress Press, 1984.

Vaca, Daniel. *Evangelicals Incorporated: Books and the Business of Religion in America*. Cambridge: Harvard University Press, 2019.

Von Kellenbach, Katharina. *Anti-Judaism in Feminist Religious Writings*. New York: Oxford University Press, 1994.

Warren, Meredith J. C. "Five Husbands: Slut-Shaming the Samaritan Woman." *The Bible & Critical Theory* 17, no. 2 (2021).

Warrior, Robert Allen. "A Native American Perspective: Canaanites, Cowboys, and Indians." In *Voices from the Margin. Interpreting the Bible in the Third World*, edited by R. S. Sugirtharajah, 287–95. Maryknoll, NY: Orbis, 2006.

Watson, Edward W., and Martin M. Culy. *Quoting Corinthians: Identifying Slogans and Quotations in 1 Corinthians*. Eugene, OR: Pickwick Press, 2018.

Weems, Renita J. *Battered Love: Marriage, Sex, and Violence in the Hebrew Prophets*. Minneapolis: Fortress Press, 1995.

———. *Just a Sister Away: A Womanist Vision of Women's Relationships in the Bible*. LuraMedia, 1988.

Whitehead, Andrew L., and Samuel L. Perry. *Taking America Back for God: Christian Nationalism in the United States*. New York: Oxford University Press, 2020.

Wimbush, Vincent L. *White Men's Magic: Scripturalization as Slavery*. New York: Oxford University Press, 2012.

Winter, Bruce. *Roman Wives, Roman Widows: The Appearance of New Women and the Pauline Communities*. Grand Rapids, MI: Eerdmans, 2003.

Wire, Antoinette Clark. *The Corinthian Woman Prophets: A Reconstruction through Paul's Rhetoric*. Minneapolis: Fortress Press, 1990.

Young, Stephen. "Biblical Inerrancy's Long History as an Evangelical Activist for White Patriarchy." *Religion Dispatches*, February 8, 2022. https://religiondispatches.org/biblical-inerrancys-long-history-as-an-evangelical-activist-for-white-patriarchy/.

———. "Revelation Naturalizes Sexual Violence and Readers Erase It: Unveiling the Son of God's Rape of Jezebel." In *Sex, Violence, and Early Christian Texts*, edited by Christy Cobb and Eric Vanden Eykel, 239–59. Lanham, MD: Lexington Books, 2022.

Young, Stephen L. "Protective Strategies and the Prestige of the 'Academic': A Religious Studies and Practice Theory Redescription of Evangelical Inerrantist Scholarship," *Biblical Interpretation* 23, no. 1 (2015): 1–35.

Index of Scriptures

Hebrew Bible/Old Testament
Genesis
1–3   129
15:16   173n40
21   174n58
34   22

Exodus
23:20–33   169n1
28   72
28:42–43   72
34:11–16   169n1

Leviticus
18   173n39

Numbers
5   22
5:11–31   194n70
25   16
25:1   16
33:50–56   169n1

Deuteronomy
7:1–5   1
7:1–26   169n1

13:16   11
20:1–20   169n1

Joshua
2   15

Judges
5:30   133
19   17, 22

2 Samuel
11   178n29

Psalms
119:105   125

Proverbs
18:7   205n73
21:9   122
21:19   122

Ezekiel
16   3

Hosea
2   3

Amos
1–2   11

New Testament
Matthew
1:1–17   124
9   26
15:21–28   46
21:28–32   57

Mark
1   25
1:13   180n41
1:16–20   32
1:21–28   38
1:27   32, 39
1:28   39
1:40–45   39
2   33
2:10   33
2:15–17   32
3:1–5   34
3:31–35   33
4:10–20   34
4:33–34   35
5   40
6:7   35
6:45   35
7   25
7:24–30   45, 182n53
9:2   35
9:10   35
10:32   35
14   36, 51

14:3–9   48
14:33   36
15:40   36
16:8   36

Luke
8:1–3   179n36
11:27–28   64

John
4   25, 52
4:27   54–55
4:39–42   55
7:53–8:11   56–57
8   59, 62
8:6   58
20:14–18   179n37

Acts
15   187n9
18:26   130
19   190n27

Romans
16:1   130
16:7   130

1 Corinthians
7   73
7:9   96
11   70, 99, 100, 104–5, 186n1
11:3   134
11:4–5   105
11:7   195n74

11:14   195n74
11:15–15a   117
14 77, 133, 140, 142, 144
14:34–35   70, 76, 112, 201n44

Galatians
1–2   187n9

Ephesians
5   128, 135, 150
5:21   150, 151
5:22   150
5:22–33   145–46
5:22–6:9   149

Colossians
3:18–4:1   145

1 Timothy
2   70, 71, 87, 96, 128, 129, 130,
    132, 133
2:11   112

2:11–12   77
5   193n58
5:9   96
5:9–11   96
5:13–14   96
6:1   196n76

2 Timothy
3:6–7   193n58
3:16–17   125

Titus
2:9–10   196n76

1 Peter
3:1   121

2 Peter
1:2–21   125

Revelation
2   22

Subject Index

abortion, 8, 92–93, 193nn55–56
academia, 158–59
adultery, 57–58, 61–62, 184n80,
  194n70
Ahmed, Leila, 187n8
Alsup, Wendy, 62, 121, 122–38,
  160, 174n58, 200n34
Anthia (Xenophon), 82–88, 89,
  192n42
apologists. *See under* Bible
  benevolence
Aristotle, 147, 149, 151–52
Artemis, 77–78, 86, 92–93,
  189n26, 190n27, 192n42
authority, 32–34, 41, 75, 96, 122,
  124, 125, 128–29

Barr, Beth Allison, 26, 47, 137–45,
  147–52, 155–60, 200n34,
  202n49, 205n73
Baugh, S. M., 190n29
behavior, evil, 12–13
Bessey, Sarah, 27, 41, 49–50,
  51–52, 54, 61, 62, 174n49
Bible benevolence, white evangelical
  Alsup, 124, 135–36
  apologists, 9–18, 44–45, 72

and badness, 3, 4–5
Barr, 139, 140–45
business, 7–9
and capitalist imperialism, 162
curiosity, 6
descriptive vs. prescriptive,
  165–66
dominance, 167
evangelical women, 117–18
good for women, 16–17, 23–25,
  32, 48, 49, 68, 69, 125,
  126–27, 130–32
gospels, 166
and history, 8, 10, 55, 69–70,
  77–80, 93–94, 109, 139, 165
and Jesus, 19, 37–45, 52, 55,
  60–62, 107–8, 147–48, 166
Jesus and women, 37–45
John, gospel of, 52
and Judaism, 55
misogyny, 23–25, 27–28, 31–32,
  104–5, 109, 167
necessity, 163
and patriarchy, 24–26, 51, 111
Paul, 93–94, 97–98, 104–5,
  106–7, 148, 166
respectability, 99, 107–9, 113–14

script, white evangelical, 9–16,
39–40, 52, 55, 62, 70, 73,
165, 167, 172n27
and shame, 63
silence of women, 73
Simon's mother-in-law, 39–40
sin, 60–61, 163–64
sin and salvation, 17–18
suffering, women's, 129
use vs. abuse/misuse, 163–65
and violence, 3, 7–10
woman with the flow of blood,
42–45
and women, 16–18, 27, 37–45,
52, 55, 60–62, 147–48,
174n58
work, 7–9, 27
Bible redemption/redeemers. *See*
benevolence of Bible
biblical exceptionalism, 151–55
Blue Parakeet (McKnight), 80–82
Butt, Kyle, 46–47

Cameron, Kirk, 197n88
Canaanites, 1, 12–14, 46, 173n44
Cato the Elder, 140–41, 143–44,
201n44
Cobern, Camden, 190n29
complementarianism, 24–25, 26,
100, 120–21, 133, 205n73.
See also egalitarianism
construct, Bible as, 161–62
context, biblical, 69, 79, 81–82
Corinthian church, 71–72, 76, 99,
101–2, 141–42

D'Angelo, Mary R., 191n35
Dawkins, Richard, 7
DeYoung, Kevin, 25–26, 205n73
Dinah, 3
Dionysius, 102
Dixon, Susanne, 93, 193n55
divorce, Alsup, 136
dog imagery, 45–47
Douglass, Frederick, 5
Driscoll, Mark, 121–25
Du Mez, Kristin Kobes,
171n23

egalitarianism, 24–25, 26, 100,
105–6, 108, 177n6, 204n66.
See also complementarianism
Ehrman, Bart, 7
endings of Mark, 36–37
Ephesus, 77–79, 190n27
Eros, 85
Evans, Rachel Held, 124–25
Eve, 5

Fall, the, 17
feminism, 49–51, 52, 54, 64, 68,
147–51
femme fatale, 82, 84, 87
fertility cult, Ephesian, 78–79
Fiorenza, Elisabeth Schüssler,
203n61
food laws, 187n9
football, 72
Friedan, Betty, 50–51

Gafney, Wil, 45

God
  agenda, 12–13
  and Canaanites, 1, 12–13
  and childbirth, 129
  goodness, 127
  husband, jealous, 3
  and Israel, 11
  New Atheists, 7
  and Paul, 204n65
  power, 204n65
  and *Veggie Tales*, 7–8
  violence, 3, 7, 10–11
God's Not Dead, 21, 23, 64–65, 67,
  187n8
"good" (term), 18, 126–27, 129,
  130–31, 162–63
good for women. *See under* Bible
  benevolence
goods, gendered, 29–30, 105–6
gospel, 98–99, 102–3, 109
grand narrative, 17
Graybill, Rhiannon, 178n29
Green, Jackie, 162
Green, Steve, 162
Grimké, Sarah, 5

Habrocomes, 83, 85, 192n42
Hagar, 174n58
hair, 99–101, 115–17, 195n74
Hays, Taylor, 119–20
health care, 39
herasure, 157
heteropatriarchy, 159
history
  Barr, 139, 158–59

and Bible benevolence, 8, 10, 55,
  69–70, 93–94, 109, 139, 165
and experience, 158
inventing, 8, 38, 43, 55, 68–70,
  77–80, 109, 139, 165
History (Livy), 141, 143–44
Hitchens, Christopher, 6–7
Hobby Lobby, 162
household codes, 145–51, 152–56
Huffaker, Vince, 190n27

impurity, ritual, 43, 44
Islam, 187n8
Israel, 1–2, 11, 16

Jairus, 40–41
Jericho, 1–2
Jesus Christ
  and anointing woman, 48–49,
    51–52
  authority, 32, 33
  Bible benevolence script, 19,
    37–45, 52, 55, 60–62, 107–8,
    147–48, 166
  Billy Graham rule, 107, 196n82
  creative interpretation, 31
  disciples, 32–33, 35
  dogs, 45–47
  feeding of crowds, 34
  and feminism, 49–50, 64
  forgiveness, 33
  gender pairs, 63
  good goggles, 31, 32, 38, 41
  goodness, 64–65
  good for women, 32, 48, 64

healing, 32–34, 38–39, 40–41
hierarchy, 34–35, 39
Jairus's daughter, 40
labor, 29, 32, 36, 38, 39
Luke, gospel of, 63–64, 185n92
Mark, gospel of, 32–37, 41, 63, 179n32
Matthew, gospel of, 46, 63
and men, 32, 35–36, 37, 38, 50, 61, 64
meta, 63
and misogyny, 30–32, 39, 46, 53–54, 61–62
non-discriminatory, 39
and patriarchy, 25–26, 30–31, 38–39, 42, 51, 61–62, 64
and Paul, 69–70
power use, 41, 53
prescriptive, 166
respectability, 107–8
resurrection appearances, 36–37, 179n37
shaming, 53–54, 58–59
Simon's mother-in-law, 38–40, 180n41
and slavery, 103, 108
speaking to women, 52–56, 147–48
Syrophoenician woman, 45–47
women at a distance, 179n35
woman at the well, 52–53
woman nearly stoned (*pericope adulturae*), 56–63
woman with the flow of blood, 40–45

and women, 25–27, 30–32, 35–64
Joshua, book of, 1, 169n2
Judaism, 43, 44, 55–56, 101, 184n73, 189n21, 202nn49–50
Juvenal, 88–89

Kimball, Dan, 26–27, 52, 55, 56, 71–73, 74–76, 77–79, 92, 93, 109–17, 164, 188nn9–10, 189n26, 197nn87–88

Levi, 3
Livy, 141, 143–44
Luke, gospel of, 63–64, 185n92

male gaze, 69
Manne, Kate, 28–30, 61, 80, 157, 178n20
Mark, gospel of, 32–37, 41, 46, 63, 179n32
marriage, 89–91, 96, 150, 198n88
Mars Hill Church, 121, 123–24
Martin, Clarice, 148–49
Mary (mother of Jesus), 64, 133
Mary Magdalene, 36–37
Matthew, gospel of, 46, 63
Matthews, Shelly, 191n35
McAfee, Lauren Green, 163–64
McAfee, Michael, 163–64
McKnight, Scot, 80–89, 91–96, 98, 190n31
McLelland, Kristi, 42, 43, 44, 58, 59–60, 62, 63

men
  assessment of women, 104
  Canaanite, 15
  goods, 29
  hair, 117, 195n74
  health care, 39
  hegemonic, 103
  interrupting, 183n70
  Israelite, 16
  and Jesus, 32, 35–36, 37, 38, 50,
    61, 64
  masculinity and evangelicalism,
    171n23
  ministry, men's, 75–76, 189n21
  and misogyny, 29–30
  power, 150
  and respectability, 103
  and sex, 22–23
  and women, 22, 29–30
Midianite women, 16
misogyny
  and adultery, 61
  Barr, 158, 160
  and Bible, 74, 109
  Bible benevolence script, 23–25,
    27–28, 31–32, 104–5, 109,
    167
  gospels, 185n92
  hair and veils, women's, 99–100
  health care, 39
  intersectionality, 178n20
  and Jesus, 30–32, 39, 46, 53–54,
    61–62
  Manne, 28–30, 31, 80
  Mark, gospel of, 46

and men, 29–30
and patriarchy, 30, 96, 167
policing, 96
Paul, 73, 79, 96, 98–100
and respectability, 99–100, 109
Roman, 141, 144
See also patriarchy; women
Museum of the Bible, 171n23

nationalism, white Christian,
  171n23
New Atheism, 6–7

Oppian Law, 140

Pastor Dave, 22, 23, 65, 67–68,
  119
patriarchy
  Alsup, 129, 131–32, 134–37
  Barr, 138–40, 143, 159–60
  Bible benevolence script, 24–26,
    51, 111
  and divorce, 136
  #EndChristianPatriarchy,
    138–40
  feminist scholars, 203n61
  good for women, 25, 120,
    131–32, 167
  hetero-, 159
  household codes, 152–55
  Jesus, 25–26, 30–31, 38–39, 42,
    51, 61–62, 64
  and kyriarchy, 203n61
  Manne, 28–30
  and misogyny, 30, 96, 167

noncompliance, Christian, 155–57

Paul, 96–97, 120–21, 134, 140, 152, 154, 156–58

respectability, 103

Roman, 144, 147, 155–56

Pattengale, Jerry, 164

Payne, Philip, 99–102, 104–6, 107–8

Paul, apostle

and Aristotle, 147, 149, 151–52

authorship, 186n2

authority, 157

Barr, 139–45, 158–60

Bible benevolence script, 93–94, 97–98, 104–5, 106–7, 148, 166

Black church, 149

and Cato, 143–44

childbirth, saved through, 129, 132–33

consistency of Bible, 73–74

and Corinthians, 71, 74, 76, 141–42

difficult passages, 127–28

and Ephesian women, 82–83, 88, 91

god, 204n65

good and bad women, 96–97

good for women, 73, 97, 104, 120

goodness, 143

hair done up, women's, 99–101

hierarchy, 149–51, 153–54

history, 8, 10, 55, 69–70, 93–94, 109, 139, 165

household codes, 145–51, 152–54

and Jesus, 69–70

leadership of women, 110–12, 130

marriage, 150

misogyny, 73, 79, 96, 98–100

modesty, 100, 103–5

motivations, 70

and noncompliance, Christian, 155–57

patriarchy, 96–97, 120–21, 134, 140, 152, 154, 156–58

policing, 96–97

pornodoxy, 80

prescriptive, 166

progressive, 106–7

recovery, historical, 79

respectability, 98–103, 106–9

and Romans, 68, 87, 88, 93, 99–101, 104, 141–44, 147

script, white evangelical, 73

and sex, 93–96

silencing of women, 70–72, 73–74, 76–77, 87, 92, 93–94, 97, 129–30, 133–34, 155–58, 197n88, 201n44, 202n50

social order, 152–53

speaks to all, 147–48

specialness, 107

submission, 150–51, 153

transgressive women, 93

veiling of women, 68–69, 99–100

widows, 94–95

Payne, Philip, 179n37, 188n18, 190n27, 195n74, 195n76, 197n86
peremption, 178n29
Perry, Samuel L., 171n23
persecution, 21–22
persona, 89
Philo, 154
Plaskow, Judith, 184nn73–75
Pliny the Younger, 155
Plotz, David, 6
Plutarch, 154
political influence, evangelical, 8–9, 164–65
pornodoxy, 80, 84, 190n30
pornography, 80
Postumus, 89
prostitution, 78–79, 190n29

race, 171n23
rape, 2, 3, 6, 17, 18
respectability, 98–103, 106–9, 113–15, 195n75
Rose, Ernestine, 5–6

Satire 6 (Juvenal), 88–92
seduction, 83, 84, 86
Seneca, 93, 193n55
sex
    desexualization, 78
    Driscoll, 121–22
    and hair, women's, 101–2
    and men, 22–23
    oversexualization, 78, 94
    and Paul, 93–96

and violence, 16
and women, 22–23, 57, 62–63, 77–79, 82, 93–96, 98, 101–2, 121–22
sexism, 23, 28–29, 204n66. *See also* misogyny
sex workers, 57
shame, 53–54, 57–59, 63
Shechem, 3
Simeon, 3
sin, 17–18, 59, 60–61, 63, 90
sin-salvation paradigm, 17–18, 59
slavery, 4–5, 72, 108, 134–35, 145–47, 148–49, 151, 163, 174n49, 195n76
Stanton, Elizabeth Cady, 6
Storkey, Elaine, 42–44
submission, 134–35, 146–47, 150–51, 153–55, 204n66
suffering, 7, 129, 137, 150–51
Swartz, Lisa Weaver, 177n6

Thomas, Christine M., 192nn42–43
translation, Bible, 141–42
Truth, Sojourner, 5

Valerius, 144
VeggieTales, 1–2, 7–8, 169n3
Vintage Faith Church, 75–76, 189n21
violence
    Bible, 3, 7–10
    Canaanites, 1, 12–14
    collateral damage, 12–13

Now truly:

"destruction," 14–15
God, 3, 7
and Israel, 11
men, 15
reality vs. exaggeration, 13–15
and sex, 16
time-bound, 10–12
white evangelicals, 7–11
and women, 16–18

Warren, Meredith J.C., 183n67
Whitehead, Andrew, 171n23
white supremacy, 171n23
whores, 124
Winters, Bruce, 191n35
Wolfe, Joanna, 183n70
Woman's Bible, The, 6
women
and abortion, 93
Alsup, 121–26
assessed by men, 104
Bible benevolence script, 16–18, 24, 27, 37–45, 52, 55, 60–63, 74, 80, 93–94
childbirth, saved through, 129, 132–33
contentious, 122
Corinthian, 71–72, 76, 99, 101–2
at a distance from Jesus, 179n35
and divorce, 136
and dogs, 45–47, 182nn55–56
Driscoll, 122–23
Ephesian, 77–79, 92
equality, 105–6

essentialism, 174n58
evangelical, 44, 59, 62–63, 117–18, 120–21
fictional, 83–84, 93, 94
givers, 29–30
good and bad, 30, 75, 80, 96–97, 123, 160
goods, 105–6
and gospel, 98–99, 102–3, 197n86
and gospels, 185n92
hair done up, 99–101
health care, 39
hierarchy, 146–47
humanity, 50–51
and husbands, 101–2, 134–35, 146–47, 150–51, 153–55
and Jesus, 25–27, 30–32, 35–64
Jesus speaking to, 52–56, 147–48
and Judaism, 56, 101, 189n21
leadership, church, 81, 110–12, 130
liberty, 105–6
Livy, 143–44
Luke, gospel of, 63–64, 185n92
Mark, gospel of, 32–37, 179n32
and marriage, 89–91, 96
and men, 22–23, 29–30, 32
ministry, women's, 75–76
modesty, 100, 103–4
power, 150
"public presence" (McKnight), 82
rabbinic views, 55–56

respectability, 99
rights, 5–6
Roman, 68, 82, 87, 88, 93,
    99–101, 104, 140–44, 147
satire, 90–91
and sex, 22–23, 57, 62–63,
    77–79, 82, 93–96, 98, 101–2,
    121–22
shaming, 53–54, 57–59, 63
silencing, 70–72, 73–74, 76–77,
    87, 92, 93, 97–98, 109–10,
    112–13, 129–30, 133–34,
    155–58, 197n88, 201n44,
    202n50
and sin, 63, 90
snatching podiums, 88–89

submission, 134–35, 146–47,
    150–51, 154–55
suffering, 129
Syrophoenician woman, 45–47
veiling, 68–69, 99–100
and violence, 16–18, 22–23
widows, 95–96
"women are people too," 50–51
woman at the well, 52–53
woman nearly stoned (pericope
    adulturae), 56–63
woman with the flow of blood,
    40–45
See also misogyny; patriarchy

Xenophon, 82–88, 192n42